D0082699

AIRLINE SAFETY

Recent Titles in
Bibliographies and Indexes in Psychology

Psychosocial Research on American Indian and Alaska Native Youth:
An Indexed Guide to Recent Dissertations
Spero M. Manson, Norman G. Dinges, Linda M. Grounds, and
Carl A. Kallgren, compilers

Research on Suicide: A Bibliography
John L. McIntosh, compiler

Books for Early Childhood: A Developmental Perspective
Jean A. Pardeck and John T. Pardeck, compilers

Family Therapy: A Bibliography, 1937-1986
Bernard Lubin, Alice W. Lubin, Marion G. Whiteford, and Rodney V. Whitlock,
compilers

States of Awareness: An Annotated Bibliography
John J. Miletich, compiler

Police, Firefighter, and Paramedic Stress: An Annotated Bibliography
John J. Miletich, compiler

AIRLINE SAFETY

An Annotated Bibliography

Compiled by
John J. Miletich

Bibliographies and Indexes in Psychology, Number 7

GREENWOOD PRESS
New York • Westport, Connecticut • London

Library of Congress Cataloging-in-Publication Data

Miletich, John J.
    Airline safety : an annotated bibliography / compiled by John J.
Miletich.
        p.   cm. — (Bibliographies and indexes in psychology, ISSN
0742-681X ; no. 7)
    Includes bibliographical references and indexes.
    ISBN 0-313-27391-X (alk. paper)
    1. Aeronautics, Commercial—Safety measures—Abstracts.
2. Aeronautics, Commercial—Accidents—Abstracts. I. Title.
II. Series.
HE9784.M56   1990
016.36312'4—dc20   90-13988

British Library Cataloguing in Publication Data is available.

Library of Congress Catalog Card Number: 90-13988
ISBN: 0-313-27391-X
ISSN: 0742-681X

First published in 1990

Greenwood Press, 88 Post Road West, Westport, CT 06881
An imprint of Greenwood Publishing Group, Inc.

Printed in the United States of America

∞

The paper used in this book complies with the
Permanent Paper Standard issued by the National
Information Standards Organization (Z39.48-1984).

10 9 8 7 6 5 4 3 2 1

To Daniel John Wilson
Idacom Electronics Ltd.

Contents

Preface

In 1983 more Americans died from bee stings than in airline crashes, yet 35 percent of Americans have a fear of flying. Prior to certification of the McDonnell Douglas DC-10, a production line DC-10 structure was subjected to the equivalent of fatigue testing of approximately forty years. But at Chicago's O'Hare International Airport on May 25, 1979, American Airlines Flight 191, a DC-10, took off and crashed seconds later because an engine fell off the plane's wing. Two hundred and seventy-three people died. Even in the mid-1970s, an aircraft took off from, or landed at, O'Hare every twenty seconds during peak hours. In spite of this increasing congestion, commercial air travel is said to be more than thirty-three times safer than automobile travel.

Before the jet age, airline travel was a faster and safer way to go from point "A" to point "B" than was travel by automobile. The number of air carrier fatalities in the U.S. rose from 144 in 1950 to 500 in 1960. The total figure for 1960 was unusually high because of a rare event—a midair collision. One hundred and thirty-four people died in December 1960 in a collision between a United DC-8 and a Trans-World Airlines (TWA) Super Constellation. The collision occurred over Staten Island, New York.

The number of airline passengers has been increasing over the years to the point where 500 million passengers depart annually from U.S. airports. One billion pieces of baggage accompany these passengers. Public apprehension has also been increasing. Hijackings, although not as frequent as during the 1960s and 1970s, still occur and are of continuing concern to airlines, governments, and the traveling public. Consumer groups express concerns about deregulation. Some deregulation critics contend that airlines de-emphasize maintenance to save money and, thereby, decrease airline safety. Metal fatigue and aging airline fleets are the focus of interest for governments and the airline industry. This concern has arisen because of passenger and crew deaths associated with the rupture of airplane fuselages during the past two years. One incident involved an Aloha Airlines 737 in April 1988. A second incident involved a United Airlines (UAL) 747 in February 1989.

More passengers, more planes, and more flights mean more crowded skies. Threat Alert Collision Avoidance System (TCAS) is an attempt to prevent midair collisions. Airport expansion

and new airports should help ease passenger and aircraft congestion on the ground. High technology devices, such as the
Thermal Neutron Analysis device (TNA), are attempts to screen
for explosives and to curb terrorist acts.

Attempts to accurately predict safety and other trends in
the airline industry, between now and the end of this decade,
will be of limited value. Observers who look back ten years
from now will have a far more complete picture of airline safety in the 1990s than those observing throughout the 1990s. Ana-
lyzing accounts of the past normally lends itself to greater ac-
curacy of results than attempts to guess what might transpire in
the future.

This bibliography consists of 650 references, covering the
time period January 1960 to May 1990. Source publications, all
of which are annotated, include books, articles, conference proceedings, theses, and government publications. Information on
obtaining government publications is available from the following: National Technical Information Service, 5285 Port Royal
Road, Springfield, Virginia, 22161.

This book, in addition to being of interest to pilots, controllers, and flight attendants—and their families and friends—
will also be of interest to a variety of individuals, beginning
with the traveling public. Specific professionals who may be interested in the volume include: aircraft mechanics, botanists,
engineers, firefighters, lawyers, legislators, meteorologists,
nurses, paramedics, physicians, police officers, psychiatrists,
psychologists, radar technicians, sociologists, and zoologists.
Librarians at university, college, special, and public libraries
can consult this publication as a reference work.

The information in this work covers, for the most part, the
following areas: business, engineering, law enforcement/security,
medicine, meteorology, psychology, and zoology. The information
emphasizes major airlines worldwide. There is relatively little
information about general aviation and commuter airlines.

I want to acknowledge the assistance of the University of
Alberta interlibrary loan staff for providing me with numerous
publications, and Edmonton Public Library staff, main branch,
for responding to my many telephone querries. Thank you to
Catherine A. Lyons, Assistant Production Editor. I especially
want to acknowledge the advice and assistance of Dr. James T.
Sabin, Executive Vice-President, Greenwood Publishing Group, Inc.

Acronyms

AAAE	American Association of Airport Executives
AAAS	American Association for the Advancement of Science
AAS	Advanced Automation System
AFA	Association of Flight Attendants
AFB	Air Force Base
ALPA	Air Line Pilots Association
ALS	Approach Light System
AMRB	Aviation Medical Review Board
AOCI	Airport Operators Council International
AOPA	Aircraft Owners and Pilots Association
ARTS-III	Automated Radar Terminal Systems-III
ASA	Anti-Static Additive
ASRS	Aviation Safety Reporting System
ATA	Air Transport Association of America
ATAC	Air Transport Association of Canada
ATARS	Automated Traffic Advisory and Resolution Service
ATC	Air Traffic Control
	Air Traffic Controller
ATCO	Air Traffic Control Officer
ATCS	Air Traffic Control Specialist
AWOS	Automated Weather Observing System
AWS	Advanced Warning System
BCAS	Beacon Collision Avoidance System

BEA	British European Airways
BIA	Bangor International Airport
BOAC	British Overseas Airways Corporation
CAA	Civil Aviation Authority
CAB	Civil Aeronautics Board
CALPA	Canadian Air Line Pilots Association
CAME	Civil Aviation Medical Examiner
CARI	Civil Aeromedical Research Institute
CAS	Collision Avoidance System
CASB	Canadian Aviation Safety Board
CASS	Coronary Artery Surgery Study
CAT	Clear Air Turbulence
CATCA	Canadian Air Traffic Control Association
CAWS	Crew Aural Warning System
CCTV	Closed-Circuit Television
CEO	Chief Executive Officer
CHD	Coronary Heart Disease
CIFRR	Common Instrument Flight Rules Room
CLC	Canadian Labour Congress
CMAC	Composite Mood Adjective Check List
COPA	Canadian Owners and Pilots Association
CP	Canadian Pacific
CPI	California Psychological Inventory
CRM	Cockpit Resource Management
CTC	Canadian Transport Commission
CVR	Cockpit Voice Recorder
DME	Designated Medical Examiner
DOT	Department of Transport
EBSC	European Bird Strike Committee

EC	European Community
ECG	Electrocardiographic
ECV	Error Check Vigilance
EEC	European Economic Community
EEG	Electroencephalogram
EPQ	Eysenck Personality Questionnaire
ETA	Estimated Time of Arrival
FAA	Federal Aviation Administration
	Federal Aviation Agency
FAR	Federal Aviation Regulations
FBI	Federal Bureau of Investigation
FDR	Flight Deck Recorder
FPL	Full Performance Level
FR	Flame-Retardant
FS	Flight Service
FSF	Flight Safety Foundation
GAMA	General Aviation Manufacturers Association
GAO	General Accounting Office
GAS	General Adaptation Syndrome
GHQ	General Health Questionnaire
HOS	Health Opinion Survey
HVL	High Voltage Laboratory
IATA	International Air Transport Association
IBM	International Business Machines
ICAO	International Civil Aviation Organization
ICI	Imperial Chemical Industries
IFALPA	International Federation of Air Line Pilots Associations
IFATCA	International Federation of Air Traffic Control Associations

IFATCA	International Federation of Air Traffic Controllers Associations
IFR	Instrument Flight Rules
IWS	International Wool Secretariat
JAL	Japan Air Lines
JAWS	Joint Airport Weather Studies
JDI	Job Description Index
KAL	Korean Airlines
LLWS	Low-Level Wind Shear
MAS	Manifest Anxiety Scale
MIT	Massachusetts Institute of Technology
MITU	Mobile Inflatable Treatment Unit
MPI	Maudsley Personality Inventory
MSLT	Multiple Sleep Latency Test
MTI	Moving Target Indicator
NAFEC	National Aviation Facilities Experimental Center
NAS	National Airspace System
NASA	National Aeronautics and Space Administration
NIOSH	National Institute of Occupational Safety and Health
NMAC	Near Midair Collision
NSF	National Science Foundation
NTSB	National Transportation Safety Board
ONA	Overseas National Airways
PATCO	Professional Air Traffic Controller's Organization
PFLP	Popular Front for the Liberation of Palestine
PSA	Pacific Southwest Airlines
PSS	Psychiatric Status Schedule
PWA	Pacific Western Airlines
PWI	Proximity Warning Indicator
RAA	Regional Airline Association

RCAF	Royal Canadian Air Force
RIM	Runway Incursion Management
RT	Reaction Time
RVR	Runway Visual Range
SAFER	Special Aviation Fire and Explosion Reduction
SAS	Scandinavian Airlines System
SCAN	System for Collection and Analysis of Near-Collision
	System for the Collection and Analysis of Near-Miss
SCL-90	Symptom Check-List 90
SODAR	Sonic Detection and Ranging
SPSS	Statistical Package for the Social Sciences
SRI	Stanford Research Institute
SSR	Secondary Surveillance Radar
STAI	State-Trait Anxiety Inventory
STM	Short-Term Memory
STPI	State-Trait Personality Inventory
TACA	Texas and Central American
TCAS	Threat Alert Collision Avoidance System
	Traffic Alert Collision Avoidance System
TF-CAS	Time-Frequency Collision Avoidance System
THC	Tetrahydrocannabinol
TNA	Thermal Neutron Activation
	Thermal Neutron Analysis
TPS	Turbulence Prediction Systems
TUC	Time of Useful Consciousness
TWA	Trans World Airlines
UAL	United Air Lines
UN	United Nations
USAF	U.S. Air Force

UTA   Union de Transports Aeriens

VFR   Visual Flight Rules

VS   Visual Search

WMO   World Meteorological Organization

AIRLINE SAFETY

1

Pilots, Controllers,
Flight Attendants

1.001   "Air Traffic Controllers Speak Out on Safety." **Canadian Labour** 14 (June 1969):   39.

Air traffic in Canada is increasing 14% annually.
Air traffic controllers (ATCs) in Montreal, Quebec
have recently been working 200 hours a month. Some
ailments—for example, ulcers and heart disease—are
ten times more common in controllers than in airline
captains in the U.S.

1.002   **Anet, P.,** H. Brouns, A. Delescluse, J. Malcolm and K.G.
Van den Abbeele. "Primary Prevention of Athero-
sclerotic Cardiovascular Disease Among Sabena Flying
Personnnel." **Aerospace Medicine** 43 (October 1972):
1147-1149.

Since 1957 Sabena Medical Services has regularly monitored the cholesterol levels of 1200 Sabena flight
personnel. Treatment was prescribed over a ten-year
period for approximately 150 men who had high cholesterol levels. Clofibrate was used to treat thirty-
two individuals during 1969-1970. There was also a
control group of twenty-nine individuals. There were
reductions, after one year, in the following: cholesterol, triglycerides, beta-lipoproteins, total lipids,
and fibrinogen. Author biographical information. Abstract. 6 figures. 3 references.

1.003   "Appeal Planned by Controller Ordered Fired in Miami
Incident." **Aviation Week and Space Technology** 112
(May 12, 1980):   33.

The Professional Air Traffic Controllers Organization
(PATCO) is defending Ronald W. Palmer, an air traffic
controller (ATC) at Miami International Airport. The
Federal Aviation Administration (FAA) wants Palmer
fired. A transcript of radio conversations between
Palmer, a Braniff flight, and a Mexicana Airlines
flight reveals the FAA's rationale for wanting Palmer
fired, part of the reason being that he vectored the
Braniff International Boeing 727 toward severe weather.

1.004   "Aviation Safety: Serious Problems Concerning the Air Traffic Control Work Force." **Government Reports Announcements and Index** 86 (August 1, 1986): 20. NTIS PB86-194586.

Remarks by the General Accounting Office (GAO) regarding the air traffic control (ATC) work force at six Federal Aviation Administration (FAA) facilities.

1.005   **Banks, Howard.** "A Shocking Charge." **Forbes** 131 (June 6, 1983): 39-40.

According to research by John Umbeck and Michael Staten, some U.S. air traffic controllers (ATCs) deliberately directed aircraft to fly illegally close together. This took place during the mid-1970s because controllers wanted to increase their chances of retiring early. The actions of the controllers caused system errors which were subsequently investigated. Controllers then claimed they were under considerable stress because of worry about the errors. The FAA (Federal Aviation Administration) was sympathetic, at the time, to the controllers. The research by Umbeck and Staten was funded by the Carthage Foundation. 1 photograph.

1.006   **Beaty, David. The Human Factor in Aircraft Accidents.** New York, NY: Stein and Day, 1969.

This book is divided into four main parts: the pilot and his environment (example: selection and training); half-hidden factors in aircraft accidents (example: saving time); hidden factors in aircraft accidents (example: pilot fatigue); and the future. 14 illustrations. 2 appendices.

1.007   **Bennett, G.** "Pilot Incapacitation and Aircraft Accidents." **European Heart Journal Supplement** G 9 (May 1988): 21-24.

A focus on: aircraft accident experience; pilot age, experience, and accident risk; in-flight incapacitation experience; accident risk from incapacitation; licensing policies and procedures; follow-up of problem cases; and licensing standards and employment standards. Author biographical information. 18 references.

1.008   "Bilcom a Threat to Public Safety." **Canadian Aviation** 49 (February 1976): 2.

An air traffic controller (ATC) in Cleveland, Ohio
noticed on his radar that two airliners, a DC-10 and a
L-1011, were approaching on a collision course. He
contacted one of the airliners and averted a midair
collision, although the airliners came within twenty
to one hundred feet of each other. The incident may
not have been averted had a language other than English also been used. There may not have been time
for effective communication. Bilingual air traffic
control (ATC) is a controversial issue in Canada.

1.009   "Bilingualism and the Issue of Safety." **Canadian
Travel News** 15 (July 22, 1976): 8.

When Canadian airline pilots and air traffic controllers (ATCs) withdrew their services—because of the
bilingual ATC issue—the economic cost to Canada was
approximately $25 million a day. To help resolve the
issue, bilingual ATC studies will be carried out in a
new simulator in Hull, Quebec.

1.010   **Billings, Charles E.** and William D. Reynard. "Human
Factors in Aircraft Incidents: Results of a 7-Year
Study." **Aviation, Space, and Environmental Medicine**
55 (October 1984): 960-965.

Human error contributes to over half of all aviation
accidents. The major obstacles to investigating human
error in aircraft accidents are: the fact that these
accidents are relatively rare events, that post-acci-
dent information in cockpit and flight data recorders
is often fragmentary or faulty, and that potential
liability hinders the investigation. Seven and a half
years after implementation of the Aviation Safety Reporting System (ASRS) in April 1976, 35,000 reports
had been submitted to the National Aeronautics and
Space Administration (NASA). More than 80% of the
reports mention human error. Altitude deviations are
the most common flight anomaly. Course deviations
are second most frequent. Aircraft design problems,
for example, are somewhat less frequent. This paper
was presented at the Thirty-first International Congress of Aviation and Space Medicine, Amsterdam, Hol-
land, September 9, 1983. Author biographical information. 1 photograph. Abstract. 7 figures. 20
references.

1.011   "Biorhythms in the Sky." **Science Digest** 77 (June
1975): 16-17.

Between 6000 and 8000 employees of United Airlines

(UAL) are participants in a biorhythm program, the results of which are being forwarded to the U.S. Naval
Laboratory for further study. Biorhythm data has been
used to decrease the number of accidents at UAL. Employee participation in the experimental program is
optional. 1 illustration.

1.012   **Blanc, C.**, E. Lafontaine and R. Laplane. "Psychiatric
and Psychological Problems in Commercial Aviation."
Aerospace Medicine 37 (January 1966):   70-73.

Air France employs more than 24,000 people. Four
hundred psychiatric studies were conducted on 250 subjects. Of the 148 flying personnel studied, thirty
were cockpit crew and 118 were cabin crew. Stewardesses made up 75% of the cabin crew. The majority of
clinical material pertained to neurotic depressive reaction and neuroses. These people appeared to be
bored with life, had difficulty sleeping, and exhibited
emotional tension. Hysteria, phobic neuroses, and ob-
sessive-compulsive neuroses were rare. Forty cases of
acute psychoses and thirteen cases of chronic psychoses
were noted. Neuropsychiatric examination is important
in pre-employment evaluation. Author biographical information. Abstract. 1 figure. 7 references.

1.013   **Blanc, C.J.**, R. Digo and P. Moroni. "Psychopathology
of Airline Stewardesses." **Aerospace Medicine** 40
(February 1969):   184-187.

One hundred and fifty-one stewardesses, employed by a
French airline, were studied during a five-year period. The most common syndromes evident in these subjects were depressive, neurotic, or psychosomatic in
nature. Problems in love life and sex life were
found in over 60% of the subjects. There was no direct relationship between these problems and professional activity. Acute psychotic conditions were
found in approximately 3% of the subjects. Author
biographical information. Abstract. 4 figures. 4
references.

1.014   **Blum, Bill** and Gina Lobaco. "Why the Skies Are Un-
friendlier." **Nation** 240 (June 1, 1985):   668-672.

On a busy day up to 25% of U.S. air traffic is in
southern and central California. In New York traffic is nearly 20% higher than before the 1981 controller strike. This is attributed to deregulation
and a better economy. Controllers in Europe usually
work thirty-two hours a week. At the Chicago En

Route Center, during the last three months of 1984,
control personnel worked more than 17,400 hours of
overtime. A report about stress and controllers was
published in 1978. The report, written by a Boston
University psychiatrist, Dr. Robert Rose, documented
high incidents of alcohol abuse, depression, and hypertension among controllers. Many heart-related
problems are common among controllers at the Los Angeles En Route Center. A controller there directs
more than twenty aircraft. Author biographical information. 1 illustration.

1.015   **Booze, C.F. Jr.** and L.S. Simcox. "Blood Pressure
Levels of Active Pilots Compared With Those of Air
Traffic Controllers." **Government Reports Announce-
ments and Index** 85 (January 4, 1985): 58. NTIS
AD-A146 645/7.

For active pilots and air traffic controllers (ATCs),
borderline and definite hypertension increased with
age. Airline pilots had lower hypertension than
ATCs.

1.016   **Booze, Charles F.** "Morbidity Experience of Air
Traffic Control Personnel—1967-1977." **Aviation,
Space, and Environmental Medicine** 50 (January 1979):
1-8.

The morbidity experience of more than 28,000 air
traffic controllers (ATCs) was examined for the time
period 1967-1977. Hypertension, hernias, uncompli-
cated ulcers, and heart murmur were the four most
frequently observed pathological conditions in these
subjects. It was also learned that the incidence of
psychoneurotic disorders is substantially higher
among ATCs than other groups. Psychiatric/psycholog-
ical and cardiovascular conditions were the two most
common reasons for the medical disqualification of
ATCs during the time period 1972-1977. Author biographical information. Abstract. 8 figures. 3 tables. 9 references.

1.017   "Boredom Spurs Pilots''Ailments.'" **Aviation Week
and Space Technology** 89 (November 18, 1968): 125-
126.

Excerpts from the remarks of Dr. Earl T. Carter, who
spoke at the Twenty-first Annual International Air
Safety Seminar of the Flight Safety Foundation, Ana-
heim, California. Dr. Carter, who is affiliated
with the Mayo Foundation, emphasized that pilot fatigue results from boredom and job dissatisfaction.

The latter two have resulted from improvements in technology. Pilot intellectual stimulation in the cockpit
is quite rare, unless, for example, an emergency arises.

1.018   **Bower, B.** "'Day After' Effects of Pot Smoking."
        Science News 128 (November 16, 1985):   310.

        Jerome A. Yesavage and colleagues tested ten experi-
        enced pilots, after each of the pilots smoked a mari-
        juana cigarette. A flight simulator was used and each
        cigarette contained nineteen milligrams of tetrahydro-
        cannabinol (THC). Yesavage and his colleagues learned
        that the pilots had difficulty, after ingestion of THC,
        correctly landing the "airplane." Persons who believe
        they are alert and normal a day after smoking a mari-
        juana cigarette may not be as alert and normal as they
        believe themselves to be, since THC metabolites can be
        found in urine for up to seventy-two hours.

1.019   **Bryant, Samuel W.** "What Jet Travel Does to Your Meta-
        bolic Clock." **Fortune** 68 (November 1963):   160-163,
        183-184 and 186.

        A number of scientists discuss bodily rhythms and cy-
        cles. Some of the scientists: Dr. Werner Menzel,
        Hamburg University; Dr. Hubertus Strughold, Brooks Air
        Force Base; Dr. Frank A. Brown, Jr., Northwestern Uni-
        versity; Dr. Franz Halberg, University of Minnesota;
        Dr. Gilbert S. Frank, Stanford University; and Dr.
        Otis Schreuder, Pan American (Pan Am) Airways. 2 il-
        lustrations.

1.020   **Buley, L.E.** "Incidence, Causes and Results of Air-
        line Pilot Incapacitation While on Duty." **Aerospace
        Medicine** 40 (January 1969):   64-70.

        Seventeen case histories of airline pilots, who died
        on-duty between January 1961 and April 1968, illus-
        trate pilot incapacitation. The pilots ranged in age
        from thirty-four to fifty-nine years. Six of the
        cases, with a total of 147 fatalities, were accidents.
        The International Civil Aviation Organization (ICAO),
        International Federation of Air Line Pilots Associa-
        tions (IFALPA), and International Air Transport Asso-
        ciation (IATA) are collaborating on a study of pilot
        incapacitation. Author biographical information. Ab-
        stract. 7 tables. 12 references.

1.021   **Burnham, Frank. Cleared to Land!: The FAA Story.**

Fallbrook, CA: Aero Publishers, Inc., 1977.

The Federal Aviation Administration (FAA) had two
predecessors: the Civil Aeronautics Administration
and the Bureau of Air Commerce. Controllers, flight
service specialists, maintenance inspectors, and engineering test pilots are a few examples of professionals
employed by the FAA. **Cleared to Land!: The FAA Story**
focuses on the experiences of these employees. Although not a history, this book is historically accu-
rate. Thirteen chapters cover 254 pages. Individual
chapters are about, among other topics, inspectors, the
academy, and the security service. 132 photographs.
Glossary of Initials and Acronyms.

1.022   **Busby, Douglas E.,** E. Arnold Higgins and Gordon E. Funk-
houser. "Protection of Airline Flight Attendants From
Hypoxia Following Rapid Decompression." **Aviation,
Space, and Environmental Medicine** 47 (September 1976):
942-944.

The subjects in this study were twenty flight attendants—ten male and ten female. They experienced a decompression environment similar to one in a DC-10 aircraft over New Mexico in 1973. Tolerances to hypoxia
were similar in both sexes. The average time of use-
ful consciousness (TUC) decreased from fifty-four
seconds at rest to thirty-three seconds, while the
flight attendants performed light-to-moderate work.
Author biographical information. Abstract. 1 figure.
2 tables. Acknowledgement. 2 references.

1.023   **Cameron, R. Graeme.** "Should Air Hostesses Continue
Flight Duty During the First Trimester of Pregnancy?"
Aerospace Medicine 44 (May 1973): 552-556.

After discussing noise and vibration, low humidity,
pressure changes, circadian rhythm, and hypoxia, the
author concludes that pregnant air hostesses should
be permitted to continue flight duty during the first
trimester of pregnancy. This paper was presented at
the Second International Meeting on Aerospace Medicine,
Melbourne, Australia, October 30-November 2, 1972.
Author biographical information. Abstract. 4 figures. 2 tables. 17 references.

1.024   **Campbell, Barbara.** "Will Flying Be Safe With French
in the Air?" **Canadian Travel News** 18 (March 15, 1979):
2.

The Canadian Air Traffic Controllers Association

(CATCA) and the Canadian Owners and Pilots Association
(COPA) are not convinced a blingual air traffic control (ATC) system in Canada is a safe system. A federal government inquiry recommended that French be
used for commercial flights over Quebec airspace.
French is already used for light planes at ten Quebec
airports.

1.025   "The Cardiovascular Fitness of Airline Pilots."
British Heart Journal 40, No. 4 (1978): 335-350.

A report by a thirteen-member working party of the
Cardiology Committee, Royal College of Physicians of
London. Seven major areas are discussed: cardiovascular examination before acceptance for training;
cardiovascular reassessment of licensed pilots; advisory panel on cardiovascular disease; advice to pilots
on maintenance of health; standards of medical examination and instrumentation; subjects for research;
and recommendations. 1 figure. 2 tables. 3 appendices. 36 references.

1.026   **Cary, Peter.** "Rough Chop Ahead for the FAA." **U.S.
News and World Report** 103 (July 6, 1987): 62-63 and
65.

Donald Engen is the outgoing FAA (Federal Aviation
Administration) Administrator, and is being replaced
by T. Allan McArtor, a Federal Express vice-president. The FAA, a guardian for airlines and passengers, was created by Congress in 1958. Senator Frank
Lautenberg (Democrat-New Jersey) and Representative
Guy Molinari (Republican-New York) want more air traffic controllers (ATCs) hired. Engen supports their
position. 2 photographs. 2 illustrations.

1.027   **Castelo-Branco, A.,** A. Cabral-Sa and J. Coelho Borges.
"Comparative Study of Physical and Mental Incapacities Among Portuguese Airline Pilots Under and Over
Age 60." **Aviation, Space, and Environmental Medicine**
56 (August 1985): 752-757.

Air Portugal pilots who died or did not fly for other reasons between 1945 and 1983 were the subjects of
this investigation. A total of 436 pilots were examined. Medical, psychological, and psychomotor tests
were administered. Incapacities due to physiopsycho-
logical reasons increased suddenly after age sixty.
Depression was common in pilots over age sixty as was
cardiovascular disease. Author biographical information. Acknowledgement. Abstract. 5 tables.

3 figures.   18 references.

1.028   "CATCA-CALPA Dispute." **Canadian Labour Comment** (July
         16, 1976):   1.

         Joe Morris, President, Canadian Labour Congress (CLC),
         believes English and French should be allowed in Quebec
         air traffic control (ATC), if ruled safe by an inquiry
         commission. The Canadian Air Traffic Control Associa-
         tion (CATCA) and the Canadian Air Line Pilots Associa-
         tion (CALPA) are engaged in a dispute with the Canadi-
         an government regarding this matter.

1.029   **Catlett, G.F.** and G.J. Kidera.   "Glaucoma in Commer-
         cial Pilots." **Aerospace Medicine** 39 (December 1968):
         1329-1337.

         Over 2000 pilots, between forty and sixty years of age,
         were examined at United Air Lines (UAL) over a period
         of ten years—more than 14,000 individual examinations.
         Confirmed ocular hypertension was detected in forty-
         nine individuals. Nine subjects had chronic simple
         glaucoma. Drug therapy was effective in certain cases
         and none of the pilots had to be grounded. Routine
         tonometry is a valuable and safe procedure in aviation
         medicine. This paper was presented at the Seventeenth
         International Congress on Aviation and Space Medicine,
         Oslo, Norway. Author biographical information. Ab-
         stract. 2 figures. 1 table. 1 appendix. 25 refer-
         ences.

1.030   **Chaitman, Bernard R.,** Kathryn B. Davis, Harold T.
         Dodge, Lloyd D. Fisher, Mary Pettinger, David R.
         Holmes and George C. Kaiser. "Should Airline Pilots
         Be Eligible to Resume Active Flight Status After Cor-
         onary Bypass Surgery?: A CASS Registry Study."
         Journal of the American College of Cardiology 8
         (December 1986): 1318-1324.

         A simulated aviator population from 10,312 consecu-
         tive patients, who underwent coronary bypass surgery
         in the Coronary Artery Surgery Study (CASS), were
         the subjects in this investigation. Research re-
         sults were reported in terms of selected clinical
         characteristics of the study population and cardiac
         event rates, and the five-year probability of remain-
         ing free of acute cardiac events stratified by age.
         Approximately twenty clinical sites cooperated in
         this study. Author biographical information. Ab-
         stract. 3 tables. 3 figures. 26 references.

1.031   **Chappell, Frank.** "Air Travelers Face Jet Lag Fa-
        tigue." **Maryland State Medical Journal** 29 (September
        1980):   33.

        How to handle jet lag. 1 illustration.

1.032   "Chuck Yeager Sees Changes in the Air." **Newsweek** 110
        (July 27, 1987):   26.

        Retired Air Force Brig. Gen. Chuck Yeager, the World
        War II ace who shattered the sound barrier, does not
        believe airline safety has declined. Yeager feels the
        problem with airlines is the bad service they are pro-
        viding passengers. He sees airline mergers as the
        root of the problem. 1 photograph.

1.033   **Cobb, Sidney.** "Illness in Air Traffic Controllers."
        Journal of the American Medical Association 225 (July
        23, 1973):   418.

        In a letter to the editor, a physician from Ann Arbor,
        Michigan discusses illness in air traffic controllers
        (ATCs) and pilots.

1.034   **Collins, W.E.,** D.J. Schroeder and L.G. Nye. "Rela-
        tionships of Anxiety Scores to Academy and Field
        Training Performance of Air Traffic Control Special-
        ists." **Government Reports Announcements and Index**
        89 (October 15, 1989):   288. NTIS AD-A209 326/8.

        The main research instrument used in this study was
        the State-Trait Personality Inventory (STPI). It was
        administered to students who entered the Federal Avi-
        ation Administration (FAA) Academy between June 1984
        and September 1985. Higher overall anxiety scores
        were associated with individuals unsucessful at the
        academy and in the field.

1.035   "Controllers Claim Safe Altitude Was 727 Crew's Re-
        sponsibility." **Aviation Week and Space Technology**
        102 (February 10, 1975):   39-40.

        A Trans World Airlines (TWA) Boeing 727-731 struck
        a Virginia mountain on December 1, 1974. All ninety-
        two on board the 727 were killed. The aircraft—it
        was not on a radar arrival—was not assigned a mini-
        mum altitude. The Federal Aviation Administration
        (FAA) and the Professional Air Traffic Controllers
        Organization (PATCO) are representing the controllers

at a National Transportation Safety Board (NTSB) inquiry. The Air Line Pilots Association (ALPA) is representing the pilots. The controller handling the
Trans World when it crashed was Merle Dameron.

1.036   "Controllers Tell Congress of Safety Concerns." **Aviation Week and Space Technology** 119 (November 7,
1983): 36.

Gregory McGuirk and Jack L. Crouse, air traffic controllers (ATCs), addressed the House Public Works and
Transportation Committee investigations subcommittee.
McGuirk and Crouse spoke about controller safety concerns. J. Lynn Helms, Federal Aviation Administration
(FAA) Administrator, also addressed the subcommittee.
Safety concerns have increased since the 1981 controllers' strike. There was a near-miss at Los Angeles
International Airport on September 27, 1983 between
a Western Airlines McDonnell Douglas DC-10 and a military transport.

1.037   **Cook, Robert H.** "Jet Engineer Fatigue Problem Reported." **Aviation Week** 73 (November 14, 1960): 42-
43.

Dr. L.J. Stutman of New York and Dr. Bruce V. Leamer
of Los Angeles studied twenty flight engineers, on be-
half of the Federal Aviation Agency (FAA). The physicians investigated mental and physical fatigue.
Personal medical history, x-ray studies, complete
blood counts, blood sugar tests, and other variables
were analyzed. The investigation, carried out over a
three-month period, focused on both domestic and international flight engineers. There was great difference in fatigue between flight engineers assigned
to piston-engine aircraft and those assigned to jet
aircraft. A fatigue questionnaire, prepared in cooperation with the Flight Engineers International Association, was sent to a separate group of 188 engineers.

1.038   **Cook, Robert H.** "Witnesses' Fate Debated in Safety
Probe." **Aviation Week and Space Technology** 77 (October 8, 1962): 42-43.

Between May 1957 and June 1961, William J. Miller,
a Trans World Airlines (TWA) flight engineer, took
298 pictures of air safety violations, without leaving his post in the cockpit. Miller's revelations
included a photograph of a donkey in the passenger
section of a TWA aircraft. The captain, according

to Miller, had permitted conventioneers to bring the animal on board at Las Vegas, Nevada. Other photographs
depicted pilots sleeping or reading at the controls.
Miller had doctored the photographs to prevent identification of flight numbers and crew facial features.
Two former hostesses—Margaret Sweet (Pan American (Pan
Am) World Airways) and Margaret M. Donofry (Eastern Air
Lines) testified, at a congressional probe of air safety
violations, they had contributed to safety violations.

1.039   **Cooper, Cary L.** and Steven J. Sloan.   "Coping With Pi-
lot Stress: Resting at Home Compared With Resting
Away From Home." **Aviation, Space, and Environmetal
Medicine** 58 (December 1987):   1175-1182.

This research, whose purpose was to study mental
health, mood, independent variables, and demographic
details, was carried out with the aid of the British
Airline Pilots Association. A total of 272 British,
commercial airline pilots were studied. The Crown-
Crisp Experiential Index, Mood Adjective Checklist
(MAC), and Statistical Package for the Social Sci-
ences (SPSS) were major research instruments used. A
biographical data questionnaire was also administered.
Author biographical information. Abstract. 7 tables.
14 references.

1.040   **Cope, F.W.**   "Idiopathic Menstrual Disorders in Airline Stewardesses: A Possible Origin From Solar Radi-
ation of Heavy Magnetic Particles." **International
Journal of Biometeorology** 25, No. 3 (1981):   219-221.

The author is affiliated with the Biochemistry Laboratory, Naval Air Development Center, Warminster, Pennsylvania. Abstract. 22 references.

1.041   **Cotton, William B.**   "Air Safety: The View From the
Cockpit." **IEEE Spectrum** 12 (August 1975):   71-74.

An airline pilot talks about three generations of air
traffic control (ATC), focusing on the Upgraded Third
Generation Air Traffic Control System. The third
generation system was prompted by a midair collision
in the late 1950s. 1 photograph. Author biographical information.

1.042   **Crump, John H.**   "Review of Stress in Air Traffic Control: Its Measurement and Effects." **Aviation,
Space, and Environmental Medicine** 50 (March 1979):

243-248.

Stress in air traffic controllers (ATCs) is examined
with a view to physiological and biochemical stress
measurement; long-term effects of stress on health;
task performance and subjective rating as measures of
stress; psychological measurement of stress; and areas
for further research. Author biographical information.
Abstract. 64 references.

1.043 **Cummings, T.W.** and Robert White. **Freedom From Fear of
       Flying.** New York, NY: Pocket Books, 1987.

       Captain Truman W. Cummings retired from a thirty-year
       career with Pan American (Pan Am) World Airways in
       1977. While with Pan Am, Captain Cummings was based
       in New York, Hong Kong, and Miami. He established a
       series of seminars, "Freedom From Fear of Flying,"
       three years before he retired. These seminars are
       now his full-time occupation.

1.044 **Cutting, Windsor C. Guide to Drug Hazards in Aviation
       Medicine.** Washington, DC: U.S. Government Printing
       Office, 1962.

       This book (97 pages) is intended as a handbook for
       aviation medical examiners. It lists drugs, their
       toxic effects, and allowable use for aviation. The
       contents of the book are divided into thirty-three
       main sections. Examples of these are as follows: an-
       tifungal agents, antiprotozoal agents, anticancer
       agents, topical agents, cardiovascular agents; anti-
       convulsants, and tranquilizers. There is a separate
       index of individual drug names.

1.045 **Dark, S.J.** "Medically Disqualified Airline Pilots."
       Government Reports Announcements and Index 85 (April
       12, 1985): 55. NTIS AD-A149 454/1.

       After an examination of the medical records of 842
       airline pilots medically disqualified by the Federal
       Aviation Administration (FAA), it was learned that
       cardiovascular diseases were the most common reason
       for disqualification.

1.046 **Dark, Shirley J.** "Medically Disqualified Airline Pi-
       lots." **Government Reports Announcements and Index**
       87 (February 1, 1987): 115. NTIS AD-A173 244/5.

During 1983 and 1984, 33% of all airline pilots medically disqualified were disqualified for cardiovascular reasons.

1.047   **Desmarais, Jack.** "We're Heading for a Mid-Air Unless Sloppy Radio Work Stops." **Canadian Aviation** 53 (September 1980): 72-73.

Both air traffic controllers (ATCs) and pilots in Canada often use only numbers, rather than call signs and numbers, when communicating by radio. This is contrary to what is specified in the **ATC Manual of Operations.** The worst infractions of proper radio procedure occur in Toronto, Ontario and Calgary, Alberta. The danger in omitting a call sign, while communicating, is that there may be two aircraft with the same number, and these aircraft might incorrectly change altitude or otherwise alter their respective positions so that a midair collision occurs. Apparently, complete call signs are used in the U.S.—even in busy cities like New York and Miami, Florida.

1.048   **Dodds, R.L.** "Airline Pilot's Views on Medical Licensing Standards." **Aerospace Medicine** 44 (October 1973): 1183-1185.

The author, for his comments, draws on his experience as Chairman, Aeromedical Committee, Canadian Air Line Pilots Association (CALPA) and his experience as Chairman, Medical Study Group, International Federation of Air Line Pilots Associations (IFALPA). Author biographical information. Abstract.

1.049   **Doty, L.L.** "Quesada Says Laxness Indicated in FAA Aviation Safety Survey." **Aviation Week** 72 (January 18, 1960): 37-38.

The comments of E.R. Quesada, Chief, Federal Aviation Agency (FAA), when he testified before the Senate Aviation Subcommittee. The head of the subcommittee is Senator A.S. Mike Monroney. One example of laxness and even defiance, on the part of an airline pilot, took place on an American Airlines flight from Tulsa, Oklahoma to New York. The pilot, Captain Clyde H. Proper, refused to pay a $1000 fine levied against him for refusing to admit an FAA inspector to his flight deck. In another incident, an FAA inspector noted that an airline crew did not use the check list during the flight. The captain of the flight later told the inspector he did not use the check list regardless of whether or not an inspector was on board.

1.050   **Dougherty, John D.** "Cardiovascular Findings in Air
        Traffic Controllers." **Aerospace Medicine** 38 (January
        1967):   26-30.

        Approximately 1200 air traffic control specialists
        (ATCS) and approximately 800 non-ATCS were compared
        regarding hypertension and electrocardiographic (ECG)
        abnormality. Journeyman radar ATCS had more ECG ab-
        normality than ATCS. Also, journeyman radar ATCS had
        more hypertension than ATCS. ECG abnormality in radar
        journeyman ATCS was greater than in non-ATCS. Author
        biographical information. Abstract. 7 figures. 2
        tables. Acknowledgements. 12 references.

1.051   **Dougherty, John D.**, David K. Trites and J. Robert
        Dille. "Self-Reported Stress-Related Symptoms Among
        Air Traffic Control Specialists (ATCS) and Non-ATCS
        Personnel." **Aerospace Medicine** 36 (October 1965):
        956-960.

        Two groups of subjects were compared: air traffic
        control specialists (ATCS) and non-ATCS. Both groups
        were studied regarding the following: headaches, high
        blood pressure, indigestion, chest pains, tranquilizer
        use, and ulcers. It was learned that the further ATCS
        progress in their careers, the more unhealthy they per-
        ceive themselves to be relative to non-ATCS. It was al-
        so learned that symptom incidence is related to experi-
        ence rather than age. Author biographical information.
        Abstract. 8 tables. 3 figures. 2 references.

1.052   **Ehret, Charles F.** and Lynne Waller Scanlon. **Overcom-
        ing Jet Lag.** New York, NY: Berkley Books, 1983.

        The first author, Dr. Charles F. Ehret, is an expert
        in chronobiology, the study of internal biological
        rhythms. This book is about a three-step program used
        by the White House, U.S. Army Rapid Deployment Force,
        and other organizations and individuals. The program—
        no drugs are used—has been tested for thirty years by
        universities. It was used by President Reagan on his
        trip to China.

1.053   **Eng, Weylin G.** "Survey on Eye Comfort in Aircraft: I.
        Flight Attendants." **Aviation, Space, and Environmental
        Medicine** 50 (April 1979): 401-404.

        A study about the eye comfort of flight attendants was
        conducted with the aid of the Association of Flight At-
        tendants. A questionnaire was developed and adminis-
        tered to the attendants. Seven hundred and seventy-four

flight attendants responded. Ninety-five percent of
the respondents were female; 70% were between twenty-
six and thirty-three years of age. Smoke was a major
cause of eye discomfort to over 90% of all respondents.
Conjunctival redness was one of the most common eye
problems reported. Smoking was the most noticeable
factor that caused eye problems. Similar eye problems
were reported in wearers and nonwearers of contact
lenses. Author biographical information. Abstract.
1 table. 3 figures. Acknowledgements. 9 references.

1.054   **Englebardt, Stanley L.** "Lessons for Everybody From
Jet Travel Fatigue." **Science Digest** 59 (March 1966):
80-84.

Noise, vibration, smoking, temperature, and humidity
are factors in fatigue experienced by jet crews and
passengers. 1 illustration.

1.055   **Fay, Raymond C.** "Air Safety and the Older Airline Pilot." **Aging and Work** 1 (Summer 1978): 153-161.

The Federal Aviation Administration (FAA) prohibits
U.S. airline pilots from being pilots after age sixty.
The age sixty criterion was medically derived from
pre-1959 data representing the general male population—not a pilot population. There is medical evidence to indicate that how well a pilot performs pro-
fessionally is not necessarily based on chronological
age. A longitudinal medical history, certain medical
tests, and absence of risk factors can establish how
well a pilot will perform. No airline pilot over age
sixty has been allowed to pilot a commercial airliner,
even though allowing them to fly could be in the public interest. Author biographical information. Abstract.

1.056   **Feldman, Charles** and Mark Diamond. "The Newest Fear
of Flying: Ear Damage." **New York** 12 (January 8,
1979): 44-46.

There are changes in air pressure as an airplane as-
cends and descends, and these changes cause, annually,
over two million cases of pressure-related sinus and
ear disorders. One disorder, aerotitis, is a mild in-
flammation/infection of the middle ear. If a person
has a cold and travels by air, he is more likely to
get barotrauma of the ear and sinuses. Even meningi-
tis can result. The problem of blocked ears can be
alleviated by chewing gum, yawning, or taking a nasal

decongestant half an hour before the airplane descends.
If a person has an upper respiratory problem and drinks
wine—especially sherry or port—this aggravates his
problem because wine contains histamines which make the
wine act as a vasodilator. Author biographical information. 2 illustrations.

1.057   "Fighting Flight Fatigue." **Financial Post Magazine**
         (November 11, 1978): 10.

         Fasting, caffeine, sleep, protein, and carbohydrates
         are the key features of a program designed to fight jet
         lag. The program was created by Dr. Charles Ehret of
         Argonne Laboratories in Chicago, Illinois. 1 illustra-
         tion.

1.058   "Four Ways to Botch a Strike." **U.S. News and World
         Report** 91 (August 24, 1981): 14-15.

         PATCO (Professional Air Traffic Controllers Organiza-
         tion) made four strategic errors, when it went on
         strike in August 1981. For example, PATCO did not
         consult other unions. Furthermore, the strike did not
         bring commercial aviation to a standstill. PATCO
         should have been more aware of President Reagan's re-
         vulsion to strikes by federal employees. Endorsement
         by PATCO in 1980 of Reagan was not a guarantee that
         Reagan would be sympathetic to PATCO's aspirations.

1.059   **Gallagher, John.** "The Perfect Pilot." **Canadian Avi-
         ation** 55 (April 1982): 40-41.

         Extra sleep, good food, and abstinence from alcohol
         are likely to help prevent a pilot from being in an
         aircraft accident. 1 photograph.

1.060   **Gavaghan, Helen.** "Computers in Cockpits Breed Pilot
         Complacency." **New Scientist** 123 (August 26, 1989):
         33.

         Comments on a NASA (National Aeronautics and Space Ad-
         ministration) report on highly automated cockpits in
         aircraft, and how these cockpits can make pilots com-
         placent and compromise safety. The McDonnel Douglas
         MD-80 and Airbus Industrie A-310 are examples of air-
         craft which have highly automated cockpits. These
         aircraft each have a crew of two because electronic
         systems have replaced the flight engineer. Many pilots
         feel excessive automation diminishes flying skills. 1

photograph.

1.061   **Gilstrap, Roderic W.** "Medical Excellence and Airline
        Pilots." **American Journal of Cardiology** 36 (October
        31, 1975): 589-591.

        Roderic W. Gilstrap, First Vice President, Air Line
        Pilots Association (ALPA), focuses—in a conference
        address—on operational considerations in air safety,
        flexibility in application of medical standards, and a
        prevention program for the airline pilot. 1 reference.

1.062   **Girodo, Michel.** "The Psychological Health and Stress
        of Pilots in a Labor Dispute." **Aviation, Space, and
        Environmental Medicine** 59 (June 1988): 505-510.

        Interviews and three research instruments—Eysenck Per-
        sonality Questionnaire (EPQ), Health Opinion Survey
        (HOS), and Symptom Check-List 90 (SCL-90)—were used in
        this study. Emotionality, extraversion, and toughmind-
        edness were compared in pilots, engineers, managers,
        and other controls. One-quarter of the pilots had ele-
        vated symptoms of anger-hostility, obsessive-compulsive-
        ness, and other indicators of psychopathology. Author
        biographical information. Abstract. 1 table. 3 fig-
        ures. 11 references.

1.063   **Gram, Dewey.** "The Bear Pit." **Newsweek** 86 (August 4,
        1975): 9.

        Stress, anxiety, and gastric ailments are common among
        air traffic controllers (ATCs). At O'Hare Internation-
        al Airport in Chicago, Illinois, the busiest airport in
        the world, two planes collided on December 20, 1972.
        Ten people died and the controller who made the error,
        which caused the accident, was under psychiatric care
        almost three years later. Nevertheless, controllers
        love their work. The average annual salary is $24,000.
        1 photograph.

1.064   **Green, R.L.** "Peptic Ulcer in Airline Stewards."
        Aerospace Medicine 4C (August 1969): 890-893.

        The Air Corporations Joint Medical Service is the med-
        ical service for both BOAC (British Overseas Airways
        Corporation) and BEA (British European Airways). BOAC
        is a long-haul airline and BEA a short-haul airline.
        Morbidity from peptic ulcer was investigated in air-
        line stewards employed by both airlines. Medical

records were examined for the years 1959-1967. Thirty-one stewards (twenty-eight BOAC and three BEA) had
ulcers. This was from a mean annual population of
1313. The peptic ulcers could not be attributed to
the occupation of airline steward. Although the eat-
ing and resting habits of stewards are disrupted—especially on long-haul flights—the members of this occupation are not unduly susceptible to peptic ulcer.
Author biographical information. Abstract. 2 tables.
1 figure. 8 references.

1.065   **Green, Roger L.**   "Cardiovascular Disease in Airline
         Stewards." **Aerospace Medicine** 40 (November 1969):
         1264-1266.

         The medical records, covering the time period 1959-
         1967, of BEA (British European Airways) and BOAC
         (British Overseas Airways Corporation), were studied.
         The mean population of these individuals numbered
         over 1300. When stewards were compared to civilian
         pilots and the general population, no evidence was
         discovered to indicate stewards were predisposed to
         heart disease. However, stewards had lower rates of
         heart disease than did pilots. There was a high rate
         of acute ischemia for stewards who were overseas. Au-
         thor biographical information. Abstract. 2 figures.
         2 tables. 6 references.

1.066   **Grose, Vernon L.**   "Coping With Boredom in the Cock-
         pit Before It's Too Late." **Professional Safety** 34
         (July 1989):   24-26.

         Boredom and work, risks and boring work, and anti-
         dotes for boredom. Author biographical information.

1.067   **Harper, C.R.** and G.J. Kidera. "Hypoglycemia in Air-
         line Pilots." **Aerospace Medicine** 44 (July 1973):
         769-771.

         The reader's attention is drawn to the physiology of
         hypoglycemia and the incidence of chemical and clin-
         ical hypoglycemia in 175 airline pilots over a time
         period of three years. Two cases are presented.
         This paper was read at the Twentieth International
         Congress of Aviation and Space Medicine, Nice, France,
         September 18-21, 1972. Author biographical informa-
         tion. Abstract. 2 tables. 20 references.

1.068   **Higgins, E.A.,** M.T. Lategola and C.E. Melton.

"Development of the Aviation Stress Protocol-Simulation and Performance, Physiological, and Biochemical
Monitoring Systems: Phase I. Assessment of Cardiovascular Function After Exposure to the Aviation
Stress Protocol-Simulation. The Relationship Between
StressoRelated Metabolites and Disqualifying Pathology in Air Traffic Control Personnel." **Government
Reports Announcements and Index** 78 (June 23, 1978):
70-71. NTIS AD-A051 690/6.

Internal body temperature, blood glucose, blood drug
level, and alcohol level were variables studied by
the authors, who are affiliated with the Federal Aviation Administration (FAA).

1.069   **Hochschild, Arlie.** "Emotional Labor in the Friendly
Skies." **Psychology Today** 16 (June 1982): 13-15.

Qualities airlines look for in prospective flight attendants, the types of passengers flight attendants
deal with, and the emotional costs of being a flight
attendant are discussed. Pan Am, Delta, United, and
Pacific Southwest Airlines (PSA) are also discussed.
1 illustration. Author biographical information.

1.070   **Hoffman, David H.** "Pilots Take Firm Stand on Safety
Margins." **Aviation Week and Space Technology** 75 (November 6, 1961): 105, 107 and 109.

Reports on the Air Line Pilots Association (ALPA) an-
nual safety forum held in Chicago, Illinois. Harry
Clark (Trans World Airlines), Sam Saint (American
Airlines), B.V. Hewes (Delta), and E.R. Watson
(Eastern Air Lines) were four of the speakers at the
three-day session. Noise abatement, air traffic,
fires, and pilot training were some of the topics
discussed. Jerome Lederer, Director, Flight Safety
Foundation, gave a progress report on Project SCAN
(System for the Collection and Analysis of Near-Miss
Reports).

1.071   **Holt, Geoffrey W.,** William F. Taylor and Earl T.
Carter. "Airline Pilot Disability: The Continued
Experience of a Major U.S. Airline." **Aviation,
Space, and Environmental Medicine** 56 (October 1985):
939-944.

Between January 1, 1975 and December 31, 1982, 368
airline pilot applicants were screened. Seventy-
three pilot applicants were rejected because of medical reasons. Forty-five of these were rejected

because of psychological reasons. After the age of
forty-five, over half of medical losses were due to
cardiovascular disease. This research was carried out
at the Mayo Clinic in Rochester, Minnesota. Author
biographical information. Abstract. 4 tables. 2
figures. 14 references.

1.072   **Holt, Geoffrey W.,** William F. Taylor and Earl T.
         Carter. "Airline Pilot Medical Disability: A Compar-
         ison Between Three Airlines With Different Approaches
         to Medical Monitoring." **Aviation, Space, and Environ-
         mental Medicine** 58 (August 1987): 788-791.

         Three major U.S. airlines, with distinctly different
         medical programs, were researched. Approximately
         12,800 pilots, representing approximately 79,800 per-
         son-years of experience, were studied. After pilots
         reached age forty-five, medical losses increased rap-
         idly in all the airlines researched. Half the losses
         were attributed to cardiovascular disease. Airlines
         with medical departments have lower pilot medical dis-
         ability rates than airlines without these departments.
         Author biographical information. Abstract. 2 tables.
         2 figures. 5 references.

1.073   **Humphries, S.V.** "Jet Lag." **Central African Journal
         of Medicine** 27 (June 1981): 122-123.

         Diminished alertness, insomnia, and irritability are
         symptoms of jet lag. These symptoms are less promi-
         nent when a person travels north or south than when he
         travels east or west. Fatigue is caused by crossing
         time zones. Circadian rhythm—a term introduced in
         1959—is disturbed when time zones are crossed. Min-
         imizing rich food and alcohol can help reduce jet
         lag. 3 references.

1.074   **Hutto, Gary L.,** Roger C. Smith and Richard I. Thack-
         ray. "Methodology in the Assessment of Stress Among
         Air Traffic Control Specialists (ATCS): Normative
         Adult Data for the State-Trait Anxiety Inventory From
         Non-ATCS Populations." **Government Reports Announce-
         ments and Index** 81 (December 18, 1981): 5484. NTIS
         AD-A103 192/1.

         This study, like the one by R.C. Smith (1980), indi-
         cates there is little evidence air traffic control
         specialists (ATCS) perform unusually stressful work.

1.075   "IFATCA Condemns Bilcom as 'Backward.'" **Canadian Aviation** 50 (July 1977):   23.

Has the text of a telegram to Canadian Prime Minister Pierre Trudeau from IFATCA (International Federation of Air Traffic Controllers Associations). The telegram protests bilingual air traffic control (ATC). A six-point IFATCA policy statement is also included.

1.076   **Iglesias, R.,** A. Terrés and A. Chavarria. "Disorders of the Menstrual Cycle in Airline Stewardesses." **Aviation, Space, and Environmental Medicine** 51 (May 1980): 518-520.

The subjects in this study, which was done in Mexico, were 200 Mexicana Airline stewardesses. Hyperpolymenorrhea was present in 20% of the stewardesses on active duty, dysmenorrhea in 17%, complete irregularity in the menstrual cycle in 16%, and hypoolygomenorrhea in 9%. There was no evidence of problems in 38% of the stewardesses. There was an increase, during flight, in the menstrual discharge of 28% of the stewardesses and a decrease in 20%. There was no change in 52%. There are five main factors which may contribute to the health problems of working stewardesses: physical (for example, noise or vibration); chemical (fog, hypoxia, fumes), biological (fungi as one example), psychosocial (crowded working conditions); and operational (strict punctuality). Author biographical information. Abstract. 4 tables. 8 references.

1.077   **Jasinski, Doris R.** "Some Health Problems of Women Flight Attendants in the Pacific." **Hawaii Medical Journal** 39 (February 1980):   39-42.

The author, who has a general practice near the University of Hawaii campus, had as patients twenty-one female flight attendants between 1973 and 1977. The women were between twenty-five and thirty-two years of age and most were employed by Pan American (Pan Am). Respiratory tract and genitourinary problems were the most frequent conditions noted by the author. Skin and gastrointestinal complaints were next in order of frequency. One flight attendant quit flying because she was afraid to fly. A version of this paper was presented at the Twenty-fifth International Congress of Aviation and Space Medicine, Helsinki, Finland, September 1977. Author biographical information. Abstract. 14 tables.

1.078   "Jet Travel and Body Clocks." **Scientific American**

214 (February 1966):   53-54.

The Federal Aviation Agency (FAA) has conducted experiments with the aid of volunteer male subjects. The
subjects travelled by air from the U.S. to such cities
as Tokyo, Japan and Rome, Italy. A control group flew
from Washington, DC to Santiago, Chile. Both these
cities are in the same time zone. Although those individuals on the Washington-to-Chile flight became tired,
those who flew to Tokyo and Rome, passing through a
number of time zones, experienced disturbed body and
mental functions for several days. This research has
implications for crew scheduling for certain international flights.

1.079   **Johnson, Geoff.**   "Controllers' 'Sleep Paralysis' Sub-
         ject of IFATCA Research." **Canadian Aviation** 61 (Feb-
         ruary 1988):   15.

         Certain people—nurses, police dispatchers, air traf-
         fic controllers (ATCs)—who work at night sometimes
         experience sleep paralysis or night shift paralysis.
         These individuals cannot move or speak for up to five
         minutes. Then the person suddenly recovers. The ex-
         perience is not an emotional response and there are no
         hallucinations. Sleep paralysis or night shift paral-
         ysis occurs when a person is struggling to remain
         awake. This condition occurs between 2:00 a.m. and
         5:00 a.m. 90% of the time. Sometimes it occurs during
         the day. The International Federation of Air Traffic
         Control Associations (IFATCA) and Sussex University
         are investigating this phenomenon. To date no air-
         craft accidents have been associated with sleep paral-
         ysis.

1.080   **Johnson, Terry E.** and Vern E. Smith.   "What's Wrong
         With Delta?" **Newsweek** 110 (July 27, 1987):   25.

         Delta Air Lines was involved in a series of unfortu-
         nate incidents during the summer of 1987. The worst
         incident occurred on July 8 over the Atlantic Ocean.
         A Delta jumbo jet came within one hundred feet of
         colliding with a Continental Airlines jet. The Delta
         aircraft was sixty miles off course. In late June,
         the pilot of another Delta jet accidentally shut off
         the engines over the Pacific. In a third incident,
         a Delta plane landed at Frankfort, Kentucky instead
         of at Lexington, Kentucky. In yet another incident—
         this one in Boston, Massachusetts—a Delta flight
         took off without authorization, almost colliding
         with a USAir Boeing 737. Also in Boston, a Delta
         jet landed on the wrong runway. 2 photographs.

1.081 **Jönsson, F.** and N. Sundgren. "Essential Hypertension in Airline Pilots." **Aerospace Medicine** 40 (January 1969): 70-75.

In this research the authors, who are with the Scandinavian Airlines System, report on eight cases of flight personnel treated for essential hypertension with Thiazide. Abstract. 4 tables. 1 figure. 8 case reports. 33 references.

1.082 **Karson, Samuel** and Jerry W. O'Dell. "Personality Makeup of the American Air Traffic Controller." **Aerospace Medicine** 45 (September 1974): 1001-1007.

In this study of over eleven thousand air traffic controllers (ATCs) and approximately 9900 applicants for air traffic control (ATC) positions, it was learned the controllers exhibited superior intelligence and attention to detail. They had the ability to be practical and free from anxiety. These controllers were not subject to flights of fancy and did not have artistic interests. Many of the applicants for controller positions were more intelligent, more practical, and more emotionally stable than the controllers. Many of the applicants had military backgrounds. The Sixteen Personality Factor Questionnaire was used in this study. Author biographical information. Abstract. 9 tables. 1 figure. 13 references.

1.083 **Kavanagh, Michael J.**, Michael W. Hurst and Robert Rose. "The Relationship Between Job Satisfaction and Psychiatric Health Symptoms for Air Traffic Controllers." **Personnel Psychology** 34 (Winter 1981): 691-707.

The subjects in this investigation were 416 air traffic controllers (ATCs), representing eight air traffic facilities in the U.S. The mean age of the subjects, all of whom were males, was 36.2 years. Average experience as ATCs was 11.2 years. Subscales of the Job Description Index (JDI), California Psychological Inventory (CPI), and the Psychiatric Status Schedule (PSS) interview were used. Author biographical information. Abstract. 4 tables. 4 reference notes. 34 references.

1.084 **Kidera, George J.** and Paul B. Gaskill. "Hearing Threshold Sensitivity in Airline Pilots." **Aerospace Medicine** 45 (July 1974): 780-781.

Over 1400 pilots employed by United Air Lines (UAL)

were administered audiograms. Results were compared
to the results of a nonpilot population group. Hearing sensitivity changes, associated with aging, were
quite similar for both groups. The results of this
study were presented at the Second International Meeting on Aerospace Medicine, Melbourne, Australia, October 30-November 2, 1972. Author biographical information. Abstract. 2 tables. 4 figures. 4 references.

1.085   **King, John K.**   "Air Safety as Seen From the Tower."
IEEE Spectrum 12 (August 1975):   67-71.

A former air traffic controller (ATC) states why air
traffic control (ATC) is changing from an accident-
preventing to an accident-causing system. He attrib-
utes the change, in part, to the following: environ-
mentalists (their call for power reduction during
takeoffs); vertical obstructions (tall buildings that
penetrate safe flight altitudes); aviation industry
compromise which favors profits rather than safety);
PATCO (Professional Air Traffic Controllers Organization); and ALPA (Air Line Pilots Association).   1
photograph.   Author biographical information.

1.086   **Kominsky, John R.,** Eric Jannerfeldt and Charles A.
Herron.   "Red Spots Among Flight Attendants: Obser-
vation—A Valuable Investigative Tool."   **American Industrial Hygiene Association Journal** 42 (April 1981):
323-324.

During January, February, and March 1980, red spots
appeared on the skin of Eastern Airlines flight attendants.   Virtually every case occurred on flights
between New York and Miami, and virtually every case
occurred on a single type of airplane.   Burning,
nausea, and headache were associated with some cases.
In most cases, however, the spots could be wiped or
washed off.   By examining the work practices of
flight attendants, it was learned that the spots
were caused by red ink, which flaked off life vests
during flight attendant preflight safety instructions.
After the vests were removed from all Eastern Airlines
aircraft, no further cases of flight attendants with
red spots were reported.   Author biographical information.   Abstract.   Acknowledgements.   3 references.

1.087   **Landsbergis, Paul.**   "Is Air Traffic Control a Stressful Occupation?"   **Labor Studies Journal** 11 (Fall
1986):   117-134.

Early research, FAA (Federal Aviation Administration)

research, 1977 NIOSH (National Institute of Occupational Safety and Health) health hazard evaluation,
FAA medical record reviews, models of job stress, economic research, Boston University health change study,
Jones Task Force Report, and current developments are
examined. Author biographical information. 71 footnotes.

1.088   **Lane, J.C.**   "Risk of In-Flight Incapacitation of Airline Pilots." **Aerospace Medicine** 42 (December 1971):
1319-1321.

Research indicates the following are causes of in-
flight incapacitation of airline pilots: uncontrolla-
ble bowel action, other gastrointestinal symptoms, ear-
ache, faintness, headache (including migraine), and
vertigo/disorientation. Author biographical information. Abstract. 1 figure. 4 tables. Acknowledgement. 7 references.

1.089   **Lategola, Michael T.**   "Changes in Cardiovascular
Health Parameters Over an Eight-Year Interval in an
ATC Population Segment." **Government Reports Announce-
ments and Index** 71 (November 10, 1971):   53.

Air traffic control (ATC) students were studied between 1960 and 1963 by the Civil Aeromedical Research
Institute (CARI). Approximately five hundred of
these individuals were studied again in 1970. Research
results indicated a susceptibility to coronary heart
disease (CHD) in the subjects of advanced age and who
were obese.

1.090   **Lavernhe, J.,** C. Blanc and J. Pasquet. "Statistical
Data on Grounding of Crew Members in an Airline Due to
Psychic Disorders." **Aerospace Medicine** 40 (August
1969):   894-895.

Between 1961 and 1968, thirty-nine Air France flight
crew members were permanently grounded for psychiatric
reasons. During the same time period, thirty members
were permanently grounded for cardiovascular illness.
The lowest incidence of psychiatric illness was in pilots, the highest in stewardesses. Author biographical information. Abstract. 3 tables. 10 references.

1.091   **Lavernhe, J.,** J. Pasquet and A. Mathivat. "Incidence
of Cardiovascular Diseases Among the Flight Deck Personnel of an Airline." **Aerospace Medicine** 40 (January

1969): 62-63.

The study population for this research consisted of
1250 Air France flight deck personnel. Sixty-four subjects gave up flying for health reasons between 1962
and 1967. Cardiovascular diseases (twenty-two cases)
were the most frequent medical reason for permanent
grounding of personnel. Psychiatric illnesses (eleven
cases) were the second most common reason. Diabetes
mellitus (five cases) was the fourth most frequent reason. Author biographical information. Abstract. 2
tables. 9 references.

1.092   "Legislators See Photos of Alleged Pilot Laxity; De-
mand Crackdown." **Aviation Week and Space Technology**
77 (September 24, 1962): 47.

D.K. Carson and William J. Miller are flight engineers
who took photographs of air crew safety violations.
Carson took the pictures in-flight between mid-1959
and mid-1961. Eastern Air Lines pilots were shown,
in the photographs, asleep or reading newspapers.
Both the Federal Aviation Agency (FAA) and Civil Aeronautics Board (CAB) were warned by Congress to improve
air crew safety standards. Carson (Eastern Air Lines)
and Miller (Trans World Airlines) complained to their
respective employers about safety, but their complaints
were ignored. Both Carson and Miller received threats,
after the existence of the photographs became known
throughout the airline industry.

1.093   **Leighton-White, R.C.**   "Airline Pilot Incapacitation in
Flight." **Aerospace Medicine** 43 (June 1972): 661-664.

The reader's attention is drawn to airline pilot incapacitation in flight with respect to: definition,
causes and effects, detection, reducing the incidence,
and dealing with incapacitation. Author biographical
information. Abstract. Acknowledgement. 6 references.

1.094   **Lowther, William.**   "Debating U.S. Air Safety."
Maclean's 97 (February 13, 1984): 8-9.

A week after members of PATCO (Professional Air Traffic Controllers Organization) illegally walked off
the job, 11,400 of them were fired by President Reagan.
The strike took place on August 3, 1981 and most of the
controllers refused to return to work. Before the
strike, the average salary of the controllers was $33,
000 a year. The union wanted shorter hours and a

$10,000-a-year raise. Controllers were said to be suf-
fering from fatigue, stress, tension. There are presently in the U.S. 85,000 flights a day. The number of
near-misses dropped from 342 in 1981 to 248 in 1983.

1.095   **MacBride, Arlene,** William Lancee and Stanley J.J.
        Freeman. "The Psychosocial Impact of a Labour Dis-
        pute." **Journal of Occupational Psychology** 54 (June
        1981): 125-133.

        There was a labor dispute in Canada in 1976 which con-
        cerned air traffic controllers (ATCs) and the implemen-
        tation of bilingual air communication in parts of Can-
        ada. The authors investigated psychological and phys-
        ical measures, including the use, by controllers, of
        medical services. Research results were reported in
        terms of: distribution of General Health Questionnaire
        (GHQ) scores during the labor dispute and during rou-
        tine operations for controllers who completed all
        three GHQs; perceived general functioning, health, and
        anxiety during the labor dispute and during routine
        operations; and mean ratings of factors which contri-
        buted to job stress during the contract dispute and
        during routine operations. Author biographical infor-
        mation. Abstract. 3 tables. 30 references.

1.096   **MacKenzie, Janet** and Julianne Lebreche. "English Only
        Spoken Here—With Near-Calamitous Results." **Maclean's**
        89 (July 1976): 19.

        Advantages and disadvantages of using both English and
        French, in air traffic control (ATC), at Dorval Air-
        port in Montreal, Quebec. 1 photograph.

1.097   **Martindale, David.** "Sweaty Palms in the Control Tow-
        er." **Psychology Today** 10 (February 1977): 70-72 and
        75.

        Chicago's O'Hare Airport, known as the "ulcer factory,"
        has 1900 flights a day and controllers have to direct
        at least a dozen aircraft at one time. In 1976 at
        least seven controllers were victims of acute hyper-
        tension. Ulcers, colitis, headaches, and high blood
        pressure are common among most of the controllers.
        Alcoholism, depression, and acute anxiety are also
        common. In 1975 about 100,000 passengers passed
        through O'Hare every day. An aircraft takes off from
        or lands at O'Hare every twenty seconds during peak
        hours. Because of stress, most controllers do not
        last five years. It was learned from a 1973 study,
        by Sidney Cobb and Robert Rose, that hypertension was

four times as common in controllers as it was in pilots. E. Elliot Benezra is a psychiatrist who has
treated numerous controllers in the Chicago area.
Benezra believes a crisis-intervention program can
help the controllers. Author biographical information. 3 illustrations. 1 photograph. 4 references.

1.098   **Martindale, David.** "Torment in the Tower." **Chicago**
         25 (April 1976): 96-101.

There is a constant pace at O'Hare International Airport in Chicago, Illinois. The runways—two for take
off, two for landing—are seldom empty. Up to forty
planes wait for take off at the same time. Up to fifty planes, flying above O'Hare, await permission to
land. There are about 135 arrivals and departures an
hour. The average age of the O'Hare air traffic controller (ATC) is twenty-six. Most have worked at
O'Hare for about five years. Their average salary is
about $24,000 annually. Challenge is the main incen-
tive for a controller transferring to O'Hare, where
there are from two to three near-misses every day. 5
photographs.

1.099   **Maxwell, Victor B.** "Hysterical Deafness: An Unusual
         Presentation of Stress in an Air Traffic Control Of-
         ficer." **Aviation, Space, and Environmental Medicine**
         57 (March 1986): 263-266.

Marital problems were associated with hysterical deafness in a forty-three-year-old, male air traffic controller (ATC) in England. Author biographical information. Abstract. 3 figures. Acknowledgements. 4
references.

1.100   **Maxwell, Victor B.,** John H. Crump and Jeff Thorp.
         "The Measurement of Risk Indicators for Coronary
         Heart Disease in Air Traffic Control Officers: A
         Screening Study in a Healthy Population." **Aviation,
         Space, and Environmental Medicine** 54 (March 1983):
         246-249.

Research results are discussed in terms of: statistical differences between air traffic control officers (ATCOs) and a reference group; risk score of
ATCOs, risk score of matched controls, and the ratio
between the two; and statistically significant differences between coronary heart disease (CHD) risk
indicators in the low risk and high risk groups. Author biographical information. Abstract. 3 tables.
1 figure. 30 references.

1.101   "McArtor Orders Industry-Wide Assessment of Pilot
        Training." **Aviation Week and Space Technology** 127
        (August 24, 1987): 20-21.

        Allan McArtor, new head of the Federal Aviation Ad-
        ministration (FAA), wants an industry-wide assess-
        ment of pilot training at U.S. airlines. McArtor, a
        decorated veteran, flew combat missions in Vietnam.
        McArtor cites increased traffic, mergers, the set-
        ting of wrong navigational coordinates, and the land-
        ing of aircraft at a wrong runway as areas of con-
        cern.

1.102   **Meadows, Edward.**   "The FAA Keeps Them Flying." **For-
        tune** 104 (December 28, 1981):   48-52.

        The U.S. air traffic control (ATC) system may be more
        efficient and more safe now than before the PATCO
        (Professional Air Traffic Controllers Organization)
        strike. One reason is that 22,000 flights a day are
        flying from the twenty-two largest airports. This is
        4000 fewer than before the strike. Another reason is
        that a controller monitors 15% fewer aircraft, at any
        one time, than before the strike. Furthermore, planes
        are required to stay apart six times the distance
        than prior to the August controller walkout. 3 photo-
        graphs.

1.103   **Melton, C.E.,** J.M. McKenzie, S.M. Wicks and J.T. Sal-
        divar. "Stress in Air Traffic Controllers: A Re-
        study of 32 Controllers 5 to 9 Years Later." **Govern-
        ment Reports Announcements and Index** 79 (July 20,
        1979): 54. NTIS AD-A065 767/6.

        Five to nine years after a group of controllers were
        originally studied, eight of the thirty-two subjects
        had noncontroller jobs. There was less stress in the
        twenty-four controllers who remained controllers than
        in the eight subjects who no longer did ATC work.
        More work experience and an improved ATC system are
        two possible explanations for less stress in the con-
        trollers.

1.104   **Melton, C.E.,** R.C. Smith, J.M. McKenzie, S.M. Hoff-
        man and J.T. Saldivar. "Stress in Air Traffic Con-
        trollers: Effects of ARTS-III." **Government Reports
        Announcements and Index** 77 (April 1, 1977): 2. NTIS
        AD-A034 752/6.

        This research investigated stress in air traffic con-
        trollers (ATCs) at Los Angeles and Oakland, Califor-
        nia before and after the installation of Automated

Radar Terminal Systems-III (ARTS-III). Physiological,
biochemical, and psychological measures of stress were
made. The State-Trait Anxiety Inventory was used.

1.105 **Melton, C.E.**, R.C. Smith, J.M. McKenzie, J.T. Saldivar
and S.M. Hoffmann. "Stress in Air Traffic Controllers:
Comparison of Two Air Route Traffic Control Centers on
Different Shift Rotation Patterns." **Government Reports
Announcements and Index** 76 (April 16, 1976): 30-31.
NTIS AD-A020 679/7.

Air traffic controllers (ATCs) at the Atlanta Air Route
Traffic Control Center, and an equal number of ATCs at
the Fort Worth Air Route Traffic Control Center, were
the subjects in this study. Stress estimates were
made on the basis of urine analysis.

1.106 **Melton, C.E.**, R.C. Smith, J.M. McKenzie, S.M. Wicks and
J.T. Saldivar. "Stress in Air Traffic Personnel: Low
Density Towers and Flight Service Stations." **Government Reports Announcements and Index** 78 (February 3,
1978): 30. NTIS AD-A046 826/4.

The popular press tends to view all air traffic control (ATC) work as unusually stressful. This is because the popular press focuses on the exceptional controller or facility—not the typical. These conclu-
sions are based on research at Fayetteville, Arkansas;
Roswell, New Mexico; and Oklahoma City, Oklahoma. Ten
air traffic control specialists (ATCSs) and twenty-
four flight service (FS) specialists participated in
the research.

1.107 **Mohler, Stanley R.** "Aging and Pilot Performance."
Geriatrics 16 (February 1961): 82-88.

A paper presented at the Seventh Annual Postgraduate
Course in Aviation Medicine, Ohio State University,
Columbus, Ohio, September 12-16, 1960. Author bio-
graphical information. Abstract. 19 references.

1.108 **Mohler, Stanley R.** "The Human Element in Air Traffic
Control: Aeromedical Aspects, Problems, and Prescriptions." **Aviation, Space, and Environmental Medicine**
54 (June 1983): 511-516.

This paper was presented at the Fifty-third Annual
Scientific Meeting, Aerospace Medical Association,
Bal Harbor, Florida, May 10-13, 1982. Author bio-
graphical information. Abstract. 2 figures. 33

references.

1.109 **Molinari, Guy V.** "How Safe Is the Air Traffic Con-
       trol System?" **USA Today** (Magazine) 116 (November
       1987): 12-14.

       Representative Guy V. Molinari (Republican-New York)
       advocates legislation to rehire certain air traffic
       controllers (ATCs) fired by President Reagan in
       1981. 1 photograph.

1.110 **Morganthau, Tom.** "The Controllers' Heavy Burden."
       Newsweek 103 (January 30, 1984): 31.

       Congress has approved the expenditure of $11 billion
       to $14 billion to modernize the air traffic control
       (ATC) system. More than half of FAA (Federal Avia-
       tion Administration) controllers have been controllers
       less than three years. During the past two and a
       half years, no commercial airline disasters in the U.S.
       were attributable to controller error. 1 photograph.

1.111 **Nagy, David.** "How Safe Are Our Airways?" **U.S. News
       and World Report** 91 (August 24, 1981): 14-17.

       U.S. airways appear to be safe, even though 12,000 air
       traffic controllers (ATCs) lost their jobs because
       they defied federal legislation. Rich Carter is a
       Continental Airlines pilot who believes it is safer
       to fly now than before the strike. Three-quarters as
       many planes are flying now. They are spaced farther
       apart in distance and time. Workers from smaller
       airport towers are being moved to major terminals,
       and the smaller towers are being shut down. Two
       thousand four hundred controller-supervisors are
       performing duties previously performed by the fired
       controllers. About one thousand military controllers
       are assisting commercial tower staff. The FAA (Fed-
       eral Aviation Administration) Academy in Oklahoma
       City, Oklahoma might triple its student enrollment by
       operating twenty-four hours a day. It would then
       graduate 4500 controllers annually rather than 1500.
       2 photographs. 1 illustration.

1.112 **Nather, David.** "Have One for the Runway." **Washing-
       ton Monthly** 21 (April 1989): 12-14 and 16.

       After six years of court battles, Northwest Airlines
       rehired one of its former pilots, Larry W. Morrison.

Morrison was fired because he had had too much to
drink in Las Vegas, Nevada in 1982. His blood alcohol
level was 0.13%. Northwest does not allow a pilot to
fly within twenty-four hours of having had a drink.
Morrison had consumed vodka less than four hours before he flew from Las Vegas to San Francisco, California. There were seventy-three passengers and six crew
members aboard the Boeing 727 which landed in San
Francisco. Eastern and United are examples of airlines which test flight crews for prescription tran-
quilizers and sedatives. Captain Edward M. Connors
was in command of Delta Flight 191 which crashed at
Dallas-Fort Worth International Airport on August 2,
1985. It was learned later that, for three years pri-
or to the crash, Connors had over a dozen prescriptions
filled for Stelazine, a powerful tranquilizer. Author
biographical information.

1.113   "New FAA Rules Require Crewmembers to Undergo Alcohol
        Tests on Request." **Aviation Week and Space Technology**
        124 (January 27, 1986): 41.

        On April 9, 1986, pilots, flight engineers, and cabin
        attendants will have to submit to a blood alcohol
        test, if requested to do so by police officers con-
        ducting an investigation. Refusal to submit to a test
        will result in suspension or loss of airmen certifi-
        cates or ratings. The previous Federal Aviation Ad-
        ministration (FAA) standard, prohibiting consumption
        of alcohol within eight hours of a flight, will re-
        main in effect. The standard which will determine if
        an air crewmember is under the influence of alcohol is
        a blood alcohol standard of 0.04% or more by weight.
        The FAA has also taken action regarding in-flight med-
        ical emergencies by requiring the installation, at one
        hundred dollars per unit, of emergency medical kits
        aboard 2300 U.S. aircraft. The kits, which have to be
        installed by August 1, 1986, will contain medication
        for treating individuals who have a heart attack,
        acute allergic reaction, or other serious medical con-
        ditions.

1.114   **Nicholson, Anthony N.** "Sleep and Wakefulness of the
        Airline Pilot." **Aviation, Space, and Environmental
        Medicine** 58 (May 1987): 395-401.

        This Stewart Memorial Lecture was presented at the
        Royal Aeronautical Society on February 11, 1986. The
        lecture focused, in part, on flight deck workload,
        short periods of sleep, circadian desynchrony, and
        two-crew operations. Author biographical information.
        Abstract. 11 figures. Acknowledgements. 18 refer-
        ences.

1.115 **Nicholson, Anthony N.** "Sleep Patterns of an Airline
       Pilot Operating World-Wide East-West Routes." **Aero-
       space Medicine** 41 (June 1970): 626-632.

       A British study in which the subject, a pilot with
       BOAC (British Overseas Airways Corporation), was ob-
       served over eighteen months. Author biographical in-
       formation. Abstract. 7 figures. Acknowledgements.
       21 references.

1.116 **Nieuwoudt, N.J.** "Editorial: The South African Aero-
       space Medical Society." **South African Medical Jour-
       nal** 52 (July 20, 1977): 137.

       An editorial about the Twenty-fourth International
       Congress of the International Academy of Aviation and
       Space Medicine, which was held in Johannesburg, South
       Africa, October 24-29, 1976. Over 300 delegates from
       thirty countries attended, over fifty papers were
       read, and two symposia were held. Some of the papers
       presented at the congress follow the editorial and
       are on pages 139-159. The Opening Address by Prime
       Minister B.J. Vorster is on page 138. Some of the
       authors of papers: Earl T. Carter (Mayo Clinic), Leo
       Schamroth (University of the Witwatersrand), Milton
       H. Gordon (Ben Gurion International Airport), R.B.
       MacLaren (British Airways Medical Service), J.P.
       Boissin (Air France), Henry J. Landry (Air Canada),
       and H. Vogel (University of Mainz).

1.117 **Nordwall, Bruce D.** "Norden Develops System to Warn
       Controllers of Runway Incursions." **Aviation Week and
       Space Technology** 130 (May 29, 1989): 28.

       RIM (Runway Incursion Management) is a system that
       manages the movement of aircraft and vehicles at air-
       ports. Developed by Norden Systems, Inc., RIM can
       warn controllers of potential conflicts. RIM can
       predict and give visual and aural warnings of hazard-
       ous situations. If RIM had existed in 1977, RIM
       might have prevented the deaths of 580 persons at
       Tenerife, Canary Islands, when two 747s collided on
       a runway. RIM can be used with the ASDE-3 high-res-
       olution ground-mapping radar system, also developed
       by Norden. The ASDE-3 system can be very useful
       when visibility is greatly restricted.

1.118 "Northwest Crew to Contest Revocation of Pilots' Li-
       censes." **Aviation Week and Space Technology** 132
       (March 26, 1990): 83.

       FAA (Federal Aviation Administration) Safety Inspector

Douglas R. Solseth arrested the crew of a Northwest
Airlines 727 in Minneapolis, Minnesota on March 8,
1990. The arrest was prompted by an anonymous tip the
crew was drunk. They tested above the legal limit for
alcohol and their licenses were revoked. Robert Kirch-
ner, Norman Prouse, and Joseph Balzer were the crew.
A hearing before the NTSB (National Transportation
Safety Board) is the first route of appeal.

1.119   "Now Air Controllers Are in the Hot Seat." **U.S. News
        and World Report** 99 (October 14, 1985): 53.

        The 14,000 air traffic controllers (ATCs) in the U.S.
        are overworked, overstressed, and poorly supervised.
        The number of runway incursions attributed to control-
        lers rose from forty-one during a six-month period in
        1984 to fifty-four during the same six-month period
        in 1985. A controller has been blamed for the aborted
        take-off of an Eastern jet at Washington's National
        Airport on September 24, 1985. The jet almost colli-
        ded with a helicopter.

1.120   "NTSB Mounts Special Probe of Controller Errors at
        O'Hare." **Aviation Week and Space Technology** 128
        (June 13, 1988): 149.

        The National Transportation Safety Board (NTSB) is in-
        vestigating operational errors at O'Hare International
        Airport in Chicago, Illinois. A four-person team from
        Washington, DC is looking into twenty operational er-
        rors recorded in five months. Twelve operational er-
        rors were recorded for all of 1987. An American Air-
        lines DC-10 and a Midway Airlines Boeing 737 were in-
        volved in an incident on June 7, 1988. The O'Hare
        tower, which should have forty-two controllers, is
        three short.

1.121   "NTSB Safety Program Would Increase Experienced Con-
        trollers at O'Hare." **Aviation Week and Space Tech-
        nology** 129 (August 15, 1988): 109.

        The National Transportation Safety Board (NTSB) is
        aware of forgetfulness, perceptual problems, excessive
        work without a break, and other problems faced by con-
        trollers at Chicago's O'Hare Airport. A day of manda-
        tory overtime a week has become necessary because of a
        controller staffing shortage. The NTSB is also aware
        of a sharp rise in controller errors. In view of
        this, the NTSB wants incentives offered to attract ex-
        perienced controllers to O'Hare.

1.122   **O'Donnell, D.R.** "The Internal Clock of the Interna-
        tional Jet Traveller." **Medical Journal of Australia**
        1 (June 5, 1971): 1227-1230.

        A paper presented at the Annual Meeting, Australian
        Society of Occupational Medicine, Canberra, Australia,
        October 2, 1970. Author biographical information.
        Abstract. 1 table. 9 references.

1.123   **Orlady, Harry W.** "Operational Aspects of Pilot Inca-
        pacitation in a Multicrew Airliner." **American Journal
        of Cardiology** 36 (October 31, 1975): 584-588.

        United Air Lines (UAL) has studied in-flight incapaci-
        tation of pilots. Maintaining control of the air-
        plane; taking care of the incapacitated crewmember;
        and reorganizing the cockpit and landing the airplane
        are the three steps to follow when a pilot becomes in-
        capacitated. Pilots become incapacitated primarily
        for cardiovascular reasons. A table indicates the
        time to initial restraint of an incapacitated crewmem-
        ber in twenty-two incidents. Author biographical in-
        formation. 4 tables. 12 references.

1.124   **Ott, James.** "FAA Chief Cites Controller Understaff-
        ing as Safety Factor." **Aviation Week and Space Tech-
        nology** 124 (March 17, 1986): 33 and 35.

        The General Accounting Office (GAO) has prepared, af-
        ter a year-long study, a report entitled **Serious
        Problems Concerning the Air Traffic Control Work-
        force.** Overworked controllers, excessive overtime
        work, inadequate training, and morale problems are
        cited in the report. However, according to Donald D.
        Engen, FAA (Federal Aviation Administration) Admin-
        istrator, the air traffic control (ATC) system is
        safe. The Senate Republican Task Force on Air Trans-
        portation Safety has been receiving testimony on ATC
        safety.

1.125   **Pauly, David,** William J. Cook and Kerry DeRochi. "An-
        ger in the Control Towers." **Newsweek** 104 (July 2,
        1984): 60.

        When air traffic controllers (ATCs) went on strike
        illegally in 1981, and were fired by President Reagan,
        11,400 controllers lost their jobs. Although air
        traffic is 8% higher than in 1981, the number of con-
        trollers has dropped about 22%. Having to work six-
        day weeks, no guarantee of vacation dates, and not
        being able to take certain breaks during their shifts

are examples of controller complaints. 1 photograph.

1.126 **Peet, Creighton.** "The Traffic Cop of the Sky." **Popular Mechanics** 130 (December 1968): 104-107 and 218.

Jim Knoetgen, age thirty-one, is an approach controller at Kennedy International Airport in New York. He works in the Common Instrument Flight Rules Room (CIFRR). From there, traffic is directed at all three of New York's major airports. Aircraft from forty-two different airlines fly in and out of Kennedy. 5 photographs.

1.127 **Peffers, A.S.R.** "Food Sanitation and Air Safety." **Aviation, Space, and Environmental Medicine** 47 (October 1976): 1107-1108.

The author, who is Deputy Director, Medical Services, British Airways, mentions six ways poor food hygiene or unsanitary food disposal can influence air safety. He also lists fifteen safety steps airlines can follow. Author biographical information. Abstract.

1.128 **Peterson, Sarah.** "A New Crop of Air Controllers Starts a Long Climb to the Towers." **U.S. News and World Report** 91 (August 24, 1981): 16.

The Federal Aviation Administration (FAA) Academy is located in Oklahoma City, Oklahoma. This is where civilian flight controllers begin their careers. After seventeen to twenty-one weeks, during which time classes last from 7:00 a.m. to 3:00 p.m., and are supplemented by evening study-time, students leave the academy. They require additional training, on-the-job, before they are fully certified. There are approximately 1500 graduates annually. Robin Nadler and Art Benzle are two new students at the academy. 1 photograph.

1.129 "Pilots Get Support From ASTA—Canada on Bilingualism." **Canadian Travel News** 14 (October 30, 1975): 3.

Canadian travel agents, in a letter to Prime Minister Pierre Trudeau, expressed their support for the Canadian Airline Pilots Association (CALPA), which opposes bilingual air traffic control (ATC) in Quebec.

1.130 **Pocock, S.J.,** A.G. Shaper, A.N. Phillips and M. Walker.

"Prediction of Men at High Risk of Heart Attack and Its
Relevance to Pilots." **European Heart Journal Supplement G** 9 (May 1988):   25-30.

Data used in this study was from the British Regional
Heart Study.   The data pertained to 7735 men between
forty and fifty-nine years of age. Results concern
risk factors and risk of ischemic heart disease; com-
bined effect of risk factors; the risk score in prac-
tice; a profile of men at high risk; and allowance for
age. Author biographical information. 6 tables. 13
references.

1.131   **Pontell, Henry N.,** Lawrence R. Salinger and Gilbert
Geis.   "Assaults in the Air: Concerning Attacks
Against Flight Attendants." **Deviant Behavior** 4 (April
1983):   297-311.

Presented at the Seventy-sixth Annual Meeting, American Sociological Association, Toronto, Ontario, August 28, 1981. Author biographical information. Abstract. Acknowledgement. 6 footnotes. 27 references.

1.132   **Powell, Stewart,** Marilyn A. Moore and Sharon F. Gold-
en.   "A 'Sick and Tired' Pilot Who Had Enough." **U.S.
News and World Report** 101 (December 22, 1986):   18-19.

At Hartsfield International Airport, in Atlanta, Georgia, on July 22, 1986, Raymond Davidson, age fifty-
nine, was the pilot of Eastern Flight 141, which was
on the ground with eighty passengers aboard. Davidson was so tired of delays he announced to his passengers he was retiring; he then took the aircraft
back to the gate and left. 1 photograph.

1.133   **Power-Waters, Brian.   Safety Last: The Dangers of
Commercial Aviation: An Indictment by an Airline Pilot.** New York, NY: Dial Press, 1972.

Includes a glossary of technical terms.

1.134   **Preble, Cecillia.**   "Growth of Air Traffic Raises ATC
Staffing Issue." **Aviation Week and Space Technology**
124 (March 31, 1986):   42-47.

In the U.S., a commercial flight takes off every six
seconds—15,000 commercial flights daily. According
to the Federal Aviation Administration (FAA), no controller should spend, without a break, more than two

hours at a radar position. However, many controllers
work more than two hours during peak air traffic periods. The controller workforce is expected to increase
by 1000 individuals during the 1986 and 1987 fiscal
years. Compared to August 3, 1981, when the controller
strike began, the percentage of full performance level
(FPL) controllers is down sharply. The National Airspace System plan will improve air traffic control
(ATC) at a cost of $11.2 billion. 3 photographs. 3
graphs. 2 tables.

1.135   **Preston, F.S.**   "Further Sleep Problems in Airline Pilots on World-Wide Schedules." **Aerospace Medicine** 44
(July 1973):   775-782.

A paper presented at the Twentieth International Congress of Aviation and Space Medicine, Nice, France,
September 1972. Author biographical information. Abstract. 6 figures. Acknowledgements. 18 references.

1.136   **Preston, F.S.**, S.C. Bateman, F.W. Meichen, R. Wilkinson and R.V. Short.   "Effects of Time Zone Changes on
Performance and Physiology of Airline Personnel."
Aviation, Space, and Environmental Medicine 47 (July
1976):   763-769.

This research was done at the Isolation Unit, Department of Physiology, University of Manchester. The
subjects were six stewardesses and ten passenger service assistants. The subjects were between twenty
and thirty-eight years of age. All were employees of
British Airways. There were four groups of four subjects, one group acting as a control group. All subjects performed the same workload tasks: adding, reaction time (RT), short term memory (STM), error
check vigilance (ECV), and visual search (VS). It
appears sleep deprivation may be the most important
factor in planning work-rest schedules for airline
crews. Author biographical information. Abstract.
5 tables. 1 figure. Acknowledgements. 5 references.

1.137   **Preston, F.S.**, S.C. Bateman, R.V. Short and R.T. Wil-
kinson.   "The Effects of Flying and of Time Changes
on Menstrual Cycle Length and on Performance in Air-
line Stewardesses." Chapter in **Biorhythms and Human
Reproduction,** edited by Michel Ferin, Franz Halberg,
Ralph M. Richart, Raymond L. Vande Wiele, Judith A.
Anderson, and Katherine F. Darabi, 501-512. New
York, NY: John Wiley and Sons, Inc., 1974.

This research investigated the effects of flying on

the menstrual cycle; the effects of time changes on the
menstrual cycle and on performance; and performance
tests (for example, addition, reaction time, short-term
memory and vigilance). The subjects were 119 BOAC
(British Overseas Airways Corporation) stewardesses.
This paper was presented at a conference sponsored by
the International Institute for the Study of Human Reproduction. Author biographical information. 3 tables. 2 figures. Acknowledgements. 21 references.

1.138   **Preston, Frank S.** "The Health of Female Air Cabin
Crews." **Journal of Occupational Medicine** 20 (September
1978): 597-600.

Over 80% of sick female cabin crewmembers, employed by
British Airways, were afflicted with upper respiratory
disease. Female cabin crewmembers were sick about
twice as often as male cabin crewmembers, and sick up
to three times as often as pilots. There are almost
5000 female cabin crew employees at British Airways.
This paper was presented at the Annual Meeting, American Occupational Medical Association, New Orleans,
Louisiana, April 11-14, 1978. Author biographical information. 4 tables. 15 references.

1.139   **Preston, Frank S.** "Twelve Year Survey of Airline Pilots." **Aerospace Medicine** 39 (March 1968): 312-314.

One thousand airline pilots, employed in the United
Kingdom between 1954 and 1965, were studied, specifically to note reasons for medical grounding. Pilots
were grounded most frequently for psychological and
cardiovascular reasons. They were grounded least
frequently because of poliomyelitis and hypertension.
Of the twenty-seven pilots who died during the period
1954-1965, twenty-two died in aircraft accidents.
One died in a traffic accident. Four died of coronary thrombosis. One took his own life. Two died of
carcinoma. Author biographical information. Abstract. 3 figures. 2 tables. Acknowledgements. 6
references.

1.140   **Proctor, Paul.** "FAA Speeds Controller Hiring to
Solve One Cause of ATC Errors at O'Hare." **Aviation
Week and Space Technology** 128 (June 27, 1988): 77
and 79.

Increased operational errors at O'Hare International
Airport in Chicago, Illinois has prompted the FAA
(Federal Aviation Administration) to streamline con-
troller hiring and training in the Great Lakes Region.

Twelve hundred operations daily, at nearby Midway Airport, has compounded the staffing problem at O'Hare.
The FAA wants the O'Hare air traffic control (ATC) facility to be an almost-error-free operation. 2 illustrations.

1.141   **Raboutet, Jean** and Philippe Raboutet. "Sudden Incapacitation Encountered in Flight by Professional Pilots in French Civil Aviation, 1948-1972." **Aviation,
Space, and Environmental Medicine** 46 (January 1975):
80-81.

Thirteen of seventeen professional airline pilots in
France—who were suddenly incapacitated between 1948
and 1972—were incapacitated because of cardiovascular
factors. The following are the ages of the pilots and,
in parentheses, the number of pilots of each age:
thirty-four (one), thirty-five (one), thirty-eight
(one), thirty-nine (one), forty (one), forty-one (two),
forty-six (three), forty-eight (one), forty-nine (one),
fifty (two), fifty-two (one), fifty-three (one), and
fifty-six (one). No accidents occurred as a result of
the incapacitation. Author biographical information.
Abstract.

1.142   **Raventos, A.** "Illness in Air Traffic Controllers."
Journal of the American Medical Association 225 (July
23, 1973):   417-418.

In a letter to the editor, a physician from Davis,
California talks about illness in air traffic controllers (ATCs) and pilots.

1.143   "Real Issue in Air Slowdown." **U.S. News and World Report** 68 (April 13, 1970):   24-26.

The Federal Aviation Administration (FAA) and the
airlines underestimated the coming boom in air travel in the early 1960s. The FAA believed it was over-
staffed with controllers. The academy for training
new controllers in Oklahoma City, Oklahoma was
closed. During the summer of 1968, members of PATCO
(Professional Air Traffic Controllers Organization)
held a work slowdown. They held another slowdown in
June 1969. The current slowdown is related to the
transfer from Baton Rouge, Louisiana by the FAA of
three controllers to other facilities. PATCO views
the latter FAA action as an anti-union move. 3 photographs. 1 illustration.

1.144   "Reducing Pilot Fatigue." **USA Today** (Magazine) 114
        (June 1986): 13.

        The Ames Research Center coordinated a study into re-
        ducing pilot fatigue with the participation and coop-
        eration of individuals and organizations worldwide.
        Among the participants were: the Institute for Aero-
        space Medicine, Cologne, West Germany; the Civil Avi-
        ation Authority, London, England; and the Stanford
        University School of Medicine, Stanford, California.
        British Airways, Japan Air Lines (JAL), Lufthansa,
        and Pan American (Pan Am) World Airways were other ma-
        jor participants. Fifty-six pilots and flight engi-
        neers volunteered to take part in the research. A key
        finding was that jet lag could be substantially re-
        duced if flight crews flying eastward, over several or
        more time zones, did not go to sleep immediately af-
        ter arriving at their destination.

1.145   **Reed, Dwayne,** Sally Glaser and John Kaldor. "Ozone
        Toxicity Symptoms Among Flight Attendants." **American
        Journal of Industrial Medicine** 1, No. 1 (1980): 43-
        54.

        More than 1300 flight attendants employed by three
        airlines—Pan American (Pan Am) World Airways, Trans
        World Airlines (TWA), and Pacific Southwest Airlines
        (PSA)—participated in this study. Six tables aid in
        reporting the results: (1) numbers of flight attend-
        ants by age and airline; (2) age-adjusted percentages
        of flight attendants reporting flight-related symptoms
        during the past twelve months, by airlines; (3) per-
        centages of flight days during which symptoms were re-
        ported by maximum cruising altitude, adjusted for
        flight duration; (4) percentages of flight days during
        which symptoms were reported, by flight duration, ad-
        justed for altitude; (5) percentages of flight days on
        which symptoms were reported by type of aircraft, ad-
        justed for altitude; and (6) multiple logistic analy-
        sis of variables independently associated with reported
        symptoms. Author biographical information. Abstract.
        Acknowledgements. 31 references.

1.146   **Reinhart, Richard O.** "'To Be or Not to Be.'" **Busi-
        ness and Commercial Aviation** 65 (August 1989): 102.

        Certain over-the-counter medications and foods (for
        example, poppy seeds) can indicate a "positive" re-
        sult in a drug-use test. This, however, does not
        prove a person uses drugs, but rather that a certain
        amount of a drug was detected. A person is designated
        as a "user" when the amount of drug in his body is
        greater than a standard unit used by a laboratory.

This approach to drug testing does not result in any false positives.

1.147   **Rockwell, Donald A.**   "The 'Jet Lag' Syndrome.   **Western Journal of Medicine** 122 (May 1975):   419.

Jet lag results from transmeridian flight.   Internal biorhythms conflict with external cues.   Fatigue, insomnia, anxiety, and gastrointestinal dysfunction are major indicators of desynchronosis.   The age of the traveller, the number of stopovers and direction of travel within the U.S. affect the signs and symptoms of jet lag.   There are at least eight ways of reducing jet lag symptoms.   1 reference.

1.148   **Rolland, Richard.**   "The Age Dilemma."   **Canadian Aviation** 55 (August 1982):   44-47.

A number of pilots in Canada have filed discrimination complaints against Air Canada and CP Air.   The complaints, for some of the pilots, concern mandatory retirement at age sixty.   For some of the other pilots, the complaints concern discriminatory hiring practices. The pilots were told they were too old to be hired. The latter pilots were between thirty-two and forty-one years of age when they applied for work.   Douglas Campbell is an Air Canada flight attendant who filed a complaint with the Human Rights Commission because Air Canada wanted him to retire at age sixty.   1 illustration.

1.149   **Rose, Robert M.**, C. David Jenkins and Michael W. Hurst.   "Air Traffic Controller Health Change Study." **Government Reports Announcements and Index** 79 (May 25, 1979):   26.   NTIS AD-A063 709/0.

Ways to predict health changes in air traffic controllers (ATCs).

1.150   **Rose, Robert M.**, C. David Jenkins and Michael W. Hurst.   "Health Change in Air Traffic Controllers: A Prospective Study.   I.   Background and Description." **Psychosomatic Medicine** 40 (March 1978):   142-165.

Five intensive examinations at Boston University, repeated field studies, and a monthly health check list were used in a study of 416 air traffic controllers (ATCs) from New York and New England.   The controllers volunteered to take part in a three-year study.   The

study concerned prediction of future physical and psychological health change. Endocrine, cardiovascular,
and work morale variables were some of the major variables studied. Author biographical information. Abstract. 2 tables. Acknowledgements. 99 references.

1.151   **Rowan, Roy.** "Jet Lag Isn't Just a State of Mind."
        Fortune 94 (August 1976):   140-145, 197-198, 200 and
        202.

        Jet lag causes a mismatch of biological and environ-
        mental rhythms to occur, but the body seeks a new
        equilibrium. It adjusts to local time over a number
        of days. Body temperature takes eight days to adjust.
        Sleep patterns may take as long as fourteen days.
        Robert W. Lundeen, John W. Laibe, Lester W. Pullen,
        and Rolf H. Towe are corporate executives who describe
        how they cope with jet lag during business trips.
        Novelist James Michener also discuses how he deals
        with this condition. Author biograhical information.
        11 photographs.

1.152   **Rowan, Roy.** "'Keep Your Watch on Home Time.'" **For-
        tune** 94 (August 1976):   197.

        Brian G. Wolfson, Chairman, Consolidated Home Indus-
        tries, and a compulsive traveller, gives tips on hand-
        ling jet lag. A few of his tips: wear loose cloth-
        ing, eat light, and do daily exercises.   1 photograph.

1.153   **Saar, John.** "Crisis of the Cluttered Air." **Life** 65
        (August 9, 1968):   38-47.

        In the U.S., there are 2450 commercial airliners and
        120,000 private planes. The lobby for the latter is
        the Aircraft Owners and Pilots Association. The
        busiest airport in the world is O'Hare Field in Chi-
        cago, Illinois. It handles 657,000 take-offs and
        landings annually. An airline captain will fly
        eighty-five hours a month and earn at least $35,000
        a year. A controller will work at least forty-eight
        hours a week and earn about $12,000 a year. Control-
        lers are represented by PATCO (Professional Air Traf-
        fic Controllers Organization).   14 photographs. 1
        illustration.

1.154   "Safety Must Receive Top Priority in Air Control,
        Says ATAC Head." **Canadian Travel Courier** 11 (May 20,
        1976):   26.

Angus C. Morrison, President, Air Transport Association of Canada (ATAC), spoke at a Special International
Air Safety Symposium in Ottawa, Ontario. Morrison emphasized that safety must be the most important consideration in air traffic control (ATC). He was referring
to the issue of bilingual ATC in Quebec. The symposium
was held with the cooperation of the Canadian Air Line
Pilots Association (CALPA) and the International Federation of Air Line Pilots Associations (IFALPA).

1.155   **Salinger, Lawrence M.,** Paul Jesilow, Henry N. Pontell
        and Gilbert Geis. "Assaults Against Airline Flight At-
        tendants: A Victimization Study." **Transportation
        Journal** 25 (Fall 1985): 66-71.

        The survey population for this research consisted of
        850 persons, who were members of the Association of
        Flight Attendants (AFA). They were surveyed via a mail
        questionnaire mailed in the spring of 1983. The re-
        sponse rate was 29.5%. Assaults were usually related
        to baggage arrangements or food or drink service. Al-
        though first-class passengers constituted a relatively
        small number of the total passengers, first-class pas-
        sengers comprised a relatively large number of assault-
        ive persons. These passengers had higher expectations
        for service than did other passengers and also had the
        opportunity for unlimited drinks. Assaults typically
        took place during take-off or landing and on weekends.
        Most assaults were verbal in nature. Author biograph-
        ical information. 25 references.

1.156   **Sasaki, Mitsuo,** Yuko Kurosaki, Atsuyoshi Mori and
        Shiro Endo. "Patterns of Sleep-Wakefulness Before and
        After Transmeridian Flight in Commercial Airline Pi-
        lots." **Aviation, Space, and Environmental Medicine
        Supplement** 57 (December 1986): B29-B42.

        There were twelve male subjects in this study: six
        pilots and six flight engineers. All were employees
        of Japan Air Lines (JAL). The age of the subjects
        ranged from thirty-seven to fifty-four years and
        their cockpit crew experience ranged from fifteen to
        twenty-nine years. Their median flying experience
        was 9300 hours, mostly in B747s and DC-8s. The sub-
        jects flew between Tokyo, Japan and San Francisco,
        California. A preliminary questionnaire, daily ac-
        tivities log, interviews, and Multiple Sleep Latency
        Tests (MSLTs) were used by the researchers. Analysis
        of sleep parameters; the mean of daily MSLTs; and cor-
        relation of prior sleep parameters and MSLT scores
        were a few of the results reported. A representative
        case study is included. Author biographical infor-
        mation. Abstract. 6 tables. 13 figures. Acknowl-
        edgements. 9 references.

1.157   **Schiele, Robin.** "Off the Cuff." **Canadian Business**
        49 (August 1976): 4.

        Other parts of the world—other than Quebec—use more
        than one language for air traffic control (ATC), but
        it is not clear how often this is done. France, Ita-
        ly, Holland, and Belgium are examples of countries in
        Europe which have bilingual ATC. The extent to which
        this is the case should be thoroughly investigated
        and related to the issue of bilingual ATC in Canada.
        1 photograph.

1.158   **Scholten, Paul.** "Pregnant Stewardess—Should She
        Fly?" **Aviation, Space, and Environmental Medicine** 47
        (January 1976): 77-81.

        Airline policy in the U.S., regarding pregnant stew-
        ardesses, has been to terminate their employment, when
        the pregnancy is confirmed. The Flint Law, however,
        is being used to challenge this policy. Pregnancy
        alone may not be sufficient reason to dismiss a stew-
        ardess from her job. Miscarriage, radiation exposure,
        fetus malformation, and abortion have, according to
        some people, been associated with stewardesses who
        continue to fly while pregnant. Pregnant stewardesses
        should be absolutely prohibited from flying after the
        twentieth week of pregnancy. Author biographical in-
        formation. Abstract. 56 references.

1.159   **Schreuder, Otis B.** "Medical Aspects of Aircraft Pilot
        Fatigue With Special Reference to the Commercial Jet
        Pilot." **Aerospace Medicine** 37 (April 1966-Section II):
        1-44.

        A number of topics are examined, including the follow-
        ing: fatigue; ozone; radiation; hypoxia; vibration;
        circadian rhythm; coronary heart disease; serum cho-
        lesterol; exercise and physical fitness; cigarette
        smoking; nutrition and diet; alcohol; and use of
        drugs. 15 tables. 241 references.

1.160   **Scott, Phil.** "Controller: The Man in the Glass
        Booth." **Flying** 115 (January 1988): 61-63.

        Mike McFayden, age thirty-four, is an air traffic
        controller (ATC), who works at Philadelphia Interna-
        tional Airport. To the east of the control tower is
        the Delaware River; to the northeast—six miles dis-
        tance—is the Philadelphia skyline. McFayden, like
        many controllers, is also a pilot. 1 illustration.

1.161   **Scott, Phil.** "Positive Control: Two TCAs, and the
        Controllers in the ATC Shuffle." **Flying** 114 (December
        1987):   30-32.

        Remarks by air traffic controllers (ATCs) in New York
        (Barry Krasner and Ed Namen), and in Charlotte, North
        Carolina (Leslie Mahaffey and Gary Chernega).   2
        photographs.

1.162   **Scott, Vernon.** "Anemia and Airline Flight Duties."
        Aviation, Space, and Environmental Medicine 46 (June
        1975):   830-835.

        Sixty-two pilots and stewardesses, at United Airlines
        (UAL), were the research subjects in this investiga-
        tion, which includes three case reports. Two of the
        case reports pertain to captains in their fifties.
        One case report pertains to a first officer, age for-
        ty. Author biographical information. Abstract. 5
        figures. 3 tables. 21 references.

1.163   **Shea, Harold.** "They Keep You Flying Safely." **Atlan-
        tic Advocate** 78 (October 1987):   27-30.

        Profile of Air Canada Captain Kingston Nener and Sec-
        ond Officer Barbara Swyers. 3 photographs.

1.164   "Should the U.S. Grant Amnesty to Air Controllers?"
        U.S. News and World Report 91 (August 24, 1981):   18-
        19.

        Moe Biller, President, American Postal Workers Union,
        believes the U.S. should grant amnesty to air traffic
        controllers (ATCs), who went on strike in defiance of
        federal law. Drew Lewis, Secretary of Transportation,
        maintains the opposite view—the controllers should
        not be granted amnesty. The comments of both men
        were made during an interview with **U.S. News and
        World Report.** 4 photographs.

1.165   "Six Traffic Controllers Subpoenaed in Probe." **Avi-
        ation Week and Space Technology** 112 (February 11,
        1980):   23.

        The FBI (Federal Bureau of Investigation) is inves-
        tigating six air traffic controllers (ATCs) regarding
        a Soviet Aeroflot flight, which landed in New York on
        January 18, 1980. The controllers were subpoenaed
        because of terminal area radar irregularities.

Soviet Ambassador Anatoly Dobrynin was aboard the Aero-
flot flight, which landed successfully at Kennedy International. The Federal Aviation Administration (FAA)
believes computer tampering was involved in the Aero-
flot incident. Premature descent of the Soviet plane
is one aspect of the investigation.

1.166   **Skrzycki, Cindy.** "Trouble in the Control Tower." **U.S.
News and World Report** 101 (July 14, 1986):   53-55.

Eight Federal Aviation Administration (FAA) air traffic
control (ATC) centers do not have as many experienced
controllers as they did in 1981:   Atlanta, Georgia;
Chicago, Illinois; Cleveland, Ohio; Indianapolis, In-
diana; Los Angeles, California; Minneapolis, Minnesota;
New York, New York; and Oakland, California. Terry
Conroy is an air traffic controller (ATC) in San Jose,
California, who has not flown since the 1981 controllers
strike because he does not feel it is safe to fly. The
FAA expects airline traffic to be 478.6 billion passenger-miles in 1997. The figure for 1986 is 279 billion
passenger-miles. 2 photographs. 1 illustration.

1.167   **Smith, Roger C.** and C.E. Melton, Jr.   "Susceptibility
to Anxiety and Shift Difficulty as Determinants of
State Anxiety in Air Traffic Controllers." **Government
Reports Announcements and Index** 74 (June 14, 1974):
32. NTIS AD-777 565/3.

Subjects were eighty volunteers administered the
State-Trait Anxiety Inventory (STAI).

1.168   **Smith, Roger C.,** C.E. Melton and Jess M. McKenzie.
"Affect Adjective Check List Assessment of Mood Vari-
ations in Air Traffic Controllers." **Government Reports Announcements and Index** 71 (November 10, 1971):
36. NTIS AD-729 832.

The Composite Mood Adjective Check List (CMACL) was
used in this study, which involved two groups of air
traffic control specialists (ATCSs) and a control
group. The subjects worked at two different facilities. Fatigue in relation to shift worked was
studied. It was fatiguing for the subjects to work
an eight-hour shift, and especially fatiguing to
work a night shift.

1.169   **Stark, Elizabeth.**   "Jet Lag: East vs. West." **Psychology Today** 20 (July 1986):   70-71.

Fatigue causes unsafe or abnormal air traffic incidents. NASA (National Aeronautics and Space Administration) received information about twenty-six such incidents between July 1980 and August 1984. R. Curtis
Graeber, a physiological psychologist, has studied the
sleep patterns of airline flight crews. The crews of
Japan Air Lines (JAL), British Airways, and other airlines spent time in sleep laboratories during lay-
overs. The pilots, copilots, and flight engineers ad-
justed more easily to westbound flights than to east-
bound flights. Graeber and his colleagues believe
crewmembers should be allowed to take scheduled naps
on-board aircraft.

1.170   **Stewart, Walter.** "We're Cracking Up Down Here!"
        Maclean's 82 (June 1969):   58-62 and 64.

        In 1962 there were 6249 registered aircraft in Canada,
        281 accidents, and 103 deaths. In 1966 there were
        8310 aircraft, 422 accidents, and 171 deaths. Accord-
        ing to the Canadian Air Traffic Control Association
        (CATCA), controllers in Canada are tense and over-
        worked. A staff shortage which existed in 1960 still
        exists nine years later. Faulty equipment is another
        problem for Canada's 1200 controllers. 4 photographs.

1.171   "Still There for the Axing at Age 60." **Flying** 116
        (September 1989):   26.

        After almost thirty years, the Federal Aviation Admin-
        istration (FAA) still maintains that the mandatory re-
        tirement age for pilots should be sixty. The retire-
        ment rule became effective on March 15, 1960. The
        FAA position has not changed, in spite of a recent or-
        der from the U.S. Court of Appeals that the FAA re-
        view its position. The FAA was not swayed by accounts
        about pilots, nearing age sixty, who averted disaster
        because of their extensive experience. Two incidents
        involved United Airlines (UAL) 747s en route to (in
        1978) and from (in 1989) Hawaii.

1.172   "Study by FAA Determines Drug Effect on Pilots." **Avi-
        ation Week and Space Technology** 128 (November 18,
        1968):   126-127.

        Reports on research conducted at the Civil Aeromedi-
        cal Institute, a facility of the Federal Aviation Ad-
        ministration (FAA) in Oklahoma City, Oklahoma. The
        subjects were forty-five males between the ages of
        eighteen and thirty-five. Three groups of subjects
        were administered Phenindamine, Chlorpheniramine, or

a placebo at three different altitudes in an altitude
chamber. The contents of the capsules and the altitude were not disclosed to the subjects. The subjects
were administered coordination tests; heart rate and
oxygen saturation were two variables monitored by the
researchers. This study revealed that some antihista-
mine compounds can impair the motor coordination of
pilots under certain conditions.

1.173 **Tashkin, Donald P.,** Anne H. Coulson, Michael S. Sim-
mons and Gary H. Spivey. "Respiratory Symptoms of
Flight Attendants During High-Altitude Flight: Possi-
ble Relation to Cabin Ozone Exposure." **International
Archives of Occupational and Environmental Health** 52,
No. 2 (1983): 117-137.

Subjects were flight attendants based in New York and
Los Angeles, who flew on Boeing 747 and 747SP aircraft.
The subjects were employed by Pan American (Pan Am)
Airlines and were surveyed via a self-administered
questionnaire. Symptoms were compared by: frequency,
severity, in-flight occurrence, and after-flight occurrence. There was greater exposure to ozone in the
higher-altitude flights of the Boeing 747SP than in
the 747. Author biographical information. Abstract.
3 tables. Acknowledgements. 46 references.

1.174 "Task Force Study Finds Controller Morale Drop."
Aviation Week and Space Technology 116 (March 22,
1982): 34.

Lawrence M. Jones is the chairman of a task force,
comprised of non-government management experts,
which made eleven recommendations regarding air traffic controllers (ATCs). The task force was established by the Transportation Department, Drew Lewis, Secretary. Controller morale related to, in part, burn-
out, as a major problem. Lewis stated the Federal
Aviation Administration (FAA) plans to implement the
recommendations within two to three years.

1.175 **Terelak, Jan.** "Alpha Index and Personality Traits
of Pilots." **Aviation, Space, and Environmental Medicine** 47 (February 1976): 133-136.

EEG (electroencephalogram) recordings from 619 pilots, between twenty and forty years of age, were
used in this investigation. The following research
instruments were also used: Maudsley Personality
Inventory (MPI), Manifest Anxiety Scale (MAS), Guil-
ford Zimmermann Temperament Survey, Thurstone Temperament Schedule, and Strelau Temperament Inventory.

Twenty-four dimensions of personality illustrate the
variance and significance of differences between means
in the low and high alpha index groups. Manifest anxiety, sociability, friendliness, and masculinity are
four of the dimensions of personality examined. Author
biographical information. Abstract. 1 table. 20 references.

1.176   **Tesh, Sylvia.** "The Politics of Stress: The Case of
Air Traffic Control." **International Journal of Health
Services** 14, No. 4 (1984): 569-587.

In 1981 when members of the Professional Air Traffic
Controllers Organization (PATCO) went on strike, they
used "stress" to describe undesirable job conditions.
PATCO appealed to experts who could, it was believed,
describe controller job-duties in scientific terms.
However, since stress can be defined in different ways,
attempts to define stress became a major problem. Furthermore, it is extremely difficult to provide virtually irrefutable evidence which links difficult working
conditions to pathological outcomes. If workers want
to win labor disputes, they should not rely on the
stress discourse. Job conditions—because they are not
the physical world—do not lend themselves properly to
methods used to investigate the physical world. An
earlier version of this paper was presented at the Annual Meeting, American Public Health Association, Dallas, Texas, November 1983. Author biographical information. Abstract. Acknowledgements. 38 references.

1.177   **Thackray, Richard I.** "Boredom and Monotony as a Con-
sequence of Automation: A Consideration of the Evidence Relating Boredom and Monotony to Stress." **Government Reports Announcements and Index** 80 (September
12, 1980): 3909. NTIS AD-A085 069/3.

On the basis of laboratory and field studies, there
is no evidence that boredom and monotony produce
stress in air traffic controllers (ATCs).

1.178   **Thomas, David.** "Into the Wild Bleu Yonder."
Maclean's 92 (September 3, 1979): 23.

Three judges have unanimously recommended that bilingual (French and English) air traffic control (ATC)
be used throughout Quebec. A dispute in 1976 between
English and French controllers brought about a shut
down, for eight days, of Canada's commercial air service. U.S. pilots who are not aware of bilingualism
at Quebec City Airport, and who land there for the

first time, are puzzled by two languages emanating from the cockpit radio speakers. 1 photograph.

1.179   **Thomas, Michael.** "Characteristics of Pilot Stress."
Chapter in **Managing Pilot Stress,** by Michael Thomas,
19-32. New York, NY: Macmillan Publishing Co., 1989.

Covers the following: intensity of the stressor;
quality of the stressor; duration and frequency of exposure to the stressor; focus of the stressor; exten-
sity of the stressor's effects; the pilot's mental and
physical condition; the pilot's ability to resist
stress; the pilot's perception of the stressor and its
potential effects; interactional effects; and positive
versus negative stress. A figure illustrates positive
and negative stress.

1.180   **Thomas, Michael.** "Conscious and Unconscious Factors."
Chapter in **Managing Pilot Stress,** by Michael Thomas,
33-51. New York, NY: Macmillan Publishing Co., 1989.

Thinking, conscious thought, unconscious thinking, perception, learning, concentration, information process-
ing, judgement, and workload are nine conscious and unconscious stress factors. Five phases of flight illustrate relationships between workload and stress: antic-
ipatory phase, high-task phase, passive activity phase,
prepatory phase, and resolution phase. 4 figures.

1.181   **Thomas, Michael.** "Environmental, Experiential, and Sociocultural Factors." Chapter in **Managing Pilot Stress,**
by Michael Thomas, 83-102. New York, NY: Macmillan
Publishing Co., 1989.

Environmental factors which contribute to pilot stress
include the work climate outside and inside the cockpit; the physical environment outside and inside the
cockpit; and the pilot's personal environment. Training, examinations, perceptions, common language, and
inner feelings are the experiential factors. Airline
deregulation is the sociocultural factor.

1.182   **Thomas, Michael.** "Exercise and Nutrition." Chapter
in **Managing Pilot Stress,** by Michael Thomas, 188-200.
New York, NY: Macmillan Publishing Co., 1989.

Looks at the benefits and types of exercise, and discusses four precautions regarding exercise. Also
discusses carbohydrates, fats, proteins, fiber, water,

vitamins, and minerals. 1 table.

1.183   **Thomas, Michael.** "Interacting With Yourself and Others." Chapter in **Managing Pilot Stress,** by Michael Thomas, 177-187. New York, NY: Macmillan Publishing Co., 1989.

Self-criticalness, who am I?, and facing one's issues are discussed in relation to interacting with oneself. Listening to others, communicating more directly, disagreement, support, and crew briefings are examined regarding interacting with others. One table presents six guidelines for effective listening. Another table is about three types of crew briefings: preflight, en route and postflight.

1.184   **Thomas, Michael.** "Life-Change and Acute Reactive Factors." Chapter in **Managing Pilot Stress,** by Michael Thomas, 103-117. New York, NY: Macmillan Publishing Co., 1989.

Life-change factors and acute reactive factors contribute to pilot stress. In-flight emergencies, occupational crisis, personal-life crisis, and post-traumatic stress disorder are examples of acute reactive factors. 5 footnotes.

1.185   **Thomas, Michael.** "Measuring Pilot Stress." Chapter in **Managing Pilot Stress,** by Michael Thomas, 137-143. New York, NY: Macmillan Publishing Co., 1989.

An examination of the Pilot Stress Inventory and the Stress Dynamics Scale.

1.186   **Thomas, Michael.** "Personality and Psychological Factors." Chapter in **Managing Pilot Stress,** by Michael Thomas, 52-67. New York, NY: Macmillan Publishing Co., 1989.

Personality profiles, norms, how pilots cope with stress, accident-prone pilots, type A personality, the pilot's identity, and mental state are discussed. A table lists twenty-seven personality traits of pilots. 1 footnote.

1.187   **Thomas, Michael.** "Physiological Factors." Chapter in **Managing Pilot Stress,** by Michael Thomas, 68-82.

New York, NY: Macmillan Publishing Co., 1989.

Cardiovascular disease, hypertension, atherosclerosis, arrhythmias, drug use, alcohol, medication, fatigue, and jet lag are physiological factors in pilot stress.

1.188   **Thomas, Michael.** "Pilot Stress." Chapter in **Managing Pilot Stress,** by Michael Thomas, 3-18. New York, NY: Macmillan Publishing Co., 1989.

The focus of this chapter is on: how pilots view stress; defining stress; the General Adaptation Syndrome (GAS); the psychological reaction pattern of pilots; and ten categories of stress factors (conscious, unconscious, personality, psychological, physiological, environmental, experiential, sociocultural, life-change, and acute reactive). A table lists thirty-five indicators of stress. There is also a figure which illustrates the GAS. 1 footnote.

1.189   **Thomas, Michael.** "Problem Solving." Chapter in **Managing Pilot Stress,** by Michael Thomas, 164-176. New York, NY: Macmillan Publishing Co., 1989.

After recognizing a problem, seven steps can be taken to solve it: define the problem; evaluate the resources available to solve the problem; examine the possible solutions; choose the best solution; implement the chosen solution by taking action; monitor the results; and make corrections as necessary.

1.190   **Thomas, Michael.** "Professional Pilots Speak on Stress." Chapter in **Managing Pilot Stress,** by Michael Thomas, 118-133. New York, NY: Macmillan Publishing Co., 1989.

Four pilots give their views on stress.

1.191   **Thomas, Michael.** "Relaxation Techniques." Chapter in **Managing Pilot Stress,** by Michael Thomas, 144-163. New York, NY: Macmillan Publishing Co., 1989.

Explains the Pilot Stress Relaxation Exercise, Lay-over Sleep-Relaxation Exercise, and relaxation inside the cockpit (breathing exercises, shoulder raise-drop, head rotation, muscle tense-release, and self-massage).

1.192   **Tillisch, Jan H.** "Medical Aspects of Safety in the

Air." **Journal of the American Medical Association** 174
(November 5, 1960): 1300-1303.

A paper presented at the 109th Annual Meeting, American Medical Association, Miami Beach, Florida, June 13-
17, 1960. Author biographical information.

1.193 "Unsafe Skies?" **Newsweek** 69 (April 3, 1967): 57.

Stanley Lyman, an air traffic controller (ATC) wants
a congressional investigation of airline safety. The
Boston-Washington corridor is especially crowded with
air traffic. Members of the National Association of
Government Employees support Lyman.

1.194 "Wacky Biological Clocks." **Science Digest** 68 (December 1970): 67.

Diplomats and businessmen are advised not to make important decisions when they arrive at their destina-
tion, after having flown through several or more time
zones: Chicago, Illinois to London; New York to Mos-
cow; San Francisco, California to Paris. Time zone
fatigue also negatively affects pilots, whose percep-
tiveness and reaction time are diminished. 1 illustration.

1.195 **Ward, Peter.** "Bilingualism, Air Traffic Controllers,
and Safety: Is There a Solution?" **Canadian Business**
49 (August 1976): 7.

The Government of Canada could, through legislation,
limit the expansion of bilingual air traffic control
(ATC). Without legislation, however, other aspects
of work in other parts of Canada could eventually require bilingualism.

1.196 **Watkin, Basil L.** "The Controller, Aviation Medicine
and Air Safety." **Aviation, Space, and Environmental
Medicine** 54 (March 1983): 263-265.

Eight areas discussed: (1) modern air traffic control (ATC), (2) the unsuspecting flying public, (3)
the statistical recording of air traffic, (4) air
safety responsibilities in New Zealand, (5) jeopard-
izing air safety, (6) controllers and DMEs (Designated
Medical Examiners), (7) aviation medical research, and
(8) controller medical problems. Author biographical
information. Abstract.

1.197 **Watkins, R.D.** "Flight-Deck Vision of Professional Pi-
       lots." **Aerospace Medicine** 41 (March 1970): 337-342.

       The author examines six aspects of the flight-deck vi-
       sion of professional pilots: (1) current near visual
       acuity standard; (2) standardization of accommodative
       amplitudes; (3) recommendations relating to the near
       vision standard; (4) working distances and recommended
       corrections; (5) lens type available; and (6) correc-
       tion for the overhead panel. Author biographical in-
       formation. Abstract. 2 tables. 23 references.

1.198 "'We Could Face the Same Explosion in Five Years.'"
       U.S. News and World Report 91 (August 24, 1981): 17.

       Interview with Dr. Robert Rose, who, for five years,
       studied air traffic controllers (ATCs) in Boston, Mas-
       sachusetts. Dr. Rose and a research team were under
       contract to the Federal Aviation Administration
       (FAA). 1 photograph.

1.199 **Weiner, Eric.** "The Long Haul." **Flying** 115 (April
       1988): 46-48, 50 and 52.

       Flight 801 is a United Airlines (UAL) New York-to-
       Tokyo nonstop flight in a 747-200. The 400-ton air-
       craft flies 6024 nautical miles through eight time
       zones and uses about 328,500 pounds of fuel. The
       most serious problems usually encountered by the
       flight crew are the English of foreign air traffic
       controllers (ATCs), exceedingly dry air in the cock-
       pit, and boredom. 4 photographs.

1.200 **Weiner, Eric.** "Official Position: 'I'm the One Who
       Closed the Corridor.'" **Flying** 114 (December 1987):
       38.

       Comments by Keith Potts, FAA (Federal Aviation Admin-
       istration) Associate Administrator. Fifty-eight-year-
       old Potts is chief architect of the U.S. air traffic
       system. Potts closed the corridor after the midair
       collision over Cerritos, California. He is also a
       general aviation pilot.

1.201 "Why Jet Travel Makes You Tired." **Science Digest**
       56 (October 1964): 25.

       Travelling by air from one time zone to another inter-
       feres with the body's biological clock by upsetting

the body's twenty-four-hour circadian rhythm. The person who flies from New York to Los Angeles, California
flies through three time zones. The person who flies
from New York to Miami, Florida stays within the same
time zone. The circadian rhythm of the latter person
is not affected.

1.202   "Why O'Hare's Controllers Quit." **Chicago** 25 (April
        1976): 101.

        At O'Hare International Airport in Chicago, Illinois—
        on December 20, 1972—a North Central DC-9 collided
        with a Delta jet. A ground controller was responsible
        for this accident, in which ten people died. This ac-
        cident and other stressful experiences account for
        controllers quitting their jobs at O'Hare. Ulcers,
        high blood pressure, anxiety, loss of appetite, and
        depression are some of the indicators of stress in
        these men. Other indicators include excessive con-
        sumption of coffee and alcohol, and chain-smoking. A
        number of ex-controllers are patients of psychiatrist
        Dr. E. Eliot Benezra.

1.203   **Wielgosz, Andreas T.** "Ensuring a Heart-Healthy Pilot
        Population." **Canadian Medical Association Journal**
        139 (November 15, 1988): 937-938.

        Civil Aviation Medical Examiners (CAMEs), the Avia-
        tion Medical Review Board (AMRB), and the Civil Avia-
        tion Tribunal are three areas of the Canadian govern-
        ment concerned with the medical fitness of Canadian
        pilots. During the time period 1977-1987, there were
        approximately 50,000 licensed male pilots in Canada.
        During this same time period, there were five fatal
        aviation accidents in Canada attributed to cardiac
        factors. Author biographical information. 5 refer-
        ences.

1.204   **Winston, Donald C.** "Senate Unit Hears Warning by
        Controllers." **Aviation Week and Space Technology** 90
        (June 30, 1969): 28-29.

        Michael J. Rock, Chairman, PATCO (Professional Air
        Traffic Controllers Organization) and George W.
        Kriske, Executive Director, Air Traffic Control Asso-
        ciation, testified before the Senate Commerce Avia-
        tion Subcommittee. They spoke about the recruitment
        and training of air traffic controllers (ATCs), and
        about technical aspects of air traffic control (ATC).
        The Federal Aviation Administration (FAA) offers a
        nine-week course in Oklahoma—a course deemed inade-
        quate by Rock. F. Lee Bailey, PATCO General Counsel,

also appeared before the subcommittee. The hearings
were convened by Senator Warren G. Magnuson (Democrat-
Washington), Chairman, Commerce Committee.

1.205   **Work, Clemens P.** "Wanted: Good Bridge Players."
        U.S. News and World Report 101 (July 14, 1986): 54-55.

All Federal Aviation Administration (FAA) controllers
are trained at the FAA Academy in Oklahoma City, Oklahoma, where there are 500 instructors. Fifteen percent
of controller candidates are women; 7% are minorities.
College education is not an indicator of success in
air traffic control (ATC) school. Being able to visu-
alize spatial relationships in three dimensions is an
asset in becoming a controller. 2 photographs.

1.206   **Yoss, Robert E.**, Norma J. Moyer, Earl T. Carter and
        William E. Evans. "Commercial Airline Pilot and His
        Ability to Remain Alert." **Aerospace Medicine** 41 (De-
        cember 1970): 1339-1346.

The ability of airline pilots to remain alert, sitting
in darkness for fifteen minutes, was studied by means
of infrared pupillography. Fifty pilots took part in
this research and their performance was rated as superior, average, marginal or unsatisfactory. Thirty-two
of the pilots were well rested. Twenty-eight of these
were rated as superior or average. Three were catego-
rized as marginal. One pilot was rated unsatisfactory.
This research indicates, in part, the importance, for
pilots, of adequate rest. Author biographical information. Abstract. 2 tables. 9 figures. 8 references.

1.207   **Zaret, Milton M.** "Air Safety: Role of Family Physi-
        cian." **New York State Journal of Medicine** 79 (Octo-
        ber 1979): 1694-1698.

Implications for airline safety of capsular cataract
in twelve air traffic controllers (ATCs) and three
airline pilots. The earliest age of onset was thirty-
three, the latest fifty-five. The family physician
should be receptive to patient remarks about looking
through a wet glass or difficulty with night driving. Author biographical information. Abstract. 1
table. 1 case report. 5 references.

2

Aircraft Maintenance

2.001   "Airlines Detail Maintenance Problems." **Air Transport World** 16 (October 1979): 27.

Forty airlines comment on their maintenance problems. About a third of the airlines reported corrosion as a problem. Aeromexico, Air Canada, Dan-Air, Frontier, National, Nordair, Olympic, Ozark, Pacific Western, Piedmont, Pioneer, and Qantas are examples of airlines commenting.

2.002   "All-Engines Power Loss Investigated." **Aviation Week and Space Technology** 108 (February 6, 1978): 28.

A National Airlines Boeing 727, while en route from Miami, Florida to Newark International Airport in Newark, New Jersey, lost power in its three engines at an altitude of 33,000 feet. The electrical system, fuel system, and fuel manifold valves were ruled out as the cause of the power loss. The airline, Federal Aviation Administration (FAA), and Boeing Co. are investigating.

2.003   "Aloha Upgrades Maintenance Program, Modernizes Fleet." **Aviation Week and Space Technology** 131 (July 24, 1989): 79 and 81.

Although an Aloha Airlines Boeing 737-200 lost the top half of a forward passenger section, only one person died—an Aloha flight attendant. The accident, which occurred on April 28, 1988, tarnished the airline's image. Aloha has, since then, spent $10 million improving its maintenance program. Maintenance inspection staff have been doubled. Heavy maintenance, which used to be done in increments at night, will be done when each aircraft is available for two to three weeks at a time. Aloha presently has thirteen aircraft and traffic and passenger revenue are higher than in 1988. Hawaiian Airlines, on the other hand, Aloha's competitor, may be sold. 2 photographs.

2.004   "Are Airliners Always Kept Fit to Fly?" **U.S. News and
        World Report** 87 (July 23, 1979):   57-58.

        A year and a half before the American Airlines DC-10
        crash in Chicago, Illinois on May 25, 1979—in which
        273 people died—Continental Air Lines discovered
        cracks in two of its DC-10 engine-mount structures.
        The Federal Aviation Administration (FAA) was not no-
        tified because the FAA allows airlines to determine
        what constitutes a major problem. Only major problems
        have to be reported. After the Chicago crash, all 138
        DC-10s operated by U.S. airlines were grounded for thir-
        ty-eight days. The FAA has only 266 inspectors to in-
        spect the work of 44,467 mechanics employed by U.S.
        scheduled airlines. At Delta Air Lines in Atlanta,
        Georgia, there are five FAA inspectors to survey 2200
        mechanics. At Eastern Air Lines in Miami, Florida
        there are four inspectors and 3800 employees. 1 photo-
        graph.

2.005   "Are Cost Cuts Hurting Air Safety?" **U.S. News and
        World Report** 100 (March 31, 1986):   71-72.

        John Nance, author of the book **Blind Trust** and also a
        former airline pilot, states, in this interview, that
        cost cuts are hurting air safety. Frank Borman, Chair-
        man and Chief Executive Officer, Eastern Air Lines, is
        also interviewed. He believes that cost cuts are not
        hurting air safety. 3 photographs.

2.006   "Asian Maintenance Centers Expand to Handle Growth in
        Airline Fleets." **Aviation Week and Space Technology**
        132 (February 12, 1990):   71-74.

        Hong Kong Aircraft Engineering Co., Aerospace Technol-
        ogies of Australia, Aircraft Maintenance and Engineer-
        ing Cooperation, and Guangzhou Aircraft Maintenance
        Engineering Co. are examples of Asian maintenance cen-
        ters expanding to handle the growth in airline fleets.
        4 photographs. 1 illustration.

2.007   "Big Is Still Safer." **Economist** 273 (December 1,
        1979):   37 and 40.

        The Federal Aviation Administration (FAA) has imposed
        fines on airlines which have breached maintenance
        rules: American Airlines ($500,000), Continental
        Airlines ($100,000), Pacific Southwest Airlines (PSA)
        ($385,000), and Braniff ($1.5 million). 1 photograph.

2.008   "British Airways 747 Sustains Damage From Loss of Flap
        Fairing on Approach." **Aviation Week and Space Technol-
        ogy** 128 (May 16, 1988): 18

        A British Airways Boeing 747-100 lost a flap fairing on
        May 9, 1988 during final approach to O'Hare Internation-
        al Airport in Chicago, Illinois. The aircraft was
        about five miles out from Runway 27L. A piece of fair-
        ing was found on a suburban street. There was damage
        to the left horizontal stabilizer and left wing spoil-
        ers.

2.009   "Civil Penalty." **Aviation Week and Space Technology**
        124 (January 27, 1986): 41.

        After Western Airlines was inspected in July and August
        1985, the Federal Aviation Administration (FAA) noted
        improper procedures regarding deferred maintenance
        items on nearly 200 separate occasions. Western is
        facing a fine of $756,000.

2.010   "Congressmen Fault FAA Safety Inspections." **Aviation
        Week and Space Technology** 123 (August 19, 1985): 36.

        Two congressmen have expressed concern about irregu-
        lar and inconsistent Federal Aviation Administration
        (FAA) safety inspections. The congressmen are repre-
        sentatives Norman Y. Mineta (Democrat-California) and
        William Lehman (Democrat-Florida). Mineta is Chair-
        man, House Public Works and Transportation Aviation
        Subcommittee. Lehman is Chairman, House Appropria-
        tions Transportation Subcommittee. Mineta and Lehman
        expressed their concerns in a letter to FAA Adminis-
        trator Donald D. Engen. According to the congressmen,
        some carriers were subjected to virtually no inspec-
        tions during the 1984 fiscal year. Federal Express
        and Aloha Airlines are examples of carriers having
        similar numbers of inspections, but large differences
        in fleet operating hours.

2.011   "Crack in Fuselage Forces 727 Landing." **Aviation
        Week and Space Technology** 128 (May 16, 1988): 18.

        Cabin pressurization was lost in an American Airlines
        Boeing 727-200 due to a fifteen-inch fuselage crack.
        American Flight 984, en route from Chicago, Illinois
        to Philadelphia, Pennsylvania, landed safely at De-
        troit Metropolitan Airport, Detroit, Michigan.
        There were no reports of injuries to the 105 passen-
        gers and seven crewmembers.

2.012   **d'Aulaire, Emily** and Per Ola d'Aulaire. "'Their Mis-
        sion: Make Damn Sure Nothing Comes Unraveled in the
        Air.'" **Smithsonian** 17 (October 1986): 48-59.

        United Airlines (UAL), the biggest air carrier in the
        U.S., has the largest private aircraft maintenance fa-
        cility in the world—the maintenance operations center
        (MOC) at San Francisco International Airport. Nearly
        8000 mechanics, electricians, and other workers work
        daily, round the clock, at the MOC. A number of these
        workers spend about three weeks "tuning up" a 747. In
        1985, 2089 people died worldwide in scheduled and char-
        tered flights which crashed. At least three of these
        crashes were maintenance related. Author biographical
        information. 14 photographs.

2.013   "Eastern Airlines Agrees to Pay Fine of $9.5 Million
        For Safety Violations." **Aviation Week and Space Tech-
        nology** 126 (February 16, 1987): 34.

        Eastern Airlines was inspected by the Federal Aviation
        Administration (FAA) from December 1985 through Janu-
        ary 1986. Over 78,000 violations were logged against
        the Miami-based carrier. Violations ranged from main-
        tenance irregularities to recordkeeping infractions.
        The fine—Eastern fought it for nearly a year—is the
        largest of its kind for safety violations.

2.014   **Eustace, Peter.** "Corrosion Worry Brings Call For
        Checks on All Aircraft." **Engineer** 266 (June 22,
        1989): 14.

        There should be mandatory corrosion checks for all
        civil aircraft in the world. Rust would hopefully be
        eliminated as a factor in metal fatigue. A steward-
        ess died in 1988, after the roof of a Boeing airliner
        was ripped off over Hawaii. 1 photograph.

2.015   "FAA Orders Lavatory Maintenance Scrutiny." **Aviation
        Week and Space Technology** 119 (July 25, 1983): 26.

        The Federal Aviation Administration (FAA) has ordered
        closer inspection of airline lavatory maintenance.
        The FAA's action follows a June 2 fire aboard an Air
        Canada DC-9-33, which made an emergency landing at
        the Greater Cincinnati Airport. The fire was in the
        aft lavatory of the DC-9. The ignition source of the
        fire remains unknown. Canadian government investiga-
        tors have examined sixty-nine flushing pump motors in
        an attempt to find the cause of the DC-9 fire. Evi-
        dence of corrosion and overheat was found in many mo-
        tors.

2.016   "FAA Probes Human Factors Affecting Aircraft Mainte-
        nance." **Aviation Week and Space Technology** 128 (May
        30, 1988):   127.

        According to FAA (Federal Aviation Administration) Ad-
        ministrator Allan McArtor, past structural inspections
        of Boeing 737s should have been more thorough.   McAr-
        tor's comments follow the structural failure of an
        Aloha Airlines Boeing 737. The forward cabin roof
        separated from that aircraft on April 28, 1988. The
        FAA is examing changes in maintenance procedures and
        will host a conference on aircraft aging.

2.017   "FAA Will Establish Confidential Hot Line For Safety
        Violations." **Aviation Week and Space Technology** 122
        (April 29, 1985):   50.

        Transportation Secretary Elizabeth Dole, while address-
        ing the Regional Airline Association, announced that a
        confidential telephone hot line will be installed at
        the Federal Aviation Administration (FAA). The hot
        line will enable individuals with knowledge of false
        recordkeeping or other safety violations to anonymous-
        ly alert federal officials.

2.018   **Fotos, Christopher P.**   "USAir Starts New Inspection
        Program to Safeguard Aging Aircraft Fleet." **Aviation
        Week and Space Technology** 132 (January 15, 1990):   66-
        67.

        USAir, which has more than seventy McDonnell Douglas
        DC-9s, has begun a structural integrity program.
        About fifty of the DC-9s will enter the program be-
        cause USAir has a relatively young fleet. The aver-
        age fleet age is 9.6 years. The structural integrity
        program is an outgrowth of the Airworthiness Assurance
        Task Force. The task force was established after the
        breakup of an Aloha Airlines 737 fuselage. 1 illus-
        tration.

2.019   **Goar, Carol.** "Making the Skies Safer." **Maclean's** 96
        (October 24, 1983):   22-23.

        Air Canada has had a series of mishaps which have af-
        fected negatively its public image. In Regina, Sas-
        katchewan, May 12, 1983: a DC-9 skidded off the run-
        way; in Cincinnati, Ohio, June 2, 1983: twenty-three
        people died in a fire which broke out in a DC-9 wash-
        room; in Gimli, Manitoba, July 23, 1983: a Boeing 767
        ran out of fuel and made an emergency landing on an
        abandoned wartime landing strip. Claude Taylor, Pres-
        ident, Air Canada, has had a nine-member panel of

experts investigate, for six weeks, Air Canada's standards and procedures. Transport Minister Lloyd Axwor-
thy has ordered Transport Canada to analyze Air Canada's operations, maintenance procedures, and safety
standards. 1 photograph.

2.020   **Gray, Robert Reed.** "Aviation Safety: Fact or Fiction." **Technology Review** 90 (August/September 1987):
32-40.

The Civil Aeronautics Act (1938) and the Federal Aviation Act (1958) governed safety in U.S. civil aeronautics. The Airline Deregulation Act (1978) contributed
to a decrease in aviation safety. U.S. airlines, pri-
or to deregulation, maintained above required levels
of safety. Between 1978 and 1984, the number of certified carriers rose from thirty-nine to 124. The
Federal Aviation Administration (FAA) decreased the
number of its inspectors from more than 2000 in 1978
to 1332 in 1983. Between 1978 and 1984, the number
of airline aircraft increased from approximately 2800
in 1978 to about 4200 in 1984. One important result
of these changes: more airplanes to inspect, but fewer
inspectors to do the work. It is difficult to find
seasoned pilots and some major airlines are reducing
age, vision, and other standards. Skilled mechanics
are, like skilled pilots, in short supply. Author
biographical information. 7 photographs.

2.021   "Growing Aircraft Maintenance Needs Press U.S. Repair
and Modification Capacity." **Aviation Week and Space
Technology** 131 (July 24, 1989): 48 and 53.

The following firms deal with the problems of growing
aircraft maintenance: Dalfort Aviation (Dallas, Tex-
as and Phoenix, Arizona); DynAir Tech of Arizona
(Phoenix, Arizona); Aerotest, Inc. (Irvine, Van Nuys,
and Mojave, California); Tracor Aviation, Inc.,
(Goleta, California); Ramcor Airline Maintenance
Corp. (Beaumont, Texas); and Lockheed Aeromod Center
(Greenville, South Carolina). 2 photographs.

2.022   **Hayes, David.** "How Safe Is Your Airplane?" **Quest**
(Toronto) 13 (November 1984): 24-26, 28, 30, 32 and
32b.

Airline aircraft maintenance and safety primarily in
a Canadian context. 2 photographs.

2.023   **Henderson, Danna K.** "Special Report: Airline M & E

Spending Up 1.6% to $9.1 Billion in 1982." **Air Transport World** 20 (July 1983):   44-48 and 112.

Maintenance and engineering expenditures by world airlines is expected to increase 6.3% in 1983 to $9.6 billion. Maintenance and engineering employment dropped 1.7% in 1982.

2.024   **Hoffer, William.**   "Horror in the Skies."   **Popular Mechanics** 166 (June 1989):   67-70, 115 and 117.

April 28, 1988: an Aloha Airlines 737 experiences a structural collapse at 24,000 feet. One person dies and sixty-one are injured. February 24, 1989: a United Airlines (UAL) 747 experiences an explosive decompression one hundred miles south of Honolulu. Nine people die and twenty-seven are injured. Both these incidents involved aging aircraft. About one-quarter of the commercial jets operated by U.S. airlines are approximately twenty years old. Aging aircraft are also known as geriatric or high-time aircraft. The Aloha Airlines 737 had logged 90,000 take-off and landing cycles. The United 747 had a history of problems. There are five ways to detect in-flight structural failures before they occur: visually, with the aid of a magnetic field, by using an electrical eddy current, with conventional x-ray, and with ultrasound. 8 photographs. 5 illustrations.

2.025   "Is Complacency Creeping Into Airline Maintenance?" **Air Transport World** 16 (October 1979):   40-41.

Examples of aircraft engine separation: an Eastern Airlines DC-8 (Houston, Texas, November 9, 1963); a National Airlines 727 (Texas, April 30, 1974); an American Airlines 707 (St. Louis, Missouri, April 5, 1977); and an Air Canada DC-8-61 (Toronto, Ontario, July 5, 1970). Engines, however, are the cause of fewer than 5% of fatal accidents. 1 photograph.

2.026   **Isgrò, Anna Cifelli.**   "The Hidden Threat to Air Safety."   **Fortune** 115 (April 13, 1987):   81-82 and 84.

Donallco, Inc. is a California company indicted for peddling reconditioned and counterfeit parts. The North Hollywood parts maker has an annual revenue of $18 million. William Allred has been Donallco's chief executive for thirty years. If convicted, he faces a prison term and fines. 3 photographs.

2.027   **Lederer, Jerome.** "Deregulation and Aviation Safety."
Chapter in **Airline Deregulation,** by Melvin A. Brenner,
James O. Leet and Elihu Schott, 125-130. Westport,
CT: ENO Foundation for Transportation, Inc., 1985.

The author, an aviation safety specialist and President Emeritus, Flight Safety Foundation, contends the
airline industry's safety record has improved under
deregulation. There was concern deregulation would
prompt or force airlines to save time and money at
the expense of safety. Between 1978 and 1983, the
number of air carriers rose from 219 to 419. Jim Bur-
nett, Chairman, National Transportation Safety Board
(NTSB), spoke about aviation safety and deregulation
on June 14, 1984, when he addressed the Subcommittee
on Government Activities and Transportation. 1 table.
Acknowledgement.

2.028   **Lindvall, Scott G.** "Aircraft Crashworthiness: Should
the Courts Set the Standards?" **William and Mary Law
Review** 27 (Winter 1986): 371-408.

Technical considerations of aircraft crashworthiness,
legal theories of recovery in crashworthiness cases,
determination of appropriate standards in aircraft
crashworthiness cases, and an effective alternative
for determining aircraft crashworthiness liability.
198 footnotes.

2.029   **Marshall, Eliot.** "Cracks in Geriatric Aircraft." **Science** 243 (February 3, 1989): 595-597.

One person died and sixty-one were injured in April
1988, when an Aloha Airlines Boeing 737 lost part of
its roof, as the aircraft reached 24,000 feet near
Maui, Hawaii. Aloha owned the most fatigued 737s in
the world. Moreover, these aircraft operated in a hot,
salty, and corrosive environment. Since the age of a
fuselage is measured in cycles and the 737 whose roof
blew apart had 89,000 cycles, an accident of the type
which took place was not unexpected. Aloha retired
its three old 737s. 1 photograph.

2.030   **Morrison, Steven A.** and Clifford Winston. "Air Safety, Deregulation, and Public Policy." **Brookings Review** 6 (Winter 1988): 10-15.

Regulatory policy and the causes of accidents; deregulation and perceptions of air safety; and policy implications are the three areas covered. Tables help
explain the text: major contributors to fatal commercial air accidents, 1965-1986; major contributors

to fatal commercial air accidents during deregulation;
characteristics of pilots and aircraft in fatal accidents; and influences on insurance expenses, 1970-1986.
Author biographical information. 1 illustration. 12
notes.

2.031   **North, David M.**   "Crash to Boost FAA Scrutiny."   **Aviation Week and Space Technology** 110 (June 4, 1979): 12-
15.

On May 25, 1979, American Airlines Flight 191 crashed
shortly after takeoff from O'Hare International Airport in Chicago, Illinois. After the DC-10's No. 1
engine broke lose, the aircraft reached an altitude of
approximately 600 feet, then crashed into a field near
the airport. Two hundred and seventy-four people died.
Investigation of the No. 1 pylon forward thrust link
attach bolt revealed a fatigue fracture. On May 29,
four days after the crash, DC-10s were grounded. The
crash and grounding will likely prompt closer scrutiny
by the Federal Aviation Administration (FAA) of maintenance procedures regarding wide-body and other aircraft. 2 photographs. 2 illustrations.

2.032   "NTSB Impounds United 767 After Engine Power Loss."
Aviation Week and Space Technology 124 (April 7,
1986): 36.

Shortly after takeoff from San Francisco International
Airport, on March 31, 1986, United Flight 310, a Boeing 767 bound for Denver, Colorado, lost power in both
its Pratt and Whitney JT9D-R4D engines. The engines
were out for approximately thirty seconds, the airplane did not lose altitude, and it returned safely to
San Francisco International. There were 183 passengers on board. On August 19, 1983, the same aircraft
experienced a dual-engine shutdown while en route from
Los Angeles, California to Denver. The 1983 and 1986
incidents do not appear to be related. The latter incident was associated with the 767's electronic engine
control (EEC) system.

2.033   "$100 Million Maintenance Base For Shannon."   **Interavia
Aerospace Review** 44 (August 1989): 764.

Irish Leasing Co., Lufthansa, and Swissair have agreed
to establish a maintenance facility in Shannon, Ireland. Initially, Boeing 737 and McDonnell Douglas MD-
80 aircraft will be serviced. The facility is expected
to employ 1000 people by 1993. The intention is to re-
cruit local staff by 1996. 1 photograph.

2.034   **O'Quigley, Sean.** "Report of a Rapid Decompression of
a Boeing 707." **Aerospace Medicine** 42 (November 1971):
1229-1230.

A Boeing 707-349C—en route from Shannon, Ireland to
London with 102 passengers and six stewardesses on
board—experienced rapid decompression on September
24, 1970. The cockpit crew began, after hearing a
muffled bang, an emergency descent to London, where
the 707 landed safely. None of the passengers or crew
had to be hospitalized, although many passengers were
shaken. A hole measuring approximately 40 inches by
36 inches was found in the main freight door. The
cause of the decompression was fatigue in rivet holes.
Author biographical information. Abstract. 2 figures. Acknowledgements.

2.035   **Ott, James.** "Inspectors Find Compliance With Safety
Standards Lacking." **Aviation Week and Space Technology** 124 (January 13, 1986): 29-30.

Six retired FAA (Federal Aviation Administration) inspectors prepared an internal report for the FAA, regarding airline safety inspections. The report contains information on more than 13,600 inspections of
327 airlines. There were safety problems in 33% of
the inspections. Airlines which received adverse
comments: Continental, Eastern, Pan American (Pan Am),
and People Express. Thirty airlines had virtually no
adverse comments.

2.036   **Proctor, Paul.** "Maintenance Technician Shortages
Constrain Growth of Australia's Airlines." **Aviation
Week and Space Technology** 131 (July 17, 1989):   98.

Airline growth and profits are being constrained in
Australia due to a shortage of maintenance technicians. Qantas, Ansett, and Australian Airlines are
being affected. Lower on-time departure rates and
increased aircraft downtime are resulting from the
worker shortage. Mechanics are being recruited overseas because of maintenance staff turnover. Qantas
could employ as many as 800 more workers. Ansett
could fill eighty vacancies. It is especially difficult to attract workers to Sydney because of the
high cost of living and housing.

2.037   **Robinson, Ruth.** "Safer Plane Travel: Still Up in
the Air." **Canadian Consumer** 19, No. 5 (1989):   50.

After the Canadian Transport Commission (CTC) was

abolished in 1988, it was replaced by the National
Transportation Act. As a result of this act, market
forces determine fares and service. A 1989 Angus Reid-
Southam News poll found that 71% of Canadians want closer regulation of air safety. According to the Law Re-
form Commission of Canada in 1989, there are as many as
ten nongovernment airline inspectors as there are federal inspectors. **The Ottawa Citizen** stated that the
number of inspectors for large commercial aircraft decreased from thirty in 1987 to twenty-two in 1989.
Forty-one inspectors were required in 1987. 1 illustration.

2.038   **Shifrin, Carole A.** "American Commits $225 Million to
Upgrade Maintenance Operations." **Aviation Week and
Space Technology** 126 (June 29, 1987): 44-46.

To upgrade maintenance operations American Airlines has
done a number of things: embarked on a multimillion
dollar capital spending program, increased maintenance
spending sharply, added more than 2200 employees, nearly doubled the number of aircraft continuously receiving heavy maintenance at Tulsa, Oklahoma, and increased
the number of cities in which American's mechanics do
maintenance work. 2 photographs.

2.039   **Skrzycki, Cindy.** "Airline Maintenance—Any Reason to
Worry?" **U.S. News and World Report** 99 (October 14,
1985): 52-53.

Although major U.S. airlines spent $3.5 billion on air-
craft maintenance in 1984, American Airlines was fined
$1.5 million in September 1985 by the Federal Aviation
Administration (FAA) for maintenance violations.
Transportation Secretary Elizabeth Dole wants Congress
to increase the penalty for violation of FAA safety
rules from $1000 to $10,000 per violation. Some of
USAir's inspection routines exceed FAA standards because USAir uses computer technology in its maintenance work. 2 photographs.

2.040   "Southwest to Pay Fine." **Aviation Week and Space
Technology** 126 (February 16, 1987): 34.

The Federal Aviation Administration (FAA) conducted an
in-depth inspection of Southwest Airlines between April
28, 1986 and May 30, 1986. Southwest will pay $402,000
in fines for violations of maintenance and safety regulations. Southwest had, for example, repeatedly de-
ferred required maintenance on some aircraft.

2.041   "Time For a New Look at Aircraft Safety." **Economist**
271 (June 16, 1979):   87-88.

The DC-10 has had four different types of disastrous
mechanical problems, involving loss of life: an engine explosion; cargo doors coming off in flight;
tire blowouts and undercarriage collapse; and engine-
pylon collapse.   Although other wide-body jets have
four hydraulic systems, the DC-10 has only three.   The
DC-10-30, unlike other DC-10s, has had few mechanical
problems. 1 photograph.

2.042   **Whittington, Hugh.**   "'System Errors' Missed DC-9
Crack."   **Canadian Aviation** 52 (November 1979):   11.

When an Air Canada DC-9-32 was at 20,000 feet over the
Atlantic Ocean—on a flight from Boston, Massachusetts
to Yarmouth, Nova Scotia—decompression blew off the
aircraft's tailcone.   This incident occurred because
technicians missed a tiny crack, which grew from one
inch in May 1979 to twelve inches in September 1979.
Similar cracks were found in the same location in other aircraft.   Air Canada now takes four separate
x-rays. 1 photograph.

2.043   "Who's Who in Airline Maintenance and Engineering."
Air Transport World 15 (September 1978):   75-77.

Maintenance and engineering personnel for seventy-nine
airlines are listed.

2.044   "Will the DC-10 Accident Affect Maintenance?" **Air
Transport World** 16 (October 1979):   26.

Twenty-nine airlines comment on future maintenance
practices, in view of the crash in Chicago, Illinois
of American Airlines Flight 191.   Air California, Air
France, Cathay Pacific, Finnair, Japan Air Lines (JAL),
Quebecair, and Republic are some of the airlines commenting.

2.045   **Woolley, David.**   "Airmec 85."   **Interavia** 40 (April
1985):   395-397.

Over 2500 visitors attended Airmec 85, where compos-
ites, airliner avionics, and aircraft life were part
of the conference program.   Agusta, Aermacchi, and
Fokker were the aircraft manufacturers present.
Qantas, Lufthansa, and British Caledonian exhibited

products. BITE (built-in test equipment) will be of
value in troubleshooting aircraft problems. Finnair
exhibited an aircraft deicing vehicle. 5 photographs.

2.046 **Woolley, David** and Dietrich Seidl. "Airmec 83." **Interavia** 38 (June 1983): 661-663.

Airmec 83, an aircraft maintenance and overhaul exhi-
bition, was held in Düsseldorf, West Germany in April
1983. It was previously held in Switzerland (twice)
and the U.S. (once). Attending Airmec for the first
time was the Hong Kong Aircraft Engineering Co. Pay-
ing visitors to Airmec 83 numbered 2500, representing
thirty-four different countries. 9 photographs.

3

Airports

3.001   **Abelson, Louis C.,** Leon D. Star and Alan S. Goldner.
"Twenty Years of Medical Support in Aircraft Disasters
at Kennedy Airport." **Aerospace Medicine** 44 (May 1973):
560-566.

Eastern Airlines, Pan American (Pan Am) Airlines,
Trans World Airlines (TWA), United Airlines (UAL),
American Airlines, the Federal Aviation Administration
(FAA), and the Port Authority of New York and New Jersey participate in the medical disaster team based
within the boundaries of Kennedy Airport. Bronx Municipal Hospital, Creedmoor State Hospital, Harlem Hospital, Kings County Hospital, and Peninsula Hospital Center are some of the hospitals with heliports or landing fields which support the Kennedy Airport disaster
plan. The U.S. Coast Guard, New York Airways, and New
York City Police provide helicopter support for the
plan. A mobile inflatable treatment unit (MITU) can
be transported to an aircraft disaster scene almost as
fast as fire equipment, and can be fully operational
in twenty minutes. Author biographical information.
Abstract. 3 tables. 4 figures. 19 references.

3.002   "Air Accident Revives Debate on Moving San Diego Airport." **Engineering News-Record** 201 (October 5, 1978):
40.

When a commercial jet and a small plane collided over
Lindbergh Field in San Diego, California, in the fall
of 1978, it was the first crash of a commercial airliner in the airport's fifty-year history. Studies
of a site for a new airport date back to 1950. Pete
Wilson, Mayor of San Diego, favors an airport sixteen miles southeast of the city.

3.003   "Air Safety." **Editorial Research Reports** 1 (June 25,
1976): 463-470.

The ten busiest airports in the U.S. in 1975 in terms
of flights in and flights out: (1) O'Hare International, Chicago, Illinois; (2) Atlanta International,

Atlanta, Georgia; (3) Los Angeles International, Los
Angeles, California; (4) John F. Kennedy International,
New York; (5) Dallas-Fort Worth Regional; (6) San Fran-
cisco International, San Francisco, California; (7) La
Guardia, New York; (8) Miami International, Miami,
Florida; (9) Logan International, Boston, Massachusetts;
and (10) Stapleton International, Denver, Colorado. The
U.S. airlines with the most major crashes between 1971
and 1976—in order of highest number of crashes: East-
ern, Pan American (Pan Am) Airlines, and TWA (Trans
World Airlines). U.S. airlines which had one major
crash between 1971 and 1976: American, Ozark, Delta,
United, Air West, and Alaska. 6 footnotes. 1 illustration.

3.004   "Air Safety's Unspent Billions." **Business Week** (Febru-
        ary 20, 1978): 55, 58 and 60.

        The Air Line Pilots Association (ALPA) states that run-
        ways can be grooved, instrument landing systems pur-
        chased, visual approach lights erected, and new approach
        lighting systems put in place to improve safety at U.S.
        airports. The airport trust fund, which will have an
        $8 billion surplus by 1985, could be used for airport
        improvements. However, unspent trust fund money can
        serve to offset the federal deficit. 1 photograph.

3.005   "Airport Runway Safety 'Reinforced' With Plastics."
        Plastics Engineering 34 (August 1978): 1.

        With the participation of the Federal Aviation Admin-
        istration (FAA), plans are under way to replace steel
        runway approach light systems (ALSs) with hollow,
        glass-fiber-reinforced structures. These structures
        will promote safety by breaking away if struck by air-
        craft which are landing. Hopefully, passengers will
        not be harmed and damage to aircraft will be minimal.
        Eighty-five airports will receive the new ALSs. De-
        troit, Michigan and Richmond, Virginia are the first
        two cities in which conversion will take place. Per-
        mali, Inc., Lev Zetlin Associates, and PPG Industries
        are also involved in this project. 1 photograph.

3.006   "Airport Snow Problems Yielding to Attack." **SAE
        Journal** 69 (March 1961): 88.

        Less than one inch of slush on an airport runway can
        make takeoff hazardous for jet aircraft. Braking
        friction coefficients in slush vary with different
        tire treads. The coefficient of friction has been
        obtained in Sweden by skidding a truck. 3 references.

3.007   "Airports Near Big Cities—How Safe?" **U.S. News and
        World Report** 92 (January 25, 1982): 54.

        When an Air Florida 737 crashed in Washington, DC on
        January 13, 1982, after taking off from National Air-
        port, the 737 came down half a mile from the Pentagon,
        a mile from the Lincoln Memorial, and a mile and a
        half from the White House. Boston, Massachusetts; Re-
        no, Nevada; Chicago, Illinois; and Los Angeles, Cali-
        fornia are other U.S. cities with airports close to
        residential areas. In 1972, while attempting to land
        at Midway Airport in Chicago, a United Airlines (UAL)
        plane crashed into a residential area. Forty-three
        on the plane and two on the ground died. Limiting de-
        velopment around airports seems virtually impossible.
        1 photograph.

3.008   **Ashford, Norman,** H.P. Martin Stanton and Clifton A.
        Moore. "Airport Aircraft Emergencies." Chapter in
        Airport Operations, by Norman Ashford, H.P. Martin
        Stanton and Clifton A. Moore, 356-394. New York, NY:
        John Wiley and Sons, Inc., 1984.

        Probability of an aircraft accident; types of emer-
        gency; level of protection required; water supply
        and emergency access roads; communication and alarm
        requirements; rescue and fire-fighting vehicles; per-
        sonnel requirements; the airport emergency plan; air-
        craft fire-fighting and rescue procedures; foaming of
        runways; and removal of disabled aircraft. 8 tables.
        5 figures. 13 references.

3.009   **Baird, David.** "Disaster on the Runway." **Maclean's**
        96 (December 19, 1983): 23.

        Ten million passengers use Barajas Airport in Madrid,
        Spain annually. This airport had a good safety rec-
        ord until recently. On November 27, 1983, a Colom-
        bian Boeing 747 slammed into a hillside while attempt-
        ing to land. Ten days later, as Iberian Airlines
        Flight 350 was taking off, its undercarriage struck an
        Aviaco Airlines DC-9, which was in the path of Flight
        350. All forty-two passengers and crew aboard the
        Aviaco died in the fiery explosion, which resulted
        from the collision. Fifty-one passengers aboard
        Flight 350 died; forty-two survived. Complaints
        about Barajas focus on radar and runway lights.

3.010   **Barbash, Gabriel I.,** Naomi Yoeli, Stephen M. Ruskin
        and Dade W. Moeller. "Airport Preparedness For Mass
        Disaster: A Proposed Schematic Plan." **Aviation,**

Space, and Environmental Medicine 57 (January 1986):
77-81.

A model based upon experience in Israel, over an
eight-year period, is applicable to any airport, and
takes into account: characteristics of airport accidents, medical resources, medical teams movement control, crash site management, and standby equipment.
Author biographical information. 1 photograph. Abstract. 1 figure. 1 table. 6 references.

3.011   Bergot, Georges P. "Disaster Planning at Major Air-
        ports." Aerospace Medicine 42 (April 1971): 449-455.

        The author conducted research at Orly Airport in Par-
        is, France and formulated a six-point plan regarding
        airport disaster planning. Author biographical infor-
        mation. Abstract. 4 tables. 8 figures. 18 refer-
        ences.

3.012   Bolton, Francis A. "Airport Earns a Fine Reputation
        For Snow Removal." Public Works 93 (December 1962):
        98-99.

        Snow, ice, and slush removal at Port Columbus Munici-
        pal Airport in Columbus, Ohio takes months of prepara-
        tion and is a year-round problem. Author biographical
        information. 2 photographs.

3.013   Bonner, C.M. "Keeping Ice Off Runways." Civil Engi-
        neering 38 (January 1968): 73.

        Urea is a deicing chemical which can also melt com-
        pacted snow. Urea is easy to store, can be spread
        easily, and prevents ice and compacted snow from stick-
        ing to pavement. Urea, furthermore, does not harm air-
        craft materials, pavement, or vegetation. Author bio-
        graphical information.

3.014   Brown, David A. "Cincinnati Crashes Not Believed In-
        volved With Design of Airport." Aviation Week and
        Space Technology 87 (December 11, 1967): 36.

        Three airline accidents at Greater Cincinnati Air-
        port apparently were not related to the design of the
        airport. On November 8, 1965, an American Airlines
        Boeing 727 crashed on approach. On November 6, 1967,
        a Trans World Airlines (TWA) 707 crashed. And on
        November 20, 1967, a TWA Convair 880 crashed. Seventy

people died in the accidents.

3.015   **Brown, F.** and L.P. Haxby. "Added Safety in Aircraft
        Fueling." **Fire Technology** 3 (August 1967): 232-240.

        Charges in flowing fluids, aircraft fueling, Shell's
        anti-static additive (ASA), ASA-3 in airport fuel sys-
        tems, and adoption of ASA-3. Presented at the Seven-
        ty-first Annual Meeting, National Fire Protection As-
        sociation, Boston, Massachusetts, May 15, 1967. Au-
        thor biographical information. Abstract. 5 figures.

3.016   **Butcher, J.N.** "The Role of Crisis Intervention in an
        Airport Disaster Plan." **Aviation, Space, and Environ-
        mental Medicine** 51 (November 1980):   1260-1262.

        The psychological crisis state usually lasts a maxi-
        mum of six weeks. It is typically characterized by
        disbelief, denial, and confusion. An individual in
        this state may have to make new adaptations to life.
        Crisis intervention provides symptomatic relief and is
        restorative and preventive. Crisis therapy helps the
        afflicted individual manage immediate life stress. In
        Minneapolis-St. Paul, Minnesota, the Metropolitan Air-
        port Disaster Crisis Intervention Program can assist
        surviving victims and family members of an airplane
        disaster. The program includes a 200-bed first-aid
        hospital. Author biographical information. Abstract.
        14 references.

3.017   "Disaster Scenario." **Aviation Week and Space Tech-
        nology** 124 (March 31, 1986):   48.

        A tornado struck the control tower at the Greater Cin-
        cinnati International Airport on March 10, 1986. A
        portable air traffic control (ATC) tower, from the
        Federal Aviation Administration (FAA) depot, was moved
        by truck to Cincinnati International. The portable
        tower was operational two days later.

3.018   **Finch, D.M.** "Runway Visibility in Thick Fog." **Jour-
        nal of the Aero-Space Transport Division** (ASCE) 90
        (October 1964):   95-121.

        Presented at the Aero-Space Transport Division Speci-
        alty Conference: Engineering For Tomorrow's Airports,
        San Francisco, California, April 22-24, 1964. Author
        biographical information. Abstract. 3 tables. 17
        figures.

3.019   "Foam Protects Aircraft From Runway Overshoot." **Modern Plastics** 47 (December 1970):   98 and 100.

The British Royal Aircraft Establishment has been using urea-formaldehyde foam to protect aircraft from runway overshoot. British Industrial Plastics uses a special spray process to apply the foam at the end of a runway. Commercial application is expected around mid-1971.   2 photographs.

3.020   "Fog Chasers." **Science Digest** 68 (December 1970):   16-17.

Fog over airports can cause air traffic jams and loss of revenue for airlines. Gene Kooser and Tom Bucchino, the owners of World Weather, Inc. of Houston, Texas, are attempting to solve the fog problem. They have developed Fog Sweep, a machine which sprays non-toxic, fog-dispersing chemicals high over airports. The chemicals turn fog into rain. 4 photographs.

3.021   **Garrison, Peter.**   "Wrong Runway Landing." **Flying** 110 (December 1983):   100-101 and 106-107.

An article based on the Air Line Pilots Association (ALPA) report of the accident in Mexico City, of a Western Airlines DC-10. The DC-10, Flight 2605, crashed on October 31, 1979, when it attempted to land on a runway under construction. The airplane struck a dump truck then a terminal building. The flight crew was among the seventy-three people aboard the airplane who died. Fifteen people survived and an undisclosed number on the ground died. ALPA prepared a report on this crash because ALPA was not satisfied with the Mexican account of the crash. The Mexican investigation had only technical support from the National Transportation Safety Board (NTSB).

3.022   **Gerdel, R.W.**   "Note on the Use of Liquefied Propane For Fog Dispersal at the Medford-Jackson Airport, Oregon." **Journal of Applied Meteorology** 7 (December 1968): 1039-1040.

Summarizes the results of a fog dispersal program at the Medford-Jackson Airport in Oregon, during the time period December 24, 1967 to February 8, 1968. Propane was used to treat twenty-five fogs and was successful in twenty-three cases. The City of Medford and the Aerojet General Corp. cooperated in this project. Author biographical information. 1 table. Abstract. 7 references.

3.023 **Gilliland, M.G.F.**, Edward T. McDonough, Roger M. Foss-
um, Graeme P. Dowling, P.E. Besant-Matthews and
Charles S. Petty. "Disaster Planning For Air Crashes:
A Retrospective Analysis of Delta Airlines Flight
191." **American Journal of Forensic Medicine and Pathology** 7 (December 1986): 308-316.

Delta Airlines Flight 191 was en route from Fort Lau-
derdale, Florida to Los Angeles, California—with a
stop at Dallas-Fort Worth, Texas—when it crashed on
Friday, August 2, 1985 on approach to Dallas-Fort
Worth. The L-1011 suddenly lost altitude and air
speed because of wind shear, struck two cars north of
the airport, then struck a large water tank. Of the
163 persons aboard the aircraft, 130 died in the crash.
A disaster plan prepared by Drs. Nizam Peerwani and
Charles S. Petty was in effect when Flight 191 crashed.
Author biographical information. Abstract. 4 figures.
Acknowledgement. An appendix lists check lists for di-
saster planning for aircraft crashes.

3.024 **Hamovitch, Eric.** "Crowded Airports, Skies Haunt Airline Executives." **This Week in Business** 1 (November 5,
1988): 4

The International Air Transport Association (IATA) is
a trade association comprised of 173 airlines. IATA
representatives discussed airports and air traffic
control (ATC) at IATA's annual meeting in Montreal,
Quebec. Three large new airports are being constructed—at Denver, Colorado; Munich, West Germany;
and Osaka, Japan. A new airport is planned for Oslo,
Norway. IATA member airlines are expected to earn in
1988 a collective profit of over $1 billion.

3.025 **Hays, Marvin B.,** John X. Stefanki and Donald H. Cheu.
"Planning an Airport Disaster Drill." **Aviation,
Space, and Environmental Medicine** 47 (May 1976):
556-560.

These recommendations for planning an airport disaster drill are based on drills at the following three
international airports: Oakland, San Francisco, and
Los Angeles. The disaster drill can be divided into
nine parts: (1) fire and rescue; (2) security; (3)
identification of the injured; (4) triage; (5) communications; (6) command post; (7) interim rescue;
(8) other modes of transportation; and (9) casualty
instructions. Author biographical information. Abstract. 7 references.

3.026 **Hicks, J.R.** "Improving Visibility Near Airports

During Periods of Fog." **Journal of Applied Meteorology** 6 February 1967): 39-42.

United Airlines (UAL) has used dry ice to disperse airport fog in the U.S. The Soviet Union claims to have used dry ice in a similar manner. Propane has been used in France at Orly Field, Paris—to disperse airport fog. Between October 6, 1964 and July 24, 1965, liquefied propane was used to disperse fogs in Greenland and the U.S. The propane was released from ground-based dispensers. Six tests were conducted at Camp Century, Greenland; six were carried out in the Hanover-Lebanon, New Hampshire area. The tests showed that liquid propane, released into fog or low stratus clouds, induced glaciation and improvement in visibility. Ten of the twelve tests were successful. Abstract. Author biographical information. 4 figures. 1 footnote. Acknowledgements. 5 references.

3.027 **Horne, Walter B.** "Skidding Accidents on Runways and Highways Can Be Reduced." **Astronautics and Aeronautics** 5 (August 1967): 48-55.

Vehicle skidding depends primarily on the interface between pavement and tires. Vehicle-operator education; vehicle design and certification; tire design and wear; and pavement design and wear are related to the alleviation of vehicle-skidding accidents. Author biographical information. 11 photographs. 5 tables. 8 figures. 7 references.

3.028 **Horne, Walter B.** and Trafford J.W. Leland. "Runway Slipperiness and Slush." **Journal of the Royal Aeronautical Society** 67 (September 1963): 559-571.

Background of U.S. research relating to runway slipperiness and fluid drag, runway-fluid effects on free-rolling wheels, and runway slipperiness effects on a braking wheel are the three major areas discussed. Author biographical information. Abstract. 34 figures. 25 references.

3.029 **Hudock, Robert P.** "Are Runways Too Short?" **Astronautics and Aeronautics** 8 (April 1970): 68-75.

The Airline Pilots Association (ALPA) has arguments which support airport certification standards. The standards are viewed as a means to the establishment of longer runways. Author biographical information. 6 photographs. 3 illustrations. 10 references.

3.030   **Jackson, Francis C.** "Airports: Thresholds of Disaster." **Journal of Trauma** 10 (July 1970): 617-618.

There are 30,000 new air travelers daily in the U.S.
Up to eighty commercial aircraft land or take off, during an hour, at a major facility in the U.S. Piloting
a large aircraft depends upon weather, avoidance of
other air traffic, pilot health, training, and other
factors. There were 189 calls for rescue and fire
equipment in 1968 at the Greater Pittsburgh Airport,
but there were no serious accidents. Disaster planning
at the Greater Pittsburgh Airport envisioned in 1961
emergency treatment prior to transfer to hospitals.
Author biographical information.

3.031   **Jeffs, Eric.** "Runway Visibility Measurement Automated."
Engineering 209 (March 27, 1970): 308.

Europe's first automatic installation for measuring
runway visual range (RVR) is in operation at Gatwick.
This parameter is essential to the operational suitability of a runway. The automatic system was developed by
Marconi Radar Systems Ltd. There are plans to provide
installations at Manchester and Liverpool, England and
at Glasgow, Scotland. Direct sunlight cannot interfere
with the automatic system and its optical system is not
impaired by debris, such as matter from aircraft exhausts. Prior to the automatic system, a man had to
examine a runway in-person. 1 illustration.

3.032   "Jet Blast Rips Asphalt Runway." **Engineering News-Record** 164 (May 26, 1960): 26.

An 80-by-110-foot section of asphalt pavement from a
runway at Stapleton Field in Denver, Colorado was
ripped up by the jet blast, as a United Air Lines
(UAL) DC-8 was preparing to take off. Similar occurrences, on a much smaller scale, have been observed at
Idlewild Airport in New York. The Stapleton Field runway was constructed during 1940-1941. Improvements
for Stapleton Field totalling $20 million have been
approved by the City of Denver. 1 photograph.

3.033   "Jet Night Landings." **Plastics World** 18 (August 1960):
11.

The Federal Aviation Agency (FAA) has been experimenting in Atlantic City, New Jersey with recessed runway
lights. These lights allow aircraft wheels to roll
over them without passengers feeling the effect of the
wheels on the lights. 1 photograph.

3.034   **Kahn, Richard S.**   "New Runway De-icer Termed 'Effective' After LaGuardia Test."   **Aviation Week and Space Technology** 92 (March 30, 1970):   34.

Union Carbide Corp. has a glycol-based product which has been used to melt compacted runway snow and loosen ice at LaGuardia Airport in New York. Edward E. Ingraham, LaGuardia Airport Manager and Chairman, Technical Committee, American Association of Airport Executives, has commented favorably on this product. Frozen runways cause aircraft diversions which are both time-consuming and expensive. With the aid of the glycol-based product, a runway can be cleared in an hour. The product was approved for testing by the Air Transport Association and can be applied with fertilizer spreading equipment. LaGuardia discontinued using a urea-based product because the product negatively affected aircraft cadmium plating.

3.035   "Lab Tests Show Salt-Seeding Could Free Airports of Fog."   **Product Engineering** 39 (February 26, 1968):   29.

Research into fog dispersal is being carried out at the Cornell Aeronautical Laboratory in Buffalo, New York. Although laboratory tests have been successful, field tests have yet to be conducted. Researchers plan to release sodium chloride of a particular size from a light airplane. The sodium chloride will fall earthward over runway approaches and through fog. The sodium chloride will attract minute droplets of water and the air over the runway will consist of drops of water. This research is applicable to warm fog only. Carbon dioxide is used to disperse cold fog—fog below freezing temperature. 4 photographs.

3.036   **Lederer, Jerome.**   "Airport Capacity and Safety." **Journal of the Air Transport Division** (ASCE) 87 (August 1961):   7-14.

Airport capacity and safety is discussed in relation to ten-year projections regarding variables such as: increases in numbers of general aviation aircraft, increases in numbers of flights annually, all-weather landings, and accidents or incidents. Satellite airports, snow removal, taxiway markings, and birds are also discussed. Author biographical information.

3.037   **Marx, Joseph Laurance.**   "How Safe Is Safe? II. On the Ground."   Chapter in **Crisis in the Skies,** by Joseph Laurance Marx, 218-253. New York, NY: David McKay Co., Inc., 1970.

Runways; snow and ice; altimeters; computers; fatalities and injuries; emergency passenger evacuation; and
accident reports are some of the topics covered.

3.038   **Marx, Joseph Laurance.** "Rating the Airports." Chap-
        ter in **Crisis in the Skies,** by Joseph Laurance Marx,
        93-107. New York, NY: David McKay Co., Inc., 1970.

        Airports in the following cities are rated: Atlanta,
        Georgia; Boston, Massachusetts; Chicago, Illinois;
        Cincinnati, Ohio; Cleveland, Ohio; Dallas-Fort-Worth,
        Texas; Denver, Colorado; Detroit, Michigan; Houston,
        Texas; Kansas City, Missouri; Los Angeles, California;
        Las Vegas, Nevada; Miami, Florida; Minneapolis-St.
        Paul, Minnesota; New Orleans, Louisiana; New York;
        Philadelphia, Pennsylvania; Pittsburgh, Pennsylvania;
        St. Louis, Missouri; San Francisco, California; and
        Washington, DC.

3.039   **McClement, Fred.** "Airport Is a Dirty Word." Chapter
        in **It Doesn't Matter Where You Sit,** by Fred McClement,
        193-211. New York, NY: Holt, Rinehart and Winston,
        1969.

        Three examples of airports with little or no fire
        equipment or rescue services are airports at Santa
        Barbara, California; Pensacola, Florida; and Corpus
        Christi, Texas. The airport at Roanoke, Virginia does
        not have fire fighting equipment, first aid or rescue
        services, yet both Eastern and Piedmont Airlines use
        this airport daily. Both airports at Washington, DC
        are top-rated. None of the commercial airports in
        Idaho have radar. The main jet runway at Cleveland,
        Ohio is 1200 feet shorter than the recommended length.
        Pittsburgh, Pennsylvania is 1300 feet short. On March
        30, 1967, a Delta Air Lines DC-8, with six crewmembers
        and a Federal Aviation Administration (FAA) inspector
        aboard, crashed near New Orleans International Air-
        port. The crew and thirteen persons in their homes
        and in a motel died. The airport, homes, and motel
        were too close to one another, illustrating poor air-
        port planning.

3.040   "New Site Tames Killer Airport." **ENR** 218 (March 12,
        1987): 14.

        Sierra Blanca Regional Airport, Ruidoso, New Mexico,
        is being relocated from a mountain valley (elevation
        7500 feet) to a mesa (elevation 6800 feet). Seventeen
        people have died at the existing airport since 1964.
        Most fatalities occurred during takeoffs. Crashes

were attributed to mountains and a single north-south
runway. Airport expansion was not possible because of
geography. Tricon-Kent, Inc. is constructing the new
airport. Future expansion of the new airport will allow accommodation of large commercial carriers. 1 illustration.

3.041   "NTSB Recommends Changes to Improve Safety of Air-
        ports." **Aviation Week and Space Technology** 120 (May 7,
        1984): 34.

        After studying airport safety for eighteen months, the
        National Transportation Safety Board (NTSB) has made
        twenty-one recommendations to the Federal Aviation Ad-
        ministration (FAA). Six recommendations deal with fu-
        eling procedures, five with firefighting and emerg-
        encies. Leaking fuel trucks and fuel trucks without
        fire extinguishers are examples of safety concerns.
        Fourteen airports were studied. Since the FAA began
        certifying airports in 1972, airport-related accidents
        have declined.

3.042   **O'Lone, Richard G.** "Chemical Seeding Disperses Air-
        port Fog." **Aviation Week and Space Technology** 88
        (January 29, 1968): 45-46.

        Fog is a liability to U.S. airlines and costs these
        airlines approximately $75 million a year. A fog-
        dispersal program in Sacramento, California is produc-
        ing encouraging results. The Air Transport Associa-
        tion contributed $100,000 to World Weather, Inc. to
        finance the program. Sacremento has a high incidence
        of warm fog. It is warm fog that shuts down most of
        the airports in the mainland U.S. Dow, Proctor and
        Gamble, and Calgon Corp. provide chemicals for the
        Sacramento tests. The National Aeronautics and Space
        Administration (NASA), in conjunction with the Cornell
        Aeronautical Laboratory at Buffalo, New York, is also
        engaged in fog-dispersal tests. In Medford, Oregon,
        the Aerojet General Corp. disperses cold fog with
        ground-based propane equipment. Propane is used for
        the same purpose at Orly Airport, Paris. 2 photo-
        graphs.

3.043   **Pixley, James I.** "Developing an Emergency Medical
        Disaster Plan For an Airport." **Aviation, Space, and
        Environmental Medicine** 51 (November 1980): 1258-
        1259.

        There are ten essential services, at Minneapolis-St.
        Paul International Airport, which can be utilized in

the event of an emergency. The services are: crash/
fire/rescue, police, medical, communications, supply
and escort, recorder, hospital, logistics, transportation, and crisis intervention. Each service has a
service chief, who has major responsibilities. The
Triage Center, originally a 200-bed military hospital,
is centrally located and is the heart of the disaster
plan. Author biographical information. Abstract.

3.044   **Proceedings of the Aircraft Ground Deicing Conference,
Denver, Colorado, September 20-22, 1988.** Warrendale,
PA: Society of Automotive Engineers, Inc., 1989.

Most of this 272-page publication consists of question-
and-answer sessions. Among the many participants:
Dick Tobiason, Air Transport Association; John H. En-
ders, Flight Safety Foundation; Dick Adams, Federal
Aviation Administration (FAA); Paavo Turtiainen, Finnair; Ralph E. Brumby, Douglas Aircraft Co.; Dave Haase,
Airline Pilots Association (ALPA); Tony Manzo, Air Canada; David L. Fitzgerald, United Airlines (UAL); and
Rudy Yates, Federal Express.

3.045   **Ramsay, W.A.** "Damage to Ottawa Air Terminal Building
Produced by a Sonic Boom." **Materials Research and
Standards** 4 (November 1964): 612-616.

On August 5, 1959, construction of the terminal building at Ottawa (Ontario) Airport was 98% complete. During the afternoon of that date, an F-104 jet fighter
was allowed by the control tower to make two low-level
passes over one of the runways. During the second
pass, when the F-104 was about 500 feet above the
ground, a shock wave occurred. All the glass in a
temporary control tower was shattered. Fortunately,
no one was injured. Walls, doorways, and ceilings
were damaged in the terminal building. Parts of walls
and ceilings were distorted. Large patches of ceiling
stucco were dislodged. Author biographical information. 9 figures. 1 footnote.

3.046   **Rebadow, Richard F.** "Improved Snow and Ice Control at
Airports: The Continuing Research." **Public Works** 102
(December 1971): 57-62.

Snow and ice control at the Greater Buffalo International Airport, Buffalo, New York. Author biographical information. 4 photographs.

3.047   "Reducing Hazards on Slippery Runways." **Engineering**

204 (December 8, 1967):   912.

The ML Aviation Co. Ltd. Mu-Meter, a three-wheeled device, is towed behind a vehicle and measures pavement
friction—dry, wet, or icy. 1 photograph. 1 illustration.

3.048   "Runway Surface Sensor Use Expands." **Aviation Week and
Space Technology** 117 (November 8, 1982):   175 and 178-
179.

Surface Systems, Inc. of St. Louis, Missouri, supplies
Scan System 16, a device comprised of sensors and a
microprocessor, which detects moisture, frost, ice,
snow, and surface temperature at airport runways. Scan
16 provides advance warning of possible slippery runways. It was recently installed at the Seattle-Tacoma
International Airport. Three people who made favorable
comments about this device: William C. Coleman, Aviation Director, Massachusetts Port Authority; Daniel C.
Orcutt, Executive Director, Indianapolis International
Airport; and Captain J.J. Ruddy, Air Line Pilots Association (ALPA). Wilson Overall, President, Surface
Systems, Inc., recommends that three sensors be installed if a runway is less than 8000 feet long. 2
photographs.

3.049   **Shpilberg, David** and Richard De Neufville.   "Best
Choice of Fire Protection: An Airport Study." **Fire
Technology** 10 (February 1974):   5-14.

Decision analysis can help illustrate tradeoffs involved in airport fire protection strategies. Strate-
gy is dependent on type and size of airport. The best
choice is not always maximum fixed fire protection.
Fixed cost of fire protection and cost of insurance
are important variables. Author biographical information. 6 figures. 2 references.

3.050   **Smith, Donald I.,** John D. Odegard and William Shea.
"Contingency Planning." Chapter in **Airport Planning
and Management,** by Donald I. Smith, John D. Odegard
and William Shea, 164-175. Belmont, CA: Wadsworth
Publishing Co., 1984.

Aspects of contingency plans; developing a contingency plan; a simple emergency plan outline; nuclear disaster response; airport emergency plan; and emergency
procedures. Emergency procedures pertaining to: structural fires; natural disasters; crowd control; radio-
logical incidents or nuclear attack; removal of dis-
abled aircraft; and medical situations. 1 table. 2

figures.

3.051   **Smith, Donald I.,** John D. Odegard and William Shea.
        "Crash, Fire, and Rescue." Chapter in **Airport Plan-
        ning and Management,** by Donald I. Smith, John D.
        Odegard and William Shea, 155-163. Belmont, CA:
        Wadsworth Publishing Co., 1984.

        Airport safety requirements, Federal Aviation Regula-
        tions (FAR), and airport fires are related to crash,
        fire, and rescue situations. 1 figure.

3.052   "Sounding Out Hazards at Airports." **New Scientist**
        91 (July 30, 1981): 288.

        SODAR (Sonic Detection and Ranging), a device which
        computes wind speed and direction above ground, is op-
        erational at Frankfurt—Main Airport. SODAR is used to
        help aircraft land more safely. 1 photograph.

3.053   **Spencer, Domina Eberle.** "Fog on Runways." **Illuminat-
        ing Engineering** 56 (July 1961): 436-442.

        Five ways of minimizing the negative effects of fog on
        illuminated runways are presented with the aid of cal-
        culations. Author biographical information. 15 fig-
        ures. 3 references.

3.054   **Unger, Harlow.** "U.S. Crashes Focus Attention on Air-
        port Safety." **Canadian Travel Courier** 17 (March 18,
        1982): 11.

        A black-star airport is an airport that has serious
        deficiencies, such as runways of inadequate length,
        dangerously congested skies or dangerous approach or
        take-off routes. There are twenty-four black-star
        airports throughout the world. Although there are no
        such airports in Canada, the only one in the U.S. is
        Los Angeles International. Some areas of the world
        are designated black star because of air traffic con-
        trol (ATC) deficiencies. Parts of Brazil, South Ko-
        rea, India, Saudi Arabia, and Indonesia are designated
        black star. Some airlines—American Airlines is an
        example—refuse to fly for safety reasons to certain
        airports.

3.055   **Willey, Fay.** "The 'Black Star' Airports." **Newsweek**

89 (April 11, 1977):   53.

The following airports are, according to the International Federation of Air Line Pilots Associations (IFALPA), seriously deficient in safety features: St. Thomas, Virgin Islands; Boston, Massachusetts (Logan); Los Angeles, California; Teheran, Iran (Mehrabad Airport); Osaka, Japan; and Colombia (seven international airports). Two of the best airports are Dulles, Washington, DC and Heathrow, London.

3.056   **Winston, Don.** "Automatic Surveyor Looks For Wavy Runways." **Control Engineering** 9 (June 1962):   149.

Waviness in runways is difficult to see. Even a pilot may not be able to detect waviness. It is important to detect flaws in runways because waviness, for example, weakens airframes and increases fuel consumption, when an airplane takes off. To address the problem of waviness, a Runway Profile Instrumentation System has been developed at the Midwest Research Institute. 1 photograph.

3.057   **Wirsch, George F.** "Jumbo Fire Protection For Jumbo Jet Hangar." **Heating/Piping/Air Conditioning** 44 (January 1972):   118-120.

The Viking Automatic Sprinkler Co. of Los Angeles, California established facilities for protecting from fire service personnel and Boeing 747s at Los Angeles County Airport. The servicing of two 747s simultaneously necessitates the protection of over $50 million in capital equipment. The 747 is the largest airplane designed for commercial use. The wing span is approximately 195 feet and the plane's overall length is about 231 feet. Author biographical information. 3 photographs.

3.058   **Woolley, David.** "Slippery Runways: Searching For a Consensus." **Interavia** 38 (July 1983):   728-730.

After a World Airways DC-10 landed at Boston's Logan International Airport on January 23, 1982, the aircraft overran the runway, ended up in shallow water, and broke up. There were 212 people on board. Only two people were not accounted for after the DC-10 was evacuated. They were presumed dead. Operating on a slippery runway, as was the World Airways DC-10, can be dangerous. Research into friction measurement will hopefully help alleviate problems encountered by aircraft taking off from or landing on slippery runways.

Two devices produced in Sweden—the Skiddometer and the Saab Friction-Tester, and one developed in the United Kingdom, the Mu-Meter—are used in friction measurement. 5 photographs. 1 illustration.

3.059 **Young, Bruce.** "Spray-On Aircraft Deicing." **Canadian Aviation** 37 (January 1964): 13.

Spray-Mat is the trade name for an invisible electric blanket used to keep parts of certain aircraft free from ice. 3 photographs.

4

Birds as Hazards
to Aircraft

4.001   **Alison, Robert M.**   "Collisions in the Sky."   **Ontario
Out of Doors** 19 (October 1987):   9 and 52-53.

According to the Federal Bird Strike Committee, there
were in 1985 767 collisions in Canada between birds
and aircraft. When a Boeing 727 struck six Canada
geese in 1986, the aircraft repair bill was $400,000.
In another incident, a hawk struck a Boeing 727. The
damage was almost $1 million. In Wabush, Newfound-
land, an engine of a Quebecair jet failed on takeoff
because a bird entered an engine. Most bird strikes
occur at airports and cause dozens of aborted takeoffs
each year. Bird strikes also cause more than one hundred precautionary landings annually in Canada. There
are about fifty bird strikes each year at Toronto's
Lester B. Pearson Airport. 1 illustration. 2 photographs.

4.002   "Bird Ingestion Confirmed as Crash Cause." **Aviation
Week and Space Technology** 77 (August 6, 1962):   45.

In Boston, Massachusetts, on October 4, 1960, an
Eastern Air Lines Lockheed Electra struck a flock of
starlings seconds after becoming airborne. The plane
then fell almost vertically into water at the edge of
Logan International Airport. This was the finding of
the Civil Aeronautics Board (CAB). Tests conducted
at the Lockheed Aircraft Corp. in California concerned
the controlled introduction of birds into an Electra's
engines. CAB was interested in improved tolerance of
turbine engines to bird ingestion. CAB also reported
on the accident of a Continental Air Lines Boeing 707
near Unionville, Missouri. A dynamite explosion in a
rear lavatory was the probable cause of this accident.

4.003   "Bird Strike Deterrent—A Feigned Falcon." **Nature
Canada** 5 (January/March 1976):   21.

Captain Robert Randall, a pilot with CP Air, built a
radio-controlled, falcon-shaped model to help solve
the bird problem at Vancouver International Airport,

Vancouver, B.C. Gas cannons, runway patrol vehicles,
and other means of bird control did not prove to be
very successful. Dunlins, gulls, and other birds
were frightened away because the shape of a predator
alerts most birds. 1 photograph.

4.004   "Bird Strikes Cause Nine Airline Accidents." **Science
News Letter** 82 (December 8, 1962):   365.

Geese, swans, ducks, and other birds have caused
varying degrees of damage to airliners. A United Airlines (UAL) Viscount, which crashed near Washington,
DC, resulted in the deaths of all seventeen people on
board. A Lockheed Electra, which took off from Boston,
Massachusetts in 1960, crashed after three of its four
engines were struck by starlings. Sixty-two people
died in that crash. The Federal Aviation Agency (FAA)
is conducting experiments in Burbank, California and
Atlantic City, New Jersey in an attempt to eliminate
the bird strike problem. Plants and food cans are removed from many airports to discourage birds from
staying at or near the airports.

4.005   "Birds Are Deaf to Jumbo Jets." **New Scientist** 97
(February 17, 1983):   441.

A bird strike is much more likely to involve a wide-
body jet (a Boeing 747) than a narrow-body jet (a
Boeing 707). Birds have more time to get away from
narrow-body jets because these airplanes are noisier
than wide-body aircraft. Joanna Burger of Rutgers
University has studied background sound levels at
J.F.K. International Airport in New York. 1 cartoon
illustration.

4.006   **Blokpoel, Hans. Bird Hazards to Aircraft: Problems
and Prevention of Bird/Aircraft Collisions.** Ottawa:
Supply and Services Canada, 1976.

An examination of: birds and bird migration; bird
strike statistics; bird-proofing of aircraft and engines; the search for on-board equipment to disperse
birds; prevention of bird strikes at airports; prevention of bird strikes away from airports; and organizations working on the bird strike hazard. Acknowledgements. 34 figures. 4 tables. 32 photographs.
11 appendices. List of abbreviations (40). 445 references.

4.007   **Brewer, George L., Jr.   "Effects of High Intensity**

Flashing Light on Pigeons." Master's thesis, University of Missouri, 1970.

Aircraft-bird collisions can and do cause loss of human life. Economic losses for the U.S. Air Force (USAF) are approximately $10 million annually. The forces involved in these collisions are so great that it is not feasible to solve this problem by strengthening engines and aircraft structures. Changing the ecology of airports—so as not to attract birds—is one way the problem has been dealt with. Falcons have been used to scare other birds. Research for this thesis indicates that a strobe acts as a stress factor to pigeons. There was decreased food consumption and increased adrenal gland weights. It may be possible to use a strobe to control birds as hazards to aircraft. 3 tables. 13 figures. 10 references.

4.008 **Buchheister, Carl W.** "Swallow Problem at Idlewild Airport." **Audubon Magazine** 62 (November/December 1960): 278-279.

A DC-7 aborted a takeoff at Idlewild International Airport in New York because the aircraft's engine air-coolers ingested birds. Runway closure was necessary in September 1960 due to tens of thousands of tree swallows resting on runways. Roland Clement, an ecologist; Clarence E. Faulkner, a biologist; and other individuals determined that the birds were attracted to the runway area by bayberries growing on bushes which had been planted to control snowdrifts and soil erosion. A suggested long-range solution to the problem is to replace the bayberry shrubs with shrubs which will control snowdrifts and soil erosion, but will not attract tree swallows. A short-term solution, for next year, is to spray the bayberry bushes to eliminate fruiting. Author biographical information. 1 photograph.

4.009 **Caithness, T.A.** "Poisoning Gulls With Alpha-Chloralose Near a New Zealand Airfield." **Journal of Wildlife Management** 32 (April 1968): 279-286.

Habitat changes; interference with nests and eggs; and elimination of nesting birds were considered as solutions to birds interfering with aircraft at Hawke Bay Airfield, Napier, New Zealand. The Wallaceville Animal Research Centre assisted in the choice of a poison. Alpha-chloralose was used because it brought about death relatively quickly and with minimal distress to the birds. Two sizes of bread were used as bait. Eighty-five percent of breeding gulls were poisoned. The number of bird-aircraft incidents dropped dramatically. Author biographical information. Abstract. 7

references. 1 figure. 2 tables.

4.010   "Cannon to Shoot Chickens." **Engineering** 210 (December 18-25, 1970): 636.

Chickens are electrocuted then kept frozen until required, for aircraft structure research, at the Canadian National Research Council. The chickens are pro-
pelled out of a cannon at aircraft structures at
speeds up to 620 miles per hour. The cannon operates
pneumatically and is about seventy feet long. 1 illustration.

4.011   **Davies, Owen.** "Unfriendly Skies." **Omni** 8 (July
1986): 84.

Bird strikes are a dangerous and costly problem to
airlines because ingestion of birds can result in engine failure and the crash of an airplane. All-Nippon
Airways is attempting to solve this problem by paint-
ing large eyes on airplane turbines. All-Nippon hopes
birds will mistake Boeing 727s and 747s for huge pred-
ators, and will avoid the aircraft. 2 photographs.

4.012   **De Jong, A.P.** "Their Airspace or Ours?" **Shell Aviation News** No. 390 (1970): 2-7.

Collisions between birds and aircraft pose a very serious safety problem. One attempt to deal with this
problem was the International Bird Strike Symposium
held in Nice, France, November 1963. As a result of
this symposium, there is international cooperation in
dealing with the bird hazard problem. West Germany,
Canada, Australia, and the Netherlands are some of the
cooperating countries. Also, the European Bird Strike
Committee (EBSC), an international committee, has been
established. Falconry has been used at the Royal Naval Air Station Lossiemouth, Scotland. However, there
are certain disadvantages in using falcons. For example, falcons function with great difficulty in strong
winds. And falcons do not perform well during moulting
period. Author biographical information. 12 photographs. 5 figures.

4.013   **Doughty, Robin W.** "Competition For Airspace: Bird
Strikes and Aircraft Operations." **Traffic Quarterly**
30 (July 1976): 449-467.

Bird strikes have blinded and killed aircraft crewmembers, and have seriously damaged aircraft. Over

half of bird strikes occur at approximately 3000 feet.
The bird strike problem has been increasing in the U.S.
Up to 150,000 Canada geese pass within seventy miles of
O'Hare Airport every year from October through December. Birds are attracted to airports because airports
are frequently located near wetlands, croplands, and
refuse dumps. Chemicals, taped distress calls of certain birds, and falconry have been used to deal with
the problem of birds at airports. Data about fourteen
significant bird strikes between 1960 and 1974 is sum-
marized in table format. Author biographical information. 5 tables. 3 figures. 15 footnotes. Acknowledgement.

4.014   "FAA Funds Engineering Study of Damage by Bird Inges-
         tion." **Aviation Week and Space Technology** 115 (August
         17, 1981): 34.

         A World Airways DC-10 ingested pigeons, at Britain's
         Gatwick Airport, as the airplane was taking off on July
         7, 1981. Damage was caused to the DC-10's General
         Electric CF6-50C2 engine. The Federal Aviation Admin-
         istration (FAA) is interested in this incident because
         the FAA is funding a study of high-bypass-ratio engines
         damaged by bird ingestion.

4.015   **Fisher, Jonathan.** "Birds and Airplanes Don't Mix."
         International Wildlife 8 (March/April 1978): 17-19.

         In 1912 in California, Cal Rodgers piloted his air-
         plane into a gull. The airplane crashed and Rodgers
         was killed. At the present time, there are 10,000
         bird strikes annually on planes worldwide. Estimated
         annual damage varies between $100 million and $1 bil-
         lion. According to John L. Seubert, U.S. Fish and
         Wildlife Service, 140 civil airports in the U.S. have
         bird problems. In incidents in the U.S., Turkey, and
         Australia in 1972 and 1973, jumbo jets lost engine
         power after collisions with birds. Bird control at
         Heathrow Airport in London is reputed to be one of the
         best in the world. A half million dollars a year is
         spent controlling birds at Kennedy International Air-
         port in New York. Falcons, recorded distress calls,
         firecrackers, shotguns, and gas cannons have been
         used worldwide to help alleviate airport bird problems.
         1 illustration. Author biographical information.

4.016   "Flying Into Birds." **Canadian Business** 40 (July
         1967): 56.

         The British Overseas Airways Corporation (BOAC) has

spent more than $3 million to repair aircraft engines
damaged in bird strikes. In Canada, the National Research Council, Royal Canadian Air Force (RCAF), and
Department of Transport (DOT) have been studying bird
density at Cold Lake, Alberta.

4.017   "Fowl Weather For Flying." **Newsweek** 70 (September 25,
        1967): 98 and 101.

        During the first nine months of 1967, there were 527
        collisions in the U.S. between commercial aircraft and
        birds. The birds ranged from sparrows to swans. In
        1960 and 1962, seventy-nine people died in commercial
        aircraft accidents caused by bird strikes. Visual
        sightings of birds and radar tracking have both been
        used to alert pilots about migrating waterfowl. High-
        intensity lights and cannon fire have been used to
        control birds.

4.018   **Garrison, Glenn.** "Crash Spurs Further Bird Ingestion
        Study." **Aviation Week** 74 (January 23, 1961): 45, 47
        and 49.

        An Eastern Air Lines Lockheed Electra crashed into Bos-
        ton harbor on October 4, 1960. When the Electra
        crashed, three of its four engines had almost full pow-
        er. A three-day Civil Aeronautics Board (CAB) hearing
        was held in that city. According to Elmer J. Briggs of
        the Federal Aviation Agency (FAA), a study to prevent
        bird ingestion and to minimize the effects of ingestion
        will be held. C.R. Mercer of Lockheed also testified
        at the hearing. 2 illustrations.

4.019   **Graham, Frank, Jr.** "Confrontation in the Skies." **Au-
        dubon** 85 (January 1983): 22 and 24.

        Gulls, doves, and ducks are examples of birds that rep-
        resent a serious threat to aviation safety at New
        York's airports, and other airports worldwide. The U.S.
        Fish and Wildlife Service states there are more than
        1400 bird strikes annually. Damage to airplanes is es-
        timated at $20 million. Shellcrackers and live ammuni-
        tion are used to scare birds away from runways. 2
        photographs.

4.020   **Great Britain. Board of Trade. Aerodromes Technical
        Directorate. Bird Control on Aerodromes.** Second Edi-
        tion. N.p., February 1969.

        Some of the topics discussed: bird behavior and visual

identification (gulls, corvids, starlings); environment control; detection, dispersal, and warning; use of
pyrotechnics and visual scares (safety, security,
storage); and the automatic gas cannon. 4 illustrations.

4.021 **Halladay, Delbert Raymond. "Avian Ecology as it Re-
lates to the Bird Hazard Problem at Vancouver Airport."**
Master's thesis, University of British Columbia, 1968.

The Vancouver Airport and its environs; faunal observations and trials; vegetation observations and trials;
and physiographic observations and trials are four major areas examined. Some of the birds identified as
"problem birds:" snowy owl, American widgeon, killdeer
plover, marsh hawk, dunlin, herring gull, barn swallow,
house finch, and American goldfinch. 16 tables. 43
figures. 107 references.

4.022 **Hunt, F.R. The Probability of Bird-Aircraft Collisions
Based on Radar Data.** N.p., November 1976.

Relationship between a bird distribution model and a
mathematical relationship between the probability of a
bird-aircraft strike and observed radar data. Abstract.
7 figures. 1 table. Acknowledgements. 14 references.

4.023 **Lansford, Henry.** "The Weird Things That Happen When
Planes and Birds Collide." **Science Digest** 65 (May
1969): 32-36.

When a flight of geese hit a DC-6 airliner over Michigan at 9500 feet, the birds made holes up to ten inches
wide in the wing. The greatest danger to aircraft is
from large birds or from large flocks of small birds.
Takeoff is when airplanes are most vulnerable. During
a two-year period, the Royal Canadian Air Force (RCAF)
lost seven fighter aircraft to bird strikes. Although
all seven pilots ejected safely from their aircraft,
all seven aircraft were destroyed. Dr. Warren L.
Flock, University of Colorado and Dr. William J. Hamilton III, University of California at Davis, are conducting research to help solve the aircraft-bird problem. 2 photographs. 1 reference.

4.024 **Line, Les.** "Fricasseed Gull." **Audubon** 85 (January
1983): 6.

A personal account of being on a Boeing 727 when it

collided with a flock of birds. The incident occurred
on April 9, 1981 over the Hudson River. The 727, an
Eastern shuttle from Washington, was at an altitude of
800 feet on final approach to La Guardia. The airplane was jarred several times, one engine was dis-
abled, and some of the landing lights were smashed.
The airplane landed safely, one engine backfiring.
There are approximately 1400 bird strikes annually in
the U.S. with damage estimated at $20 million. On No-
vember 28, 1982, there were two incidents involving
bird strikes at New Orleans International Airport. A
Delta DC-9 and a Republic DC-9 struck gulls.

4.025   **Matazzoni, Joe.** "Share the Air: Israelis Take Rap-
tors Under Their Wing." **Sierra** 72 (November/December
1987):   17.

There used to be hundreds of collisions between birds
and aircraft in Israel, but collisions are now a rare
occurrence. The Israel Air Force, during the last decade, lost more jets in bird strikes than in combat
with Arab forces. The reason for the dramatic decrease in bird strikes is associated with the Israel
Raptor Information Center and the center's profile of
bird migration in Israel. Aircraft can now avoid mi-
gratory flyways. 1 cartoon illustration.

4.026   **McMahon, Patrick.** "Determined Ducks Defy Deportation."
Canadian Audubon 29 (January/February 1967):   8-10.

Ducks, mostly mallards, were a serious hazard to aircraft landing at and taking off from McCall International Airfield in Calgary, Alberta. Personnel from
the Canadian Wildlife Service designed special nets in
which to capture the ducks. The ducks were banded and
their underbellies painted yellow. Then the ducks
were placed in crates and flown in an Air Canada transport to Vancouver, B.C. This was not an effective way
of dealing with the duck problem because banded ducks
with yellow underbellies were again found in Calgary.
5 photographs.

4.027   **Murton, R.K.** and E.N. Wright. Editors. **The Problems
of Birds as Pests.** London: Academic Press, Inc.,
1968.

This book consists of two main parts. The first part
is about birds and aircraft; the second part is about
birds and agriculture. This book is also entitled
Symposia of the Institute of Biology No. 17. The entire book contains the proceedings of a symposium held

at the Royal Geographical Society, London, September
28-29, 1967. The first part consists of six papers:
(1) "Birds and Aircraft: the Problems" by E.R. Stables
and N.D. New; (2) "Prospective Considerations Concerning Bioacoustics in Relation to Bird-Scaring Techniques" by R.G. Busnel and J. Giban; (3) "Recent Developments in Bird Scaring on Airfields" by T. Brough;
(4) "Bird Recognition by Radar: A Study in Quantita-
tive Radar Ornithology" by G. Schaefer; (5) "A Bird
Warning System For Aircraft in Flight" by W.W.H. Gunn
and V.E. Solman; and (6) "Modification of the Habitat
as a Means of Bird Control" by E.N. Wright.

4.028   "Preventive Bird Control Can Reduce Costly, Dangerous
          Bird Airplane Collisions." **Pest Control** 35 (September
          1967): 12-16 and 18.

          Noise stimuli, lasers, and avicide are three methods
          used to control birds at airports. The names of twen-
          ty-nine types of birds involved in bird airplane colli-
          sions are listed. A table lists bird control methods
          used at airports in the western U.S. 7 photographs. 2
          illustrations.

4.029   **Proceedings of the World Conference on Bird Hazards to
          Aircraft, Kingston, Ontario, September 2-5, 1969.** N.p.,
          1969.

          During September 2-5, 1969, 141 men and women, repre-
          senting twenty-one countries, met in Kingston, Ontario.
          Australia, Canada, Denmark, Italy, Poland, Sweden, and
          the U.S. were some of the countries represented. Ten
          major areas of concern were discussed: (1) the problem
          of bird hazards to aircraft (fourteen papers); (2) air-
          port surveys (three papers); (3) ground cover and
          earthworms (three papers); (4) dispersal of birds (six
          papers); (5) bird migration studies (fourteen papers);
          (6) airworthiness (three papers); (7) identification
          of bird remains (one paper); (8) population control
          (two papers); (9) exchange of information (two papers);
          and (10) conclusions and recommendations. The follow-
          ing are some of the authors who participated: J.G.W.
          Brown, W. Keil, J.D. Romer, V.E. Jacoby, J. Hild, C.W.
          Stortenbeker, E.N. Wright, G.A. Richardson, R.S. Cox,
          and H.L. Cogswell.

4.030   **Reed, Arthur.** "Bird-Strike Study." **Air Transport
          World** 19 (March 1982): 65.

          There are fewer bird strikes if an airliner has wing-
          tip-mounted strobe lights. This conclusion was reached

by B.J. Zuur of the Swiss Ornithological Station, Sem-
pach, Switzerland. Zuur carried out research in 1980
with thirty-six Swissair DC-9s. Fourteen of the aircraft were fitted with strobes; twenty-two did not
have strobes. There were 145 bird strikes among the
thirty-six aircraft. 1 table. 1 illustration.

4.031   **Roberts, Carman.**   "The Birds."   **Canadian Aviation** 57
        (February 1984):   71-73.

The first bird strike took place in 1912. Now there
are 10,000 bird strikes annually worldwide. Dollar
costs range between $100 million and $1 billion each
year. The Royal Air Force began using falconry to
control nuisance birds in 1947. In Canada, falconry
was first used in the early 1960s. The number of bird
strikes at Toronto International Airport varied from
forty-seven in 1976 to ten in 1978. Author biographical information. 2 photographs.

4.032   **Saul, E.K.**   "Birds and Aircraft: A Problem at Auck-
        land's New International Airport."   **Journal of the
        Royal Aeronautical Society** 71 (May 1967):   366-376.

Auckland International Airport in New Zealand is located in an area of farmland, tidal mudflats, and a
harbor. Birds are attracted to this area by a vast
supply of marine invertebrates and vegetation. Gulls,
terns, swans, and herons are examples of birds which
pose a threat to aircraft. Four major methods have
been used to manage the bird problem: environmental
control; supplying alternative habitat; scaring; and
evaluation and prediction. The following are specific examples of these methods: elimination of shelter,
long/short grass, artificial roosts, hawk shapes, and
daily observations. A table depicts bird incidents
at Auckland International between August 1965 and July 1966, indicating strikes, near-misses, and types
of birds. Author biographical information. Abstract.
1 table. 6 figures. Acknowledgements. 8 references.

4.033   **Smith, Donald I.**, John D. Odegard and William Shea.
        "Bird Control." in **Airport Planning and Management,**
        by Donald I Smith, John D. Odegard and William Shea,
        179-182. Belmont, CA: Wadsworth Publishing Co.,
        1984.

Reduction of the bird food supply; hawk and owl trap-
ping; earthworm and gull control; drainage; and fo-
liage removal are ways of controlling birds at airports. 1 figure.

4.034   **Solman, V.E.F.**   "Bird Control and Air Safety." in
          Transactions of the Thirty-third North American Wild-
          life and Natural Resources Conference, Houston, Texas,
          March 11-13, 1968, edited by James B. Trefethen, 328-
          336. Washington, DC: Wildlife Management Institute,
          1968.

          The author who is Staff Specialist, Migratory Bird
          Habitat, Canadian Wildlife Service, talks about bird
          control and air safety in Canadian and non-Canadian
          contexts. 3 references. Discussion.

4.035   **Solman, Victor E.F.**   "Photography in Bird Control For
          Air Safety." **Journal of the Biological Photographic**
          Association 37 (July 1969):   150-155.

          The problem of bird damage to aircraft in Canada be-
          came so serious that, in 1962, the National Research
          Council of Canada began to investigate the situation.
          The Associate Committee on Bird Hazards to Aircraft
          was subsequently formed. The Canadian Airline Pilots
          Association (CALPA) and the Canadian Wildlife Service
          were two of a number of organizations which sent per-
          sonnel to serve on the committee. It was immediately
          realized that birds pose a threat to aircraft at two
          particular times. The first is at airports—when
          planes are moving on the ground or when they are land-
          ing or taking off. The second is when birds migrate
          to and from their breeding grounds. Photography of
          radar screens showing migratory birds came to be a
          useful way of studying their movements. Author bio-
          graphical information. 5 figures. 4 references.

5

Aircraft Fires

5.001   **Abelson, Louis C.,** Leon D. Star and John X. Stefanki.
        "Passenger Survival in Wide-Bodied Jet Aircraft Acci-
        dents vs. Other Aircraft: A Comparison." **Aviation,**
        Space, and Environmental Medicine 51 (November 1980):
        1266-1269.

        Improvement in occupant restraint systems, fire sup-
        pression, and suppression of toxic fumes are three of
        the reasons for passenger survival in wide-bodied jet
        aircraft accidents. A mobile emergency hospital at
        Kennedy Airport in New York can be used in tandem,
        and brought to the scene of an airplane crash. The
        condition of crash victims can be monitored by New
        York Medical College. Author biographical informa-
        tion. Abstract. 3 tables. 6 figures. 12 references.

5.002   "Air Canada Introduces Aircraft Safety Measure." **Ca-**
        nadian Travel News 23 (February 9, 1984): 6

        Air Canada, which has 17,500 seats in its airline
        fleet, is replacing up to 500 seat cushions a month,
        with more fire-resistant, polyurethane cushions. The
        changeover is expected to take approximately three
        years and was prompted by a fire aboard an Air Canada
        flight on June 2, 1983. The DC-9 made an emergency
        landing at Cincinnati, Ohio.

5.003   "American 767-200ER Returns to Frankfurt Following En-
        gine Fire." **Aviation Week and Space Technology** 127
        (August 24, 1987): 25.

        On August 16, 1987, an American Airlines Boeing 767-
        200ER made an unscheduled landing at Frankfurt-Main
        International Airport. Shortly after takeoff, an en-
        gine caught fire on the aircraft which was bound from
        Frankfurt to Chicago, Illinois. The pilot made a
        single-engine landing. There were 173 passengers and
        nine crew aboard the airplane.

5.004   "A Bit Buffeted." **Economist** 287 (June 11, 1983): 26

and 29.

An Air Canada jet makes an emergency landing at Cincinnati, Ohio and twenty-three passengers die in the on-
board fire.   An Eastern Airlines L-1011 en route from
Miami, Florida to the Bahamas, comes close to being
ditched in the Atlantic because of engine trouble.   A
Republic Airlines DC-9—bound from Fresno, California
to Phoenix, Arizona—comes to within a few gallons of
running out of fuel in mid-air.   In spite of these incidents, passenger airline safety in the U.S. is very
good.   There were no fatal airline crashes there in
1980 and 1981.   The Air Line Pilots Association (ALPA)
wants to make flying safer by having airlines install
less combustible interiors.   1 photograph.

5.005   **Chicarello, Peter J.** and David C. Shpilberg.   "Minimum
Extinguishment Area Required For Safe Escape of Aircraft Occupants During a Fuel Spill Fire."   **Fire Technology** 12 (November 1976):   276-289.

How to determine the minimum fire area that must be ex-
tinguished to delay fuselage burn-through long enough
to allow aircraft occupants to escape.   Author biographical information.   Abstract.   7 figures.   7 references.

5.006   "FAA Multi-Faceted Aircraft Fire Safety Effort."   **Interavia** 35 (October 1980):   879.

The Federal Aviation Administration (FAA) is involved
in research to eliminate or reduce aircraft fires.
Seconds are important in evacuating a burning airplane.
Cabin fire safety can be improved by replacing polyure-
thane foams used in seating.   These foams, when burned,
produce toxic gases.   The FAA also wants to see a more
flame-resistant cabin window.   Acrylic plastic is presently used.   Experiments are also being carried out
with an anti-misting additive for Jet A aircraft fuel.
2 photographs.

5.007   "FAA Proposes Rulemaking Aimed at Fire Suppression."
Aviation Week and Space Technology 121 (October 22,
1984):   41.

The Federal Aviation Administration (FAA) wants to reduce the likelihood of aircraft post-crash ground
fires.   There would be protection against fuel tank
explosions; there would be assurance of engine fuel
supply shutoff.   The latter would reduce fire hazard
from spilled fuel.   The FAA recommendations are based
on research by the Special Aviation Fire and Explosion

Reduction (SAFER) Advisory Committee. This committee
was established in 1978.

5.008   "FAA Takes Unified Look at Cabin Fires." **Aviation
Week and Space Technology** 107 (September 26, 1977):
40.

The Federal Aviation Administration (FAA) is conducting research into aircraft cabin fires and occupant
survivability. Part of the research is being done at
the National Aviation Facilities Experimental Center
(NAFEC). Other research is being carried out at the
Civil Aeromedical Institute. Heat, smoke density,
and gas anlysis are being studied. Public hearings
are scheduled in Washington, DC.

5.009   "FAA to Consider Changing Aircraft Evacuation Rules."
Aviation Week and Space Technology 123 (September 9,
1985): 34.

A post-crash fire can limit the number of exits available for passenger evacuation of an aircraft. This
was illustrated on March 1, 1978 in Los Angeles, California and on November 12, 1975 in New York. Both incidents involved DC-10 aircraft. The National Transportation Safety Board (NTSB), in a letter to the Federal Aviation Administration (FAA), expressed opposi-
tion to the reduction of exits on Boeing 747 aircraft.

5.010   "Fell-Fab Improves Aviation Safety." **Canada Commerce**
(Fall 1986): 15-16.

Fell-Fab Products is a Hamilton, Ontario company, some
of whose products are endorsed by Air Canada and the
Aerospace Industries Association of Canada. Fell-Fab
produces Fire-Bloc, a concept which involves protecting airline seat cushions with a fire-resistant fab-
ric shield. A Boeing 747 can be refitted in one week.
Fell-Fab is also involved in satellite components. 4
photographs.

5.011   "Fire Cited in Varig 747 Crash Near Orly." **Aviation
Week and Space Technology** 104 (April 12, 1976): 20-
21.

A Varig jet—en route from Rio de Janeiro, Brazil to
Paris, France on July 11, 1973—was at 8000 feet and
preparing to land at Orly Airport, when fire broke
out in the rear toilet area. Heavy smoke was asphyx-
iating passengers as the crew began an emergency

descent.   Soon there was heavy black smoke in the cockpit.   As the aircraft landed in a field three miles
from the runway, the landing gear collapsed, and the
aircraft skidded almost 2000 feet before coming to
rest.   Eight crewmembers escaped through the side window of the cockpit.   Two other crewmembers escaped
through doors at the forward section.   Although firefighters arrived about six minutes after the crash,
123 people died on board the aircraft.

5.012   "Fire Fighting, Life Support Systems Getting Improvement at Air Canada." **Canadian Aviation** 60 (March 1987):
7.

Air Canada is spending millions of dollars to improve
fire safety aboard its airplanes.   This action is being
taken because of a fire aboard an Air Canada DC-9 in
1983.   Twenty-three passengers died after the DC-9 made
an emergency landing at Cincinnati, Ohio.   Passenger
and crew smokehoods, Halon fire extinguishers, and washroom fire detectors are part of the efforts to improve
fire safety.   1 photograph.

5.013   **Fittes, D.W.**, D.J. Griffiths and P. Nash.   "The Use of
Light Water For Major Aircraft Fires." **Fire Technology**
5 (November 1969):   284-298.

Presented at the Seventy-third Annual Meeting, National
Fire Protection Association, New York, May 12, 1969.
Author biographical information.   Abstract.   7 tables.
9 figures.   2 references.   Acknowledgements.

5.014   "FR Treatment Boosts Wool's Use in Aircraft." **Textile
World** 136 (March 1986):   27.

The Wool Bureau sponsored "Fly More Safely With Wool,"
a seminar in Atlanta, Georgia.   Zirpro wool treated
with flame-retardant (FR), developed by the International Wool Secretariat (IWS), was discussed at the
seminar.   When this type of wool was tested regarding
burning behavior, toxicity, and other factors, it had
distinct advantages over other types of FR fibers.
Zirpro-treated wool can help increase the amount of
time aircraft passengers have to vacate an aircraft
should fire occur.

5.015   "A Fuel Additive Flunks Its Test." **Chemical Week** 135
(December 12, 1984):   16 and 18.

A Boeing jet, piloted by remote control, crashed and

caught fire at Edwards Air Force Base in California on
December 1, 1984. The jet was part of a joint venture
of the National Aeronautics and Space Administration
(NASA), the Federal Aviation Administration (FAA), and
Imperial Chemical Industries (ICI). The plane was carrying 12,000 gallons of fuel containing an anti-misting
jet fuel additive. ICI had spent $15 million on the
additive over seventeen years. The Air Transport Association (ATA) feels a drawback of the additive is its
high sodium content, which can lead to engine corrosion.
Dow Chemical and Conoco have also developed anti-misting
agents. 1 photograph.

5.016   **Fulton, H.B., Jr.** "A Pilot's Guide to Cabin Air Quality and Fire Safety." **New York State Journal of Medicine** 85 (July 1985): 384-388.

Ventilation on board aircraft; cigarette smoking and
on-board fires; and pilot health are the subjects covered in this article. Includes eight photographs of
magazine ads which portray flight crews as heroes who
smoke cigarettes. The ads were published between 1940
and 1985. Author biographical information. 3 figures.

5.017   **Gallagher, John.** "PWA Passengers Owe Their Survival
to Shift Change." **Canadian Aviation** 60 (August 1987):
11.

The pilots of a Pacific Western Airlines (PWA) Boeing
737-200 heard a loud bang, during the aircraft's takeoff roll, at Calgary International Airport on March
22, 1984. They realized, almost two minutes later,
they had a major fire—not a blown tire. There was no
engine fire warning. All the passengers were evacuated safely and only five people were injured. There
were no children, physically handicapped, or elderly on
board because Flight 501 was a commuter flight. Most
of the passengers were business people. All were
able-bodied and evacuated the airplane quite easily.
Eleven firefighters fought the fire because the firefighters were changing shifts when the fire broke out.
1 illustration.

5.018   **Gavaghan, Helen.** "Slapdash Welding Sparked Aircraft
Fire at Manchester." **New Scientist** 121 (March 18,
1989): 28.

Carbon monoxide and hydrogen cyanide were responsible
for the deaths of forty-eight out of fifty-five people, who died in a fire on a British Airways Boeing
737. The accident occurred at Manchester in 1985.

This and other information is contained in a report issued by the Department of Transport Accident Investigation Branch. An inadequate exchange of information between British Airways and Pratt and Whitney was instru-
mental in contributing to the cause of the fire. The
report, which also discusses smokehoods and water spray
systems, makes a total of thirty-one safety recommendations. 1 photograph.

5.019 **Godson, John. Clipper 806: The Anatomy of an Air Disaster.** Chicago, IL: Contemporary Books, Inc., 1978.

Pan American (Pan Am) Flight 806, a Boeing 707, departed Sydney, Australia and was en route to San Francisco,
California. On a rainy night in January 1974, Flight
806 landed in the jungle near Pago Pago. Initially,
no one was injured seriously in the relatively gentle
landing. However, because of the ensuing fire—and
specifically the toxic fumes which followed—ten of the
101 people aboard the 707 got out of the plane alive.
Four survived.

5.020 **Hill, I.R.** "The Immediate Problems of Aircraft Fires."
American Journal of Forensic Medicine and Pathology 7
(December 1986): 271-277.

The crash fire environment (ignition, temperature intensity, and toxic gases and synthetic materials) and
the accident experience (the possibility of escape,
pulmonary impairment, and flammable materials and their
toxic products) should be included in a discussion of
aircraft fires. Author biographical information. Abstract. 3 tables. Acknowledgement. 38 references.

5.021 **Jaglowski, Joseph J., Jr.** "Improving Emergency
Egress." **Fire Technology** 2 (November 1966): 273-275.

Blasting additional openings in fuselage walls may be
a way to evacute more people from aircraft than is
presently possible. Presented at the Seventieth Annual Meeting, National Fire Protection Association,
Chicago, Illinois, May 17, 1966. Author biographical
information. Abstract.

5.022 **Jeffs, Eric.** "Airport Fire: Services Criticised."
Engineering 208 (August 15, 1969): 155.

On April 8, 1968, a British Overseas Airways Corporation (BOAC) 707—it took off from Heathrow Airport in

London—crashed shortly after takeoff, due to an engine fire resulting from compressor disc failure.
The 707 was carrying 116 passengers and a crew of
eleven. A stewardess and four passengers were killed.
Inadequate deployment of equipment, equipment failure,
and insufficient foam were among the shortcomings of
the fire services at the airport. 1 photograph.

5.023 **Marcy, John F.** "Interior Material Finishes." **Fire
Technology** 2 (November 1966): 263-273.

Flammability of materials used in furnishings and as
finishes in transport aircraft. Presented at the Seventieth Annual Meeting, National Fire Protection Association, Chicago, Illinois, May 17, 1966. Author biographical information. Abstract. 2 tables. 10 figures. 7 references.

5.024 "Mineta Claims Airlines Resist Safety Improvements."
Aviation Week and Space Technology 123 (October 7,
1985): 27.

Representative Norman Y. Mineta (Democrat-California)
is Chairman, House Aviation Subcommittee. Representative John Paul Hammerschmidt (Republican-Arkansas) is
the ranking minority member of the subcommittee. They
have approached Transportation Secretary Elizabeth
Dole and FAA (Federal Aviation Administration) head
Donald Engen about cabin safety regulations. The regulations concern smoke detectors, fire extinguishers,
and improved seat cushions. Mineta is also concerned
about the excessive amount of carry-on luggage being
brought on board by passengers.

5.025 **Neal, Molly.** "Fighting Airport Fires." **Engineering**
211 (September 1971): 630-633.

If firefighters cannot get to and control an aircraft
fire within five minutes, the chances of passengers
and crew surviving are poor. Fire trucks, helicopters,
and hovercraft are used in airport fire situations in
the United Kingdom (UK), Canada, and New Zealand. The
Department of Trade and Industry is responsible for
checking the efficiency of airport fire services in
the UK. This department also maintains the Fire Service Training School. The Fire Service Training Aircraft Pool is located at Glasgow Airport in Glasgow,
Scotland. Author biographical information. 8 figures. 1 table.

5.026 **Nolan, David.** "Airline Safety: The Shocking Truth."
       Discover 7 (October 1986): 30-33, 36-44 and 48-53.

       Seat failure is a common cause of airline passenger in-
       juries, as exemplified by an Air California Boeing 737,
       which skidded to a stop on its belly in 1981 at John
       Wayne Airport. Thirty-three passengers were injured,
       four seriously. Rear-facing seats and shoulder har-
       nesses would reduce passenger injuries. Flames and
       smoke kill twice as many passengers in survivable ac-
       cidents as does the impact. FM-9, a jet fuel additive,
       can apparently minimize the likelihood of fire. Ure-
       thane foam covers airplane seat cushions and interior
       upholstery, and although cheap and light, it not only
       burns easily, it also gives off thick smoke and lethal
       gases. Smokehoods, which passengers would put on if
       a fire broke out, would extend passenger breathing time.
       Smokehoods might have saved lives on June 2, 1983, when
       fire broke out on an Air Canada flight, which made an
       emergency landing in Cincinnati, Ohio. Twenty-three
       people were asphyxiated in their seats. 4 illustra-
       tions. 25 photographs.

5.027 "NTSB Recommends L-1011 Inspections After Singapore Ac-
       cident." **Aviation Week and Space Technology** 123 (Decem-
       ber 9, 1985): 33.

       On October 18, 1985, there was a fire on board an Alia
       Royal Jordanian Airlines L-1011, as it was descending
       to land in Singapore, Malaya. The National Transpor-
       tation Safety Board (NTSB) wants, as a result of this
       incident, the Federal Aviation Administration (FAA) to
       review the design of the L-1011 oxygen system, and also
       to review the design of the aircraft's door opening
       mechanism.

5.028 **Ott, James.** "Smoke Detectors Start Conflict." **Avia-
       tion Week and Space Technology** 121 (September 24, 1984):
       27-28.

       The Air Line Pilots Association (ALPA) is only one or-
       ganization which questions the adequacy and reliability
       of house-hold-type smoke detectors in aircraft. Under-
       writers Laboratories, Inc. is concerned about the ef-
       fects of long-term vibration on these smoke detectors.
       Although household detectors can cost as little as $10,
       aviation purpose detectors can cost between $800 and
       $1300 each. There is the real possibility of theft of
       batteries from household detectors. Pyrotronics, of
       Cedar Knolls, New Jersey, offers a smoke detection
       system, which, over a twenty-year period, would be
       less costly than maintaining single-station smoke de-
       tectors. Air Canada's experience has included missing

batteries and missing detectors. Pan American (Pan Am)
World Airways has had favorable experiments with resi-
dential-type smoke detectors.

5.029   "Pan Am Engine Fire." **Aviation Week and Space Technology** 122 (July 1, 1985): 34.

A Pan American (Pan Am) World Airways Boeing 747, on a
flight from Los Angeles, California to London with 354
passengers on board, made an emergency landing at
Prestwick, Scotland, June 20, 1985, after an engine
fire.

5.030   **Pane, Gregg A.,** Stanley R. Mohler and Glenn C. Hamilton.
"The Cincinnati DC-9 Experience: Lessons in Aircraft
and Airport Safety." **Aviation, Space, and Environmental Medicine** 56 (May 1985): 457-461.

On June 2, 1983, Air Canada Flight 797, a DC-9, was en
route from Dallas, Texas to Toronto, Ontario. A flight
attendant noted a fire in the aft washroom. The fire
seemed to subside after carbon dioxide was discharged
into the washroom. The DC-9 then made an unscheduled
landing at the Greater Cincinnati International Airport. It was learned later that the twenty-three persons who died in the airplane had high blood levels of
carbon monoxide, cyanide, and fluoride. Toxic fumes—
not burns—killed the victims. Protective smokehoods,
modern plastics for aircraft interiors, emergency aisle
lighting, fire proofed inflatable slides, and smoke
detectors in lavatories are recommended to improve aircraft safety. Author biographical information. Abstract. 4 figures. 17 references.

5.031   **Quinn, Hal.** "A Burning Nightmare at 31,000 Feet."
Maclean's 96 (June 13, 1983): 19.

Richard Forrest, age sixty-three, was aboard Air Canada Flight 797, when a fire broke out on the DC-9, which
was headed from Dallas, Texas to Toronto, Ontario on
June 2, 1983. After the plane made an emergency landing at Greater Cincinnati International Airport, Forrest, a management consultant, crawled through thick
dark smoke to an exit, then slid down an escape chute.
He and fourteen other passengers were treated later in
hospital for smoke inhalation and minor injuries.
When Captain Donald Cameron was landing the plane, his
chair was on fire and the cockpit was full of smoke.
First Officer Claude Ouimet escaped through a smashed
window, his uniform on fire. 2 photographs.

5.032   **Quintiere, James G.** and Takeyoshi Tanaka. "Some Anal-
        yses of the FAA Post Crash Aircraft Fire Scenario."
        Fire Technology 19 (May 1983): 77-89.

        Wind effects, simulation of a post crash fire scenario,
        flow measurements, and estimation of doorway mass flow-
        rates by temperature data are examined. Author bio-
        graphical information. Abstract. 8 figures. 3 tables.
        9 references. Acknowledgements.

5.033   **Russell, Ralph A.** "Reducing Fuel Hazards by Gelling."
        Fire Technology 2 (November 1966): 276-278.

        Reports on Federal Aviation Agency (FAA) research into
        the use of gels to reduce flammability and flame spread
        of jet fuel. Presented at the Seventieth Annual Meet-
        ing, National Fire Protection Association, Chicago, Il-
        linois, May 17, 1966. Author biographical information.
        Abstract.

5.034   "Sprinklers Under Study." **New Scientist** 123 (July 8,
        1989): 43.

        Research is under way regarding fine mist water sprin-
        klers, which would protect passengers in burning air-
        planes. The Civil Aviation Authority (CAA), Boeing,
        and Transport Canada are involved in the research.
        Research is focusing on the advantages and disadvan-
        tages of water droplet size. One group of researchers
        feel passengers would breathe in more toxic gases more
        readily if the inside of the airplane were sprayed
        with fine mist water. Another group of researchers
        supports the opposite view—large drops of water would
        mean inhalation of fewer toxic gases.

5.035   **Woolley, David.** "Airliner Interiors: Safety in the
        Melting Pot." **Interavia** 40 (December 1985): 1349-
        1351.

        Numerous airlines in the U.S. and Europe are taking
        steps to make the interiors of their aircraft safer
        and more fire resistant. Delta, United, Western,
        American, Air France, British Airways, KLM, and Luf-
        thansa are some of these airlines. Curtailing toxic
        gas emission from burning seat cushions is a major
        safety concern. This concern is understandable in
        view of a fire in a British Airtours 737 at Manchester,
        England in September 1985. 4 photographs.

6

Weather and Aircraft

6.001   "Airborne Infrared System Provides Advance Warning of
Turbulence." **Aviation Week and Space Technology** 130
(June 19, 1989): 130-131.

Turbulence Prediction Systems (TPS) has developed the
Advanced Warning System (AWS) to warn pilots of turbulence. Research into this type of system stems from
airline accidents caused by wind shear and microbursts.
The cause of or contributing factor in approximately
42% of weather-related incidents between 1962 and 1974
was air turbulence. The August 1985 crash in Dallas,
Texas of Delta 191 is one example. The Federal Aviation Administration (FAA) ruled in September 1988
that all commercial jet aircraft must have a wind
shear detection and flight-guidance system installed.
Air turbulence is classified as either low-level wind
shear (LLWS) or clear air turbulence (CAT), LLWS considered as the most hazardous. CAT encounters cause
passenger injury and airframe fatigue, and are responsible for course alterations and landing diversions.
1 illustration.

6.002   "Aircraft Icing Protection Conference." **Aircraft
Engineering** 32 (July 1960): 206.

Abstracts of five papers presented at an international conference held at Luton Airport in Great Britain
on June 14, 1960. The papers: (1) "The Icing Research Aircraft (B.T. Cheverton); (2) "Clouds and
Aircraft Icing" (R.F. Jones); (3) "Airline Ice Protection Requirements" (B. Briggs and G. Hinton-Lever);
(4) "Results of Experimental Flights in Natural Icing Conditions and Operations of Aircraft Thermal Ice
Protection Systems" (O.K. Trunov and M.S. Egorov);
and (5) "Icing Problems of High Speed Aircraft" (C.K.
Rush).

6.003   "Airframe Icing Has Posed Problems For DC-9-10 Aircraft." **Aviation Week and Space Technology** 127 (November 23, 1987): 36.

Airframe icing has been responsible for non-fatal
take-off accidents in McDonnell Douglas DC-9-10 series
aircraft. However, increased take-off speeds do reduce risk of stall with undetected ice. Boeing conducted tests with simulated frost and snow in the early
1980s, following incidents of near-stall after liftoff
of the Boeing 737.

6.004   "Atmospheric Visibility Is Decreasing in the Eastern
        United States." **Weatherwise** 25 (June 1972): 134-135.

        Visibility is a major factor in the safe visual landing
        of airplanes. Visibility improved in three different
        sections of the U.S. between approximately 1930 and
        1965. A major reason for the improvement was the wide-
        spread conversion from coal to gas and oil. Three me-
        teorologists (M.E. Miller, N.L. Canfield, and T.A. Rit-
        ter) and a statistician (C.R. Weaver) demonstrated that
        visibility is becoming poorer east of the Mississippi
        River. These researchers did research at three air-
        ports in Ohio, Kentucky, and Tennessee. 3 figures. 1
        reference.

6.005   **Collins, Richard L.** "Act of God? Or Man?" **Flying**
        110 (August 1983): 34.

        Comments on the exoneration by the National Transpor-
        tation Safety Board (NTSB) of the pilot of a Pan Ameri-
        can (Pan Am) World Airways 727 which crashed near New
        Orleans, Louisiana due to a microburst. The author
        contends that the exoneration of the pilot is a depar-
        ture from past NTSB practice. Virtually all general
        aviation accidents involving thunderstorms were attri-
        buted to pilot judgement.

6.006   **Covault, Craig.** "Heavy Rain Danger Called Greater
        Than Wind Shear." **Aviation Week and Space Technology**
        114 (January 26, 1981): 50-51.

        The University of Dayton Research Institute in Dayton,
        Ohio has been conducting research for the National
        Aeronautics and Space Administration (NASA). The re-
        search is indicating that heavy rain is as great a
        danger or even greater to aircraft—in the approach
        phase—than is wind shear. This finding has implica-
        tions for the Federal Aviation Administration (FAA)
        wind shear detection and avoidance program. James K.
        Luers and Patrick A. Haines have presented research
        results at the Nineteenth Aerospace Sciences Meeting,
        American Institute of Aeronautics and Astronautics.

6.007   "Danger—Slush!" **Aircraft Engineering** 33 (April
        1961):   93.

        Slush affects an airplane's take-off performance in
        three ways. Slush causes excess drag because the air-
        plane's wheels have to force slush aside. Secondly,
        slush impairs an airplane's directional control. And
        thirdly, slush causes loss of thrust. This happens,
        for example, when slush is ingested into engine in-
        takes.

6.008   "Delta DC-8 Skids Off Dallas Runway." **Aviation Week**
        74 (February 13, 1961):   42.

        On February 6, 1961, a Delta Air Lines DC-8 skidded
        off the runway after landing at Love Field in Dallas,
        Texas. There was only minor damage to the aircraft;
        no injuries were reported. The DC-8, Flight 921,
        had originated in Atlanta, Georgia and was carrying
        109 persons. There was snow at Love Field and the
        runway was wet and slushy. The airplane was not evac-
        uated until half an hour after it stopped in the mud.

6.009   "Electra Wing Broke in Storm Turbulence." **Aviation
        Week and Space Technology** 88 (May 13, 1968):   43.

        On May 3, 1968 approximately nine aircraft were in
        the vicinity of Dawson, Texas during a thunderstorm.
        Most aircraft diverted east to avoid the storm. An
        Electra, Braniff Flight 352, bound to Dallas from
        Houston, was one of the aircraft which diverted west.
        The Electra descended from 20,000 to 5000 feet and
        crashed about twelve minutes before estimated time of
        arrival (ETA). Eighty-five people—eighty passen-
        gers, five crew—were killed. The right wing, which
        broke from the aircraft, was the cause of the crash.

6.010   **Few, A.A.** "Lightning and the New-Generation Air-
        craft." **Science** 168 (May 22, 1970):   1011-1012.

        Lightning strikes to aircraft merit further investi-
        gation, especially since new-generation aircraft,
        such as jumbo jets, use more sophisticated hardware
        than did earlier aircraft. Author biographical in-
        formation. 1 reference.

6.011   **Gallagher, J.D.** "Storm Check List For Pilots." **Ca-
        nadian Aviation** 39 (July 1966):   24-25.

A thirty-two-point check list regarding general flight
planning; thunder rain showers (TRWs) and turbulence;
lightning strikes; hail damage; and other meteorological information pilots should be familiar with regarding safety. 2 photographs.

6.012   **Gallagher, John.** "Would Color Radar Have Saved This
        DC-9?" **Canadian Aviation** 58 (August 1985): 13.

The pilot of a USAir DC-9 who encountered wind shear,
while attempting to land at Detroit, Michigan in 1984,
might have piloted the DC-9 differently had his black-
and-white radar display been a color display. The DC-9
touched down about 2500 feet beyond the threshold on a
10,000-foot runway, skidded about 3800 feet, then left
the runway, coming to a stop on grass. The aircraft
was evacuated successfully and there were no injuries.
1 illustration.

6.013   **Garrison, Peter.** "Ash-Blasted." **Flying** 111 (August
        1984): 26-27.

On a summer evening in 1982 the air was clear at 37,000
feet over the Indian Ocean. A British Airways Boeing
747 was at 37,000 feet and en route from Kuala Lumpur,
Malaya to Perth, Australia. Then the flight deck crew
and passenger cabin crew began noticing bluish smoke
inside the aircraft. Soon all four engines were out.
The 747 glided to 13,000 feet before the crew could re-
start the number four engine. Five minutes later all
four engines had been restarted and the plane began to
climb. The 747 eventually made an uneventful landing
at Jakarta, Indonesia on three engines. The entire
incident was due to a cloud of volcanic ash. "Flight
Operation in Volcanic Dust" was published by Boeing
in April 1983 as an operations manual bulletin.

6.014   **Garrison, Peter.** "Dark Day at New Orleans." **Flying**
        110 (August 1983): 92-95.

An account of the crash at New Orleans, Louisiana of
a Pan American (Pan Am) World Airways Boeing 727.
Flight 759 crashed shortly after takeoff due to wind-
shear. No mechanical failure was involved. There
were moderate thunderstorms in the area and erratic
winds, but no lightning. The 727's ascent was arrested and, just as the airplane was about to climb,
it struck trees along Williams Avenue. Seconds
later it crashed into a residential area. All aboard
and eight people on the ground were killed. A transcript of comments by the following are included in

the article: captain, first officer, flight engineer,
ground control, other aircraft, Pan Am Operations Office, cabin public address system, and the tower.

6.015   **Gavaghan, Helen.** "Computers Keep the Airlanes Open."
        New Scientist 114 (June 18, 1987): 40.

        The National Airspace System (NAS) plan, which began
        in 1982 and involves $16 billion, will improve air
        traffic control (ATC) and the updating of weather re-
        ports. Computers are essential to the NAS plan and
        will be located at twenty centers throughout the U.S.
        Donald D. Engen, head of the Federal Aviation Adminis-
        tration (FAA) was in Seattle, Washington, where he
        formally switched on the first of the computers. Sen-
        sors which detect windshear at airports are also part
        of the NAS plan. Since airspace close to airports is
        where 90% of near-misses occur, the FAA will make col-
        lision-avoidance systems mandatory. 2 photographs.

6.016   **Goff, R. Craig.** "Characterization of Winds Potential-
        ly Hazardous to Aircraft." **Journal of Aircraft** 19
        (February 1982): 151-156.

        This paper was presented as Paper 81-0387 at the Nine-
        teenth AIAA Aerospace Sciences Meeting, St. Louis,
        Missouri, January 12-15, 1981. The paper presents
        fourteen months of meteorological tower wind observa-
        tions with particular reference to the wind's verti-
        cal component. Author biographical information. Ab-
        stract. 3 tables. 3 figures. Acknowledgments. 12
        references.

6.017   "Helping Pilots Avoid Volcanic Clouds." **Science
        News** 125 (March 10, 1984): 152.

        The National Aeronautics and Space Administration
        (NASA) and the Federal Aviation Administration (FAA)
        are interested in using satellites to monitor volcan-
        ic activity. This is because the jet engines of
        Boeing 747s stalled over Indonesia due to dust clouds
        from Galunggung, an erupting volcano. Stalling oc-
        curred twice in 1982 at an altitude of 30,000 feet.
        Fortunately, the engines were restarted at a lower
        altitude. Nimbus 7 is one satellite NASA is using to
        make airline travel safer.

6.018   **Klass, Philip J.** "Microburst Radar May Spur Review
        of Tower's Role in Aborting Landings." **Aviation Week**

and Space Technology 130 (May 1, 1989):   79 and 81.

The flight crew of United Airlines (UAL) Flight 863
chose not to land at Stapleton International Airport
in Denver, Colorado on July 11, 1988 because the Denver tower had detected a severe microburst. The radar
which detected the microburst was developed by Lincoln
Laboratory. The microburst situation at Stapleton
brings to light the issue of whether or not a controller should recommend to a flight crew that it abort a
landing. Traditionally, the flight crew has made
such decisions. UAL now has a policy that its flight
crews not land when alerted about microbursts. 1 illustration.

6.019   "Larger, Faster Aircraft More Likely to Be Struck."
        Aviation Week and Space Technology 96 (January 31,
        1972):   56.

        Because of their greater size, speed, use of non-metal-
        lic materials, and miniaturized avionics, advanced
        technology aircraft—the Boeing 747 is an example—may
        be more vulnerable to lightning strikes than were
        their predecessors. This view was expressed by Dr.
        Edward T. Pierce, Stanford Research Institute (SRI).
        Dr. Pierce addressed the American Association for the
        Advancement of Science (AAAS).

6.020   "Lightning Research Network Helping Controllers Make
        Air Travel Safer." **Bulletin of the American Meteoro-
        logical Society** 65 (March 1984):   245-246.

        Richard E. Orville is an atmospheric scientist, who
        started the lightning observing network, on the U.S.
        east coast. Orville started the network in 1982 with
        financial assistance from the National Science Founda-
        tion (NSF). The network enables air traffic control-
        lers (ATCs) at Leesburg, Virginia know more reliably—
        than with radar or satellites—the location of thunder-
        storms. The lightning location network can alert con-
        trollers about storms up to half an hour earlier than
        can other methods. The National Aeronautics and Space
        Administration (NASA), Niagara Mohawk Power Corp., Na-
        tional Weather Service, and Electric Power Research
        Institute also support the network.

6.021   "Manufacturers Issue Volcano Advisories." **Aviation
        Week and Space Technology** 112 (June 9, 1980):   41 and
        43-45.

        Boeing, Lockheed, McDonnell Douglas, General Electric,

Pratt and Whitney, and Rolls-Royce have announced special precautions to airlines who could come into contact with volcanic material erupting from Mount St.
Helens. The precautions concern a variety of things,
including contaminated runways, braking, compressor
airfoil erosion, and oil system contamination.

6.022 **McCarthy, John** and Robert Serafin. "The Microburst:
Hazard to Aircraft." **Weatherwise** 37 (June 1984):
120-127.

Six areas are covered: what is a microburst?; microburst visual characteristics; microburst facts and
figures; what can be done to improve safety?; detection systems; and maintaining a vigilance. Author
biographical information. 14 photographs. 3 illustrations. Acknowledgements.

6.023 **McClement, Fred.** "Clear Air Turbulence." Chapter in
It Doesn't Matter Where You Sit, by Fred McClement,
54-70. New York, NY: Holt, Rinehart and Winston,
1969.

Clear Air Turbulence (CAT) is illustrated by the July
12, 1963 incident involving United Air Lines (UAL)
Flight 746. This flight left San Francisco International Airport and was headed for O'Hare Field in Chicago, Illinois. There were fifty-three passengers
and six crew aboard the Boeing 720B. The flight deck
crew consisted of Captain Lynden Duescher, forty-two;
First Officer Eric Anderson, thirty-four; and Second
Officer Ervin Rochlits, forty-one. E.P. Aiken, another United pilot, was also on board. Flight 746
was tossed about and plummeted to 14,000 feet before
the crew could bring the aircraft under control.

6.024 **McClement, Fred.** "The Danger That Radar Cannot See."
Chapter in **It Doesn't Matter Where You Sit,** by Fred
McClement, 38-53. New York, NY: Holt, Rinehart and
Winston, 1969.

On August 6, 1966 Braniff Airways Flight 250 crashed
near Falls City, Nebraska. The aircraft was a BAC-111
built by the British Aircraft Corp. The captain was
Donald G. Pauly, age forty-seven; the copilot was
James A. Hilliker, age thirty-nine. Two stewardesses
and thirty-eight passengers were also on board. Before Flight 250 crashed, it was at an altitude of
5000 feet, and there was no lightning near it. The
right wing and tail were broken off in flight. Investigators concluded the cause of the crash was a pulsa-
ting burst of wind that caved in the aircraft. The

velocity of the wind was thought to be 140 foot-sec-
onds.

6.025   **McClement, Fred.** "Geostrophy and the Montreal Air
        Crash." Chapter in **It Doesn't Matter Where You Sit,**
        by Fred McClement, 71-89. New York, NY: Holt, Rine-
        hart and Winston, 1969.

        On November 29, 1963 an Air Canada DC-8F crashed near
        Montreal, Quebec. There were 118 persons aboard Flight
        831. All 118 died in the crash. The Montreal area was
        experiencing a bad storm which included torrential rain
        showers. The flight deck crew consisted of Captain
        John Snider, forty-seven; First Officer Harry Dyck,
        thirty-five; and Second Officer Edward Baxter, twenty-
        nine. Geostrophic convection was the likely cause of
        the crash. Although the U.S. instituted the use of
        flight recorders in 1958, flight recorders became man-
        datory for Trans-Canada Airlines after the November 29
        crash.

6.026   **McClement, Fred.** "The Phenomenon of Lightning." Chap-
        ter in **It Doesn't Matter Where You Sit,** by Fred McClem-
        ent, 17-37. New York, NY: Holt, Rinehart and Winston,
        1969.

        After a Pan American (Pan Am) World Airways 707 Jet
        Clipper crashed near Elkton, Maryland on December 8,
        1963, the Civil Aeronautics Board (CAB), which investi-
        gated the accident, attributed the crash to turbulence.
        It was learned later that lightning caused the 707 to
        explode because the 707 did not have static wicks. A
        National Airlines DC-8, which was also struck by
        lightning at almost the same moment as the 707, did
        not explode. The National was equipped with static
        wicks. Many years earlier, on August 31, 1940, a
        Pennsylvania Central Airlines DC-3 was struck by
        lightning over Lovettsville, Virginia. The DC-3 plum-
        meted to the ground.

6.027   **Monastersky, Richard.** "Mastering the Microburst."
        Science News 131 (March 21, 1987): 185-187.

        A microburst is a short-lived pattern of intense winds
        which descend from rain clouds in spring and summer.
        When the microburst hits the ground, the falling air
        fans out horizontally. The microburst causes wind
        shear, a quick change in wind speed or direction.
        Huntsville, Alabama, a humid area, will spawn wet mi-
        crobursts. Denver, Colorado, an arid area, will spawn
        dry microbursts. Unexpected, dramatic changes in wind

direction or speed pose serious problems for airplanes
which are landing or taking off. That is what happened
on August 2, 1985 at the Dallas-Fort Worth Airport.
Delta Flight 191, on descending, flew through a microburst and crashed. The generally acknowledged leading
expert on microbursts is T. Theodore Fujita of the
University of Chicago. He first noted the phenomena
of microbursts in 1974. 7 illustrations.

6.028   **Mordoff, Keith F.** "Researchers Study Methods to Combat
        Effects of Wind Shear." **Aviation Week and Space Tech-
        nology** 118 (February 21, 1983): 40-42.

        FWG Associates, Inc., which specializes in environmen-
        tal effects on engineering systems, has studied wind
        shear recovery for aircraft, using a model of a Boeing
        727. The FWG research simulated the 727 taking off
        through a severe downburst, and crashing shortly after-
        wards. Walter Frost, FWG President, is also affiliated
        with the University of Tennessee Space Institute. 6
        photographs. 2 illustrations.

6.029   "1989 World Meteorological Day Celebrates Meteorology
        in the Service of Aviation." **Bulletin of the American
        Meteorological Society** 70 (April 1989): 414-415.

        Comments by Godwin O.P. Obasi, Secretary-General, World
        Meteorological Organization (WMO).

6.030   "No More 'Wing and Prayer' Weather Reports." **Design
        News** 42 (October 20, 1986): 31.

        The AWOS I (Automated Weather Observing System) broad-
        casts weather reports from airport touchdown zones,
        minute-by-minute, twenty-four-hours a day. Wind di-
        rection, wind speed, temperature, dew point, and other
        information is provided. AWOS I is available from
        Handar, Inc. and the purchase price varies from ap-
        proximately $20,000 to more than $100,000. The pri-
        mary market for this product are the 6000 publicly-
        accessible airports in the U.S. 1 photograph.

6.031   **O'Lone, Richard G.** "Volcanic Eruption Disrupts Air
        Traffic." **Aviation Week and Space Technology** 112
        (May 26, 1980): 18-21.

        On May 18, 1980 Mount St. Helens volcano, located in
        southwest Washington, erupted, spewing highly acid
        volcanic ash. About 1200 feet of mountaintop was

blown away and ash soared higher than 70,000 feet.
Numerous airports were closed, including airports at:
Spokane, Washington; Lewiston, Idaho; and Kalispell,
Montana. One example of ash damage to aircraft was
abrasion to the engine compressor blades of a Hughes
Airwest DC-9, which left San Francisco, California en
route to Calgary, Alberta. The Federal Aviation Administration (FAA) warned general aviation the ash could
lead to engine failure. Hughes Airwest, United, Western, and Northwest cancelled numerous flights. 7
photographs.

6.032 **Ott, James.** "Improved Weather Alerts Offset by Poor
       Delivery to Cockpit." **Aviation Week and Space Tech-
       nology** 127 (October 5, 1987): 33-34.

       According to Patrick W. Clyne of Northwest Airlines
       and the Air Line Pilots Association (ALPA), the Feder-
       al Aviation Administration (FAA) weather services pro-
       gram has improved hazard detection. What has not im-
       proved, however, is delivery of weather information to
       the cockpit. Clyne addressed a House subcommittee
       chaired by Representative Dave McCurdy (Democrat-Okla-
       homa). 1 table.

6.033 **Shaw, Adam. Sound of Impact: The Legacy of TWA
       Flight 514.** New York, NY: Viking Press, 1977.

       The winds were fierce and the rain heavy around 11:00
       a.m. on December 1, 1974, as a TWA (Trans World Air-
       lines) Boeing 727 was on approach to Dulles Airport.
       Flight 514—which was flying from Columbus, Ohio to
       Washington, DC—with eighty-five passengers and a
       crew of seven crashed into a mountain twenty-three
       miles west of Dulles. Flight 514 could not land, as
       initially planned, at National Airport because of bad
       weather. Captain Richard Brock, First Officer Leonard
       Kresheck, Flight Engineer Tom Safranek, and eighty-
       nine others aboard the 727 died in the crash. 3 dia-
       grams.

6.034 **Simon, C.** "Record-Breaking Microburst Near Air Force
       1." **Science News** 125 (January 21, 1984): 36.

       Six minutes after Air Force One, the presidential
       jet, landed at Andrews Air Force Base, the strongest
       microburst ever recorded occurred. Since 1964 eight
       aircraft accidents have been linked to microbursts.
       To detect microbursts the Federal Aviation Adminis-
       tration (FAA) plans to install Doppler radar at more
       than seventy airports in the U.S.

6.035   **Stanton, William.** "Hail-Stoned." **Flying** 111 (January
        1984): 92-93.

        Captain William Stanton, First Officer Don Heisley, and
        Flight Engineer Verne Yates were to fly a Japan Air
        Lines (JAL) DC-8-61 from Tokyo to Chitose, Japan—one
        hour and fifteen minutes north of Tokyo. Flight 519
        departed Tokyo International Airport with eighty-nine
        passengers and five stewardesses on board. The DC-8-61
        was suddenly struck by lightning, heavy hail, and tur-
        bulence. It was learned later the hailstones had var-
        ied in diameter from 1.5 to 2.25 inches. Part of the
        windshield was shattered, there was loss of airspeed
        indication, and the plane became almost uncontrolla-
        ble. However, Flight 519 managed to land safely back
        at Tokyo. 1 illustration.

6.036   "Weather Cited as Major Factor in Three N.Y. Runway
        Overruns." **Aviation Week and Space Technology** 80
        (April 13, 1964): 41.

        Within approximately twelve hours, a Pan American (Pan
        Am) World Airways Boeing 707, an El Al Israel Airlines
        Boeing 707, and an American Airlines Lockheed Electra
        turboprop overran runways in New York. Two of the ac-
        cidents occurred at Kennedy International Airport; one
        accident occurred at La Guardia. In all three accidents
        runways were wet, fog was present, and instrument ap-
        proaches were used. Forty-nine persons were injured in
        the Pan Am incident. Civil Aeronautics Board (CAB) in-
        vestigators speculated that aquaplaning was associated
        with at least two of the accidents. It may be neces-
        sary to install arresting devices which halt airliners
        at the ends of runways.

6.037   "Weather Cited in Two DC-9 Crashes." **Aviation Week
        and Space Technology** 108 (February 6, 1978): 35.

        The National Transportation Safety Board (NTSB) has
        linked weather to two DC-9 crashes. On June 23, 1976,
        an Allegheny Airlines DC-9 crashed at Philadelphia In-
        ternational Airport. Although there were no fatali-
        ties, eighty-seven persons on board were injured. On
        April 4, 1977, a Southern Airways DC-9 crashed near
        New Hope, Georgia. Sixty-two of eighty-five persons
        on board were killed. Nine persons on the ground also
        died in the accident. The ingestion of water and hail
        brought about loss of thrust followed by severe stall-
        ing of the Southern Airways DC-9. Wind shear near the
        ground caused the Allegheny DC-9 to crash.

6.038   "Wind Shear Microbursts Focus of Weather Study."

Aviation Week and Space Technology 116 (June 14, 1982): 41 and 43.

Denver, Colorado has an average of sixty-five thunderstorms annually. For this reason, Denver was chosen for the Joint Airport Weather Studies (JAWS) project. The project is studying microbursts identified by T. Theodore Fujita of the University of Chicago. Microbursts cannot be identified by conventional radar, but can be detected by Doppler radar. The crash of an Eastern Airlines Boeing 727 at John F. Kennedy Airport on June 24, 1975 and the crash of a Continental Airlines 727 at Stapleton Airport on May 7, 1975 were attributed by Fugita to microbursts. One hundred individuals are involved in JAWS, which is expected to last three months. The primary funding agency is the National Science Foundation (NSF). 1 photograph.

6.039   **Yaffee, Michael L.** "New Studies Explore Lightning." **Aviation Week and Space Technology** 96 (January 31, 1972):   51 and 54-56.

In Pittsfield, Massachusetts, the General Electric High Voltage Laboratory (HVL) is conducting research on lightning effects on aircraft for NASA (National Aeronautics and Space Administration). The HVL began this type of research in the early 1930s, with studies of the Douglas DC-3. A commercial transport will be struck by lightning approximately once a year. The HVL is engaged in five research programs. 5 photographs.

7

Emergency and
Hard Landings

7.001 "Boeing 737 Makes Emergency Landing After Losing Power
       in Hail Storm." **Aviation Week and Space Technology** 128
       (May 30, 1988): 123.

       A TACA International Airlines Boeing 737-300 was fly-
       ing in severe hail near New Orleans, Louisiana, when it
       lost power in both engines. The 737 was en route from
       Belize in Central America to New Orleans. The airplane
       landed beside a levee. There were no injuries to pas-
       sengers or crew. 1 photograph.

7.002 **Burrows, William E.** "A Slight Breakdown in Communica-
       tion." **Psychology Today** 16 (November 1982): 44-45.

       On May 8, 1978, National Airlines Flight 193, a Boeing
       727, left Mobile, Alabama and headed for Pensacola,
       Florida. There were fifty-two passengers and a crew
       of six on board. The pilot was George T. Kunz; the
       co-pilot, Leonard G. Sanderson, Jr.; and the flight
       engineer, James Stockwell. At 9:20 p.m. the 727 began
       descending through fog and haze four miles from Pensa-
       cola Regional Airport. National 193 landed in twelve
       feet of water three miles short of Runway 25. Three
       passengers drowned. It was learned later the pilot
       had misread the altimeter and was not wearing his
       glasses. 1 photograph.

7.003 "The Close Call in Boston." **Newsweek** 99 (February 1,
       1982): 22.

       World Airways Flight 30 originated in Honolulu, Ha-
       waii and made what appeared to be a normal landing at
       Logan International Airport in Boston, Massachusetts.
       But the DC-10, with 208 passengers and crew on board,
       continued down the icy runway until the aircraft's
       nose broke off and the DC-10 ended up in Boston har-
       bor. Some members of the flight crew were pitched
       into the harbor. Although approximately seventeen
       people were rushed to hospitals, there were no seri-
       ous injuries. 1 photograph.

7.004   "Eastern DC-9 Splits Open in Hard Landing at Pensacola." **Aviation Week and Space Technology** 128 (January
4, 1988): 68-69.

An Eastern Airlines McDonnell Douglas DC-9-31 bounced
as high as forty feet in the air when it made a hard
landing at Pensacola Regional Airport, Florida. The
incident took place on December 27, 1987. There were
ninety-nine passengers and five crew on board. Three
passengers were slightly injured. The fuselage, between rows twenty-one and twenty-two, broke open when
the plane landed at 11:39 p.m. None of the tires
ruptured, there was no apparent leakage of fuel, and
no fire. This was the sixth hard landing accident of
a DC-9 since it went into scheduled service in 1965.
The other five incidents took place between 1969 and
1977, and involved four other airlines. 1 photograph.

7.005   **Götestam, Bengta,** K. Gunnar Götestam and Lennart Melin.
"Anxiety and Coping Behavior During an Emergency Landing." **Behavior Modification** 7 (October 1983): 569-
575.

A fire broke out in a Boeing 747 which was en route
from London to New York, necessitating an emergency
landing in Labrador. Two psychologists and a psychiatrist were among the 370 passengers. During a stop-
over of approximately seventeen hours, the psychologists and psychiatrist collected data for a survey of
anxiety and coping behavior during the emergency
landing. Two findings: a higher proportion of women
than men chose cognitive strategies, and a lower proportion of women than men chose drugs to cope with
anxiety. Author biographical information. Abstract.
1 figure. 1 table.

7.006   "NTSB Investigates 747 Takeoff Abort." **Aviation Week
and Space Technology** 121 (November 26, 1984): 34.

A United Airlines (UAL) Boeing 747 aborted its takeoff from Honolulu, Hawaii on November 16, 1984, after
the crew heard a loud noise. There were two blown
tires and leakage of jet fuel in the incident. Thirty-six passengers were injured. A National Airlines
Boeing 747 charter landed shortly after takeoff from
Las Vegas, Nevada on November 18, 1984, after an engine fire. The 747, which was bound for Detroit,
Michigan, made a precautionary landing. There were
468 passengers and twenty crew on board.

7.007   **Ott, James.** "Air Canada 767 Lands Dead Stick After

Flameouts." **Aviation Week and Space Technology** 119
(August 1, 1983): 24-26.

At Gimli, Manitoba, which is approximately sixty miles
north of Winnipeg, Air Canada Flight 143 landed, at a
former Canadian Armed Forces air base on July 23,
1983. Flight 143, a Boeing 767, originated in Montreal, Quebec and was en route to Edmonton, Alberta via
Ottawa, Ontario. Captain R.O. Pearson and First Officer Maurice Quintal landed the aircraft after both engines flamed out. There were sixty-one passengers and
six other crewmembers on board. The abandoned runway
the 767 landed on is used for automobile racing. The
airplane came to a stop about 1000 feet from parked
vehicles. People were preparing for the next day's
races. 3 photographs. 2 illustrations.

7.008   "Overflight at JFK." **Newsweek** 103 (March 12, 1984):
37.

An SAS (Scandinavian Airlines System) DC-10 touched
down at Kennedy Airport in New York and came to the
end of an 8400-foot runway, finally stopping in shallow water, after overshooting the runway. The DC-10
had arrived from Oslo, Norway with 177 people on
board. Eight received minor injuries. Bad runway
conditions, mechanical failure, and pilot error were
reasons cited for the mishap. 1 photograph.

7.009   "Safety of Aging Aircraft Undergoes Reassessment."
Aviation Week and Space Technology 128 (May 16,
1988): 16-18.

On April 28, 1988, an Aloha 737-200 lost the top half
of a fuselage section at an altitude of 24,000 feet.
The airplane made an emergency landing on Maui. One
flight attendant died and sixty-nine passengers were
injured. Aloha has since then retired four 737-200s.
Representative Dan Glickman (Democrat-Kansas) began
preparing legislation that would require enhanced inspection of older aircraft. 2 photographs. 1 illustration.

7.010   "727 Damage Slight After Dive Incident." **Aviation
Week and Space Technology** 110 (April 23, 1979): 29.

On April 4, 1979, near Flint, Michigan, a Trans
World Airlines (TWA) Boeing 727 plunged from 39,000
feet to approximately 6000 feet. The aircraft, piloted by Captain Harvey Gibson, went into a spiral-
ing, out-of-control dive. Captain Gibson managed to

make an emergency landing at Detroit Municipal Airport. Damage to the airplane was relatively light,
with no evidence of overstress, such as popped rivets.
There was, however, damage to the main landing gear
and gear doors, and fuel leaks required repairs.
Langhorne Bond, Federal Aviation Administration (FAA)
Administrator, was one of the people who examined the
727. 1 photograph.

7.011   "Spantax DC-10 Crashes After Aborted Takeoff." **Aviation Week and Space Technology** 117 (September 20,
1982): 36.

On September 13, 1982, a Spantax McDonnell Douglas DC-
10-30 crashed at Malaga, Spain, after an aborted takeoff. There were 380 passengers and thirteen crew on
board. The initial death toll was fifty-one dead or
missing. An engine was torn off the right wing, when
the engine struck a concrete ground facility building.
Some rear exits could not be used after the airplane
came to rest. The DC-10, built in 1977, was used initially by Overseas National Airways (ONA). The airplane was to have flown from Madrid to Malaga to New
York.

8

Collision Avoidance

8.001   "Air Canada's New Fleet Safety Device." **Canadian
         Transportation and Distribution Management** 92 (June
         1989): 16.

         Air Canada is the first airline in Canada which will
         be equipped with TCAS (threat-alert collision avoid-
         ance system). The airline's entire fleet will be
         equipped with the system.

8.002   **Beaudet, Richard.** "Midair." **Canadian Aviation** 62
         (January 1989): 37 and 48.

         A Canadian Aviation Safety Board (CASB) report states
         that, between 1985 and 1987, air traffic controllers
         (ATCs) were responsible for 11.2% of near-collision
         incidents in Canada, pilots for 45.3%, and ground ve-
         hicle operators for 37.5%. A phraseology quality as-
         surance program, which contributes to better communi-
         cation at airports in Quebec, has dramatically de-
         creased the number of safety-related incidents.
         Technology is viewed as backing up—not replacing—
         the see-and-avoid concept of collision avoidance. 4
         photographs. Author biographical information.

8.003   **Beringer, Dennis B.** "Collision Avoidance Response
         Stereotypes in Pilots and Nonpilots." **Human Factors**
         20 (October 1978): 529-536.

         Midair collisions are a real and present danger.
         They are likely to occur when a pilot is responsible
         for maintaining separation by visual means. The pi-
         lot must perform certain tasks to maintain adequate
         separation. Pilots and nonpilots were tested in a
         flight training simulator. Nonpilots preferred to
         turn left to avoid a head-on collision. Pilots gen-
         erally turned right. However, 25% of pilots also
         preferred to turn left. Author biographical infor-
         mation. Abstract. 5 figures. Acknowledgements.
         15 references.

8.004   "CASB to Hold Public Hearings on Near-Misses Near Air-
        ports." **Canadian Aviation** 59 (March 1986):   3-4.

        Eight areas of concern regarding near-misses near air-
        ports in Canada are to be discussed in May 1986, when
        the Canadian Aviation Safety Board (CASB) holds public
        hearings. The number of near-misses tripled between
        1973 and 1985. One topic to be examined in May is the
        marking of airside maneuvering areas. 1 table.

8.005   **Collins, Richard L.** "Avoidance Tactics." **Flying** 114
        (June 1987):   76-77 and 81.

        Airspace in cities as different as New York and Lex-
        ington, Kentucky. The Grand Canyon (1956) and San Di-
        ego, California (1978) as locations of aircraft colli-
        sions. "See" and "Be Seen" as forms of collision
        avoidance. Helicopters, high-wing airplanes, and un-
        controlled airports are also discussed. 2 illustra-
        tions.

8.006   **Doty, L.L.** "Near-Miss Rate Spurs European Concern."
        Aviation Week and Space Technology 85 (December 12,
        1966):   44-45.

        Expresses concern about reducing near-misses between
        military and commercial aircraft in parts of Europe.
        Talks about Eurocontrol, an air traffic control (ATC)
        organization in which seven European nations partici-
        pate. There were in 1965 113 near-misses in Eurocon-
        trol airspace. Upper airspace, once occupied solely
        by military aircraft, has become crowded since air-
        lines have increased the number of jets in their
        fleets. Projected increases for the number of com-
        mercial aircraft operating above 20,000 feet are giv-
        en.

8.007   "FAA, ATA Shown Anti-Collision System." **Aviation
        Week and Space Technology** 78 (April 15, 1963):   105,
        107, 109 and 111.

        The Sperry Gyroscope Co. demonstrated an anti-colli-
        sion system to the Federal Aviation Agency (FAA) and
        the Air Transport Association. The airborne system
        is similar to systems developed by two other compa-
        nies: Bendix Radio and the National Co. The Sperry
        system is a collision avoidance system (CAS) and a
        proximity warning indicator (PWI). The key issue in
        collision avoidance is the ability to differentiate
        threatening from non-threatening aircraft, and—when
        necessary—to take the proper evasive maneuver. An

important feature of the Sperry system is its useful-
ness in situations where two aircraft are changing altitude. 5 illustrations.

8.008   "FAA Orders Expansion of Los Angeles TCA." **Aviation
Week and Space Technology** 127 (August 24, 1987):   23-
24.

Allan McArtor, FAA (Federal Aviation Administration)
Administrator, announced emergency air traffic rules
for the Los Angeles International Airport. McArtor
wants to assure the public safety is being maintained
in that airspace. Among the critics of McArtor's
move are the California Aviation Council and the Experimental Aircraft Association. Between August 1,
1986 and August 1, 1987, there were fifty-one near-
collisions reported in the Los Angeles basin. This
number was three times higher than the previous year.
1 illustration.

8.009   "FAA Revises 1984 Near Midair Reports Upward From 299
to 592." **Aviation Week and Space Technology** 122 (June
17, 1985):   37.

There were in 1984 57 million takeoffs and landings at
airports where the Federal Aviation Administration
(FAA) has control towers. Partly because of doubts,
on the part of the Aviation Consumer Action Project,
regarding the number of reported near midair collisions, the FAA revised its totals upwards for 1983 and
1984:   478 instead of 286 for 1983, and 592 instead of
299 for 1984. The total for the first quarter of 1985
has also been revised upwards: 154 instead of 141.
The first-quarter total for 1984 was ninety-eight.

8.010   **Graham, Walton** and Robert H. Orr.   "Terminal Air
Traffic Flow and Collision Exposure." **Proceedings of
the IEEE** 58 (March 1970):   328-336.

Seven sections comprise this article: introduction,
definitions, parameters, model derivation, effect of
users sharing same airport, exceptional terminals,
and midair collisions and NMACs (near midair collisions). Abstract. Author biographical information.
14 figures. 2 tables. 3 references.

8.011   **Hoffman, David H.**   "Study Shows Problem of Midair
Collisions Is Far From Solved." **Aviation Week and
Space Technology** 77 (October 15, 1962):   42.

Comments, with the aid of numerous statistics, on
Project Scan, a report about midair collisions. The
report was published by the Federal Aviation Agency
(FAA). Pilots and air traffic controllers (ATCs) reported 3126 incidents involving risk of midair collision during the fiscal year 1962. Midair collisions
in 1961 claimed twenty-one lives. The Flight Safety
Foundation (FSF) made a number of recommendations to
the FAA about minimizing midair collisions. One rec-
ommendation concerned continuation of collecting anonymous near collision reports.

8.012   "Increasing Near-Midair Incidents Spur Drive to Im-
         prove ATC Performance." **Aviation Week and Space Tech-**
         nology 127 (August 24, 1987):   21-23.

         According to the Federal Aviation Administration (FAA),
         there were 758 near-collision reports filed in 1985
         and 828 in 1986. To deal with the increasing numbers
         of incidents, an FAA team meets weekly to examine new
         near-collision reports. Impact '88 is an FAA program
         whose aim it is, in part, to accelerate testing of a
         traffic alert collision avoidance system. Recent
         near-collisions have occurred near La Guardia Airport
         and John F. Kennedy International Airport. 1 illus-
         tration.

8.013   **Jones, Richard B.** and Frederick H. Lutze, Jr.   "Com-
         puter Simulation of Near Midair Collisions in the Ter-
         minal Environment." **Journal of Aircraft** 11 (August
         1974):   457-459.

         Introduction, analysis, numerical procedure, and re-
         sults and conclusions of computer simulation of near
         midair collisions in the terminal environment by two
         author/researchers from Virginia Polytechnic Insti-
         tute and State University. Abstract. 3 figures. 5
         references.

8.014   **Julian, Ken.** "Preventing Midair Collisions." **High**
         Technology 5 (July 1985):   48-53 and 72.

         Piedmont Airlines is testing TCAS (threat-alert colli-
         sion avoidance system). TCAS, an invisible radar
         shield, backs up ground-based radar, computers, and
         human air traffic controllers (ATCs). The backup is
         accomplished by surrounding the airplane with the in-
         visible radar shield. TCAS scans a range of fifteen
         miles every second. If TCAS "decides" other aircraft
         in the area pose a collision threat, TCAS alerts the
         flight crew and the crew, with the aid of data provided

by TCAS, takes evasive action. The origins of TCAS date back to 1955 and the Air Transport Association of America (ATA). Collins Radio, McDonnell Douglas, and Honeywell each tried developing a successful TCAS. Now, Bendix Transportation Avionics and Dalmo Victor provide the FAA (Federal Aviation Administration) with TCAS. Lincoln Laboratory is attempting to produce a low-cost TCAS for small aircraft. 1 illustration. 5 photographs. Author biographical information. 6 references.

8.015   **Kanafani, Adib.** "The Analysis of Hazards and the Hazards of Analysis: Reflections on Air Traffic Safety Management." **Accident Analysis and Prevention** 18, No. 5 (1986): 403-416.

Air traffic safety; risk analysis and its pitfalls; a framework for air traffic safety management; air traffic control (ATC) and collision safety; and synthesis are the major areas examined. Author biographical information. Abstract. 2 figures. 19 references.

8.016   **Linsley, Clyde, Jr.** "Sorting Out the Crowds in the Sky." **Transportation USA** 5 (Winter 1979): 18-21.

BCAS (Beacon Collision Avoidance System) and ATARS (Automated Traffic Advisory and Resolution Service) are attempts by the FAA (Federal Aviation Administration) to prevent aircraft collisions. 7 photographs. Author biographical information.

8.017   **Lowenhar, Herman.** "Collision Avoidance: How? When?" **Space/Aeronautics** 53 (March 1970): 20-28.

Three devices can aid in preventing aircraft from colliding: the Time-Frequency Collision Avoidance System (TF-CAS), the Secant-B, and Xenon flashers. The respective costs of these devices are: TF-CAS (at least $4000), Secant-B ($500), and Xenon flashers ($200). Most airliner collisions involve light aircraft, but TF-CAS is too expensive for general aviation. McDonnell Douglas, Bendix, and Sierra-Wilcox are involved in producing a collision avoidance device. Collins gave up after twelve years of effort. 6 illustrations. 2 photographs.

8.018   **Macburnie, Eric.** "CASB Urges Greater Vigilance to Reduce Risk of Ground Collisions." **Canadian Aviation** 60 (November 1987): 8-9.

According to the Canadian Aviation Safety Board (CASB), the Canadian government should implement forty-seven measures to reduce collision risk at civil airports. For example, improving visibility from some control towers should be done as soon as possible. Further-more, some poor practices followed by pilots should be rectified, poor radio discipline being one such prac-tice. At civil airports in 1985 there were over 200 conflicts involving aircraft or vehicles and aircraft. Forty-three people died near the airport at Cranbrook, B.C. in 1978, when a Pacific Western Airlines (PWA) Boeing 737 crashed, after the pilot aborted a landing because he thought he was going to collide with a snow-sweeper on the runway.

8.019   **Machol, Robert E.** "An Aircraft Collision Model." **Management Science** 21 (June 1975): 1089-1101.

When systems analysis was used to improve navigation standards of jet aircraft flying over the North Atlan-tic Ocean, cost was minimized at the same time safety was maximized. The standards were improved because of a 1960's controversy between airline owners and pilots. Author biographical information. Abstract. 7 figures. 5 references.

8.020   **Marx, Joseph Laurance.** "In Control, Out of Control?" Chapter in **Crisis in the Skies,** by Joseph Laurance Marx, 108-132. New York, NY: David McKay Co., Inc., 1970.

A look at air traffic control (ATC); midair collisions; commercial airports and radar; the Federal Aviation Ad-ministration (FAA); air traffic controllers (ATCs); and transponders.

8.021   **McClellan, J. Mac.** "The Grand Delusion." **Flying** 114 (June 1987): 72-74.

Pilots, controllers, radar, and the Federal Aviation Administration (FAA) as variables in preventing air-craft collision. 1 illustration.

8.022   **McClellan, J. Mac.** "TCAS." **Flying** 114 (June 1987): 82 and 84.

TCAS (Traffic Alert Collision Avodiance System) is a device for "backing up" a pilot's eyes and a control-ler's separation. The need for TCAS arose after the

collision, over the Grand Canyon, between two airliners in 1956. The high-speed computer portion of TCAS
plots the bearing and distance to transponder-equipped
airplanes. TCAS then plots the closure rate of airplanes which are a "threat," and advises the pilots of
TCAS-equipped airplanes how to avoid a collision.
Three types of TCAS—TCAS I, TCAS II, and TCAS III—
were to be developed, TCAS I representing the lowest
level of sophistication and TCAS III representing the
highest level. According to Bendix, TCAS II will cost
about $125,000. 1 illustration.

8.023   "Midair-Collision Risk Increases." **Astronautics and
Aeronautics** 11 (January 1973):   14-15.

On June 6, 1971, at 15,000 feet in good weather near
Duarte, California, there was a midair collision between a Hughes Air West DC-9 and a U.S. Marine Corp.
F-4B. The DC-9 was flying IFR (Instrument Flight
Rules), the F-4B, VFR (visual flight rules). According to research by the National Transportation Safety Board (NTSB), most midair accidents in 1969-1970
occurred at an altitude of one hundred feet or less
and between general aviation aircraft. Generally
speaking, most midair collisions occur at or near airports and at low closure speeds. Pilots of every level of experience can be involved in this type of accident. The see-and-avoid concept can be used to prevent
midair collisions.

8.024   **Morganthau, Tom,** Bob Cohn, Richard Sandza and Andrew
Murr. "Year of the Near Miss." **Newsweek** 110 (July
27, 1987):   20-24 and 26-27.

According to the Federal Aviation Administration (FAA),
there is more than one near-miss a day involving U.S.
commercial flights. On the other hand, there were
0.92 fatalities per 100,000 hours flown in 1986. The
figure was 1.72 in 1978. And the airline death toll
for 1986 was 86 compared to 197 in 1985. Transportation Secretary Elizabeth Dole has approved the hiring
of 580 controllers. Doppler radar, which detects wind
shear, is expected to make flying safer as is TCAS
(traffic alert and collision avoidance system) technology. 5 photographs. 4 illustrations.

8.025   "NASA Shuttle Commander Involved in Near Collision
With Pan Am A310." **Aviation Week and Space Technology** 130 (May 22, 1989):   105.

On May 16, 1989, a T-38 jet trainer and a Pan American

(Pan Am) World Airways Airbus Industrie A310-200 almost
collided. The pilot of the T-38 was astronaut David M.
Walker. There were 166 passengers and a crew of ten on
the Pan Am flight. The incident took place near Dulles
International Airport. Both aircraft were flying IFR
(Instrument Flight Rules). The T-38 came within approximately 500 feet of the Airbus, which was en route to
Paris. Walker had left Houston, Texas and was headed
for Washington, DC. A Pan Am Safety spokesman said the
near-collision indicates the need for T/CAS (traffic
alert/collision avoidance system).

8.026   "Near-Miss Statistics." **Aviation Week and Space Technology** 96 (May 22, 1972):   79.

In 1971, forty-four near-midair collisions were due to
system errors. For the first three months of 1972,
there were five such incidents.

8.027   "New Collision Study Prepared." **Aviation Week and
Space Technology** 90 (June 30, 1969):   28.

It has been announced that a midair collision study
will be published in July 1969 by the National Transportation Safety Board (NTSB). This study will be
compared with a near-midair collision study published
by the Federal Aviation Administration (FAA) in 1968.
Only three midair collisions in 1968 involved a commercial carrier. Most of the accidents occurred below
5000 feet during the summer or on a weekend. Air traffic control (ATC) was a factor in 20% of collisions.

8.028   "New Scare Over Near Misses by Jets." **U.S. News and
World Report** 79 (December 22, 1975):   36.

Airliners in the U.S., when flying between cities, fly
above 18,000 feet in exclusive airspace. Vertical
separation between aircraft is 1000 feet; horizontal
separation is five miles. A near-miss typically occurs at lower altitudes within thirty miles of a major airport. One hundred and twenty-three people lost
their lives in U.S. airline accidents as of December
12, 1975. The total for 1974 was 467. It was 499 in
1960. 1 illustration.

8.029   **Noland, David.**   "Fearless Flying." **Discover** 9 (November 1988):   44-45.

In 1986 a Piper Archer unknowingly entered restricted

airspace over Cerritos, California. The single engine aircraft collided with an Aeromexico DC-9 and eighty-two people died. A Traffic and Collision Avoidance System (TCAS) would very likely have prevented the collision. By the early to mid-1990s, all airliners are expected to be equipped with TCAS 3. Later all small aircraft will have a Mode C transponder. This device will inform controllers and airline pilots of the small plane's position and the evasive action the large plane can take, if necessary. The Advanced Automation System (AAS) is a $3.6-billion IBM (International Business Machines) project, expected to be operational in 1998. The AAS will, among other things, warn pilots of potential collision courses and calculate flight paths up to half an hour ahead. 2 illustrations.

8.030   **Ratcliffe, S.** "Devices For the Avoidance of Collision in the Air." **Electronics and Power** 31 (July 1985): 515-518.

Between 1946 and 1981, the annual rate for midair collisions, for the world's airlines, was about 2.4 collisions per year. In the U.S., midair collisions constitute about 1% of all civil aircraft accidents and involve two aircraft. These collisions, however, account for about 5% of all civil aviation fatalities. Furthermore, these collisions occur under VFR (visual flight rules) conditions. Collision-avoidance devices include MTI (moving target indicator), SSR (secondary-surveillance radar), and TCAS (traffic alert and collision-avoidance system). 3 illustrations. 1 photograph. 12 references. Author biographical information.

8.031   "Safer Skies?" **Scientific American** 259 (September 1988): 29-30.

Reported midair near-collisions rose from 311 in 1982 to 1063 in 1987—more than threefold. Most of the near-collisions included noncommercial aircraft flying visual flight rules (VFR). A Mode C transponder reports altitude automatically when it is querried by ground radar. Controllers can see if an aircraft with a transponder is a safety threat to other aircraft. A new Federal Aviation Administration (FAA) rule requires use of Mode C transponders by all aircraft within thirty miles of the 138 busiest airports in the U.S.

8.032   "The Safety Factor." **Newsweek** 58 (July 10, 1961): 38.

In December 1960, 134 people lost their lives in a midair collision over Staten Island, New York. The Flight

Safety Foundation (FSF) has initiated SCAN (system for collection and analysis of near-collision) reports to avert such collisions. There were only twenty midair collisions involving scheduled airlines between 1948 and 1959. There were four to five near-collisions a day in 1954 reported by commercial pilots. In 1956 there were 11.5 billion passenger miles without any fatalities. 1 photograph.

8.033   **Scherschel, Patricia M.** "Crowded Skies—And a Big Push For Air Safety." **U.S. News and World Report** 88 (March 10, 1980): 57-58.

Three hundred million passengers were carried by U.S. domestic airlines in 1979. This represents an increase of 75% since 1969. The total number of passengers by 1990 is expected to exceed 500 million. There are fears of midair collisions because the number of reported near-misses between 1973 and 1978 rose from 275 to 504. Since the Pacific Southwest Airlines (PSA) disaster over San Diego, California on September 25, 1978, there have been more than a dozen reported near-misses over San Diego. Many near-misses are attributed to an increase in the number of planes not subject to ground control. Many general aviation aircraft, numbering 193,000, fall into this category. 2 photographs. 1 illustration.

8.034   **Schneider, Charles E.** "ATC Hazards Feared Overlooked." **Aviation Week and Space Technology** 96 (May 22, 1972): 78-79.

On December 31, 1971, the Federal Aviation Administration (FAA) terminated its near-miss reporting program. The program guaranteed immunity to pilots who reported near-misses. Since the termination of immunity, the number of reports of near-misses has dropped sharply. The Air Line Pilots Association (ALPA) wants pilots to report near-misses. Some individuals believe hazardous situations are being overlooked because immunity no longer exists.

8.035   "Search For Safety in the Skies." **Life** 50 (February 10, 1961): 66-78.

The Federal Aviation Agency (FAA) has a research budget of approximately $62 million—90% budgeted for midair collision research. One hundred and twenty-eight people died in a midair collision over the Grand Canyon on June 30, 1956. One hundred and thirty-four died in a midair over New York on December 16, 1960.

More than 100,000 planes—2000 of them commercial carriers—use U.S. air lanes. The National Aviation Facilities Experimental Center in Atlantic City, New
Jersey is the location for elaborate air safety tests.
12 photographs.

8.036   **Steinberg, Herbert A.**   "Collision and Missed Approach
Risks in High-Capacity Airport Operations." **Proceedings of the IEEE** 58 (March 1970):   314-321.

A risk model for airport landing operations is discussed in this article, which consists of eight main
sections: (1) introduction, (2) historical background,
(3) general description, (4) turn-on, (5) approach,
(6) missed approach, (7) conclusion, and (8) appendix:
requirements for model implementation. Abstract. List
of symbols. Author biographical information. 5 tables. 1 figure. 10 references.

8.037   **Stephenson, James.**   "Air Misses." **New Statesman and
Society** 1 (August 26, 1988):   32.

According to the Civil Aviation Authority (CAA), there
were sixty-one near-misses involving commercial aircraft in the United Kingdom (UK) in 1986, and fifty-
five near-misses in 1987. The Joint Airmiss Working
Group, which publishes near-miss statistics, accepts
accounts of near-misses only from air crews. The
London Air Traffic Control Centre handled over a million flights in 1987. 4 graphs.

8.038   **Vincent, T.L.**, E.M. Cliff, W.J. Grantham and W.Y.
Peng. "Some Aspects of Collision Avoidance." **AIAA
Journal** 12 (January 1974):   3-4.

Four authors examine aspects of collision avoidance
regarding two vehicles: a light aircraft designated
as "pursuer" and a commercial aircraft designated as
"evader." The likelihood of collision varies in each
of three zones: "green," "yellow," "red." Author
biographical information. 4 figures. 6 references.

8.039   **Weiner, Eric.**   "Pressure Groups." **Flying** 114 (June
1987):   69 and 71.

The viewpoints of major aviation groups regarding
collision avoidance, including the General Aviation
Manufacturers Association (GAMA), Air Transport Association (ATA), Air Line Pilots Association (ALPA),

and Aircraft Owners and Pilots Association (AOPA).   1
illustration.

8.040   **Whittington, Hugh.**   "More Recommendations on Near Mid-
Air."   **Canadian Aviation** 61 (September 1988):   5.

Two wide-body jets nearly collided over the North Atlantic Ocean on July 8, 1987:   a Continental Airlines
Boeing 747 and a Delta Airlines Lockheed L-1011.   The
Canadian Aviation Safety Board (CASB) issued three
safety recommendations because of this incident.

8.041   **Work, Clemens P.**   "The Gremlins in the Sky." **U.S.
News and World Report** 103 (July 20, 1987):   12-13.

Delta Pilots were involved in four near-disasters between June 18 and July 8, 1987.   In one incident, a
Delta jet came to within 600 feet of the Pacific Ocean,
after the crew accidentally shut off the plane's engines.   The pilot, however, managed to restore power
before the jet hit the water.   In another incident,
near Newfoundland, a Delta jet missed by one hundred
feet a Continental Airlines jet.   The Delta jet was
sxity miles off course.   1 photograph.

9

Security and Air Piracy

9.001   "Airline, Airport Security Bolstered in Face of Pending Labor Disputes." **Aviation Week and Space Technology** 128 (February 29, 1988): 62.

Northwest Airlines and Pan American (Pan Am) World
Airways are facing pending labor disputes. Northwest
has hired guards for facilities at the Minneapolis-St.
Paul International Airport. The International Broth-
erhood of Teamsters might strike against Pan Am.
Federal Aviation Administration (FAA) surveillance
was being increased for these reasons.

9.002   "Airline, Airport Security Rules Are Consolidated,
Toughened." **Canadian Aviation** 61 (February 1988): 3.

The Air Carrier Security Regulations replace the Civil Aviation Security Measures and Foreign Aircraft Security Measures Regulations. This change is expected
to contribute to enhanced security for Canadian airports and airlines.

9.003   "Airport Security Increased For Convention." **Aviation
Week and Space Technology** 121 (July 9, 1984): 30.

An airspace restriction is being sought around Moscone
Center in San Francisco, California, which is site of
the forthcoming Democratic National Convention. There
will also be increased security at San Francisco International Airport. Airport police will be at full
strength. If backup is required, it will be provided
by the California Highway Patrol and other police
forces. American Airlines will transport most of the
25,000 delegates.

9.004   **Anderson, Harry,** Theodore Stanger, Dorinda Elliott and
John Barry. "The Agony of Pan Am Flight 73." **Newsweek** 108 (September 15, 1986): 20-24 and 26.

Pan Am (Pan American) Flight 73 arrived in Karachi,

Pakistan from Bombay, India and was to depart for
Frankfurt, West Germany and New York. As passengers
were boarding in Karachi, four Arabic-speaking terrorists seized control of the plane. The Pan Am's flight
crew managed to escape through an escape hatch. The
hijackers demanded to be flown to Larnaca, Cyprus in
order to release terrorists in prison in Cyprus. The
hijackers paniced and began shooting. Sixteen passengers and crew died and approximately fifty were seriously wounded. 4 photographs. 2 illustrations.

9.005   "Angry Men, Desperate Days." **Newsweek** 76 (September
        21, 1970): 22-26.

        Three airplanes—Trans World Airlines (TWA) Flight
        741, Swissair Flight 100, and British Overseas Airways
        Corporation (BOAC) Flight 775—were hijacked to Jordan
        by members of the Popular Front for the Liberation of
        Palestine (PFLP). The hijackers were not successful
        in hijacking El Al Flight 219. 9 photographs.

9.006   **Ashford, Norman,** H.P. Martin Stanton and Clifton A.
        Moore. "Airport Security." Chapter in **Airport Opera-
        tions,** by Norman Ashford, H.P. Martin Stanton and
        Clifton A. Moore, 243-265. New York, NY: John Wiley
        and Sons, Inc., 1984.

        Structure of planning for security; responsibility and
        organization; airside security procedures; landside
        security procedures—passenger terminal; landside pro-
        cedures—cargo terminal; security equipment and sys-
        tems; and security operations. 2 tables. 1 figure.
        3 references. 1 appendix.

9.007   "Asian Carriers Have Long-Term Commitment to Security
        Programs." **Aviation Week and Space Technology** 130
        (May 8, 1989):   77.

        An emphasis on airline security in Japan, South Korea,
        and Taiwan. Specific reference is made to the x-ray-
        ing of baggage by Cathay Pacific and the bombing in-
        flight in 1987 of a Korean Air Boeing 707. Passengers
        in Asia may be subject to a second body search if they
        stop at a duty-free shop.

9.008   "At Dawson Field: Life as a Hostage." **Newsweek** 76
        (September 21, 1970):   23B.

        Sylvia Jacobsen (Tallahassee, Florida); June Haesler

(Bay View, New Jersey); Naomi Feinstein (New York); Sarah Raab (Trenton, New Jersey); and Sally Schindler (Worcester, Massachusetts) were a few of the hostages held in the desert in Jordan, after members of the Popular Front for the Liberation of Palestine (PFLP) hijacked three airliners. 1 photograph.

9.009   **Ben-Porat, Yeshayahu,** Eitan Haber and Zeev Schiff. **Entebbe Rescue.** New York, NY: Delacorte Press, 1977.

Air France Flight 139 originated in Tel Aviv, Israel on June 27, 1976. While on the Athens-to-Paris part of its journey, Flight 139 was hijacked by terrorists. Flight 139 was commandeered to Entebbe, Uganda—over 2500 miles from Israel. The leader of the hijackers was a German man. The Israeli government examined options on how to deal with the hijacking, and decided on a top secret hostage rescue plan—Operation Thunderball. On July 3, 1976, Lieutenant Colonel Jonathan Netaniahu, commander of Israeli paratrooper raiding forces, led his men, late at night, in a surprise attack against the terrorists and Ugandan soldiers. Netaniahu and his men had rehearsed the rescue in Israel before boarding four Hercules transports and flying to Uganda. In the ensuing gun battle at Entebbe International Airport, 105 hostages were rescued. Lieutenant Colonel Netaniahu died in the attack. Dora Bloch, a seventy-five-year-old Israeli, was the only hostage left behind. She was later executed by Ugandan secret police on orders from Idi Amin. Twenty Ugandan soldiers died in the shooting. Idi Amin had the four air traffic controllers (ATCs) at Entebbe shot, charging they had cooperated with Israel. 36 photographs. The following are other book-length accounts of the raid on Entebbe: **Operation Thunder: The Entebbe Raid** (1976) by Yehuda Ofer (8 photographs); **Counterstrike Entebbe** (1976) by Tony Williamson (4 illustrations); and **90 Minutes at Entebbe** (1976) by William Stevenson (32 photographs. 3 illustrations).

9.010   **Blank, Joseph K.** "Airport Security: Is It in the Bag?" **Security Management** 30 (February 1986): 73-75.

Metal detectors, x-ray devices, dogs, vapor analyzers, nuclear magnetic resonance, and thermal neutron activation are used in air travel safety. Three treaties pertain to international policy regarding air piracy. 1 illustration. Author biographical information. 9 references.

9.011   "Bombing Poses Threat to Pan Am Recovery." **Aviation**

Week and Space Technology 130 (January 2, 1989):   32.

Terrorism was responsible for a $400-million loss in
1986 for Pan American (Pan Am) World Airways. The
downing by a bomb of Pan Am Flight 103 on December 21,
1988 over Lockerbie, Scotland is expected to delay Pan
Am's financial recovery.

9.012   **Brown, David A.** "Bomb Destroys Pan Am 747 in Blast
Over Scotland." **Aviation Week and Space Technology** 130
(January 2, 1989):   28-29.

On December 21, 1988, Pan American (Pan Am) Flight 103—
while cruising at 31,000 feet over Lockerbie, Scotland—
exploded, and broke into at least five major parts. All
passengers and crew—259 individuals—and at least elev-
en persons on the ground died. A bomb likely made from
Semtax, an odorless plastic explosive made in Czechoslo-
vakia caused the explosion. Some pieces of wreckage
were found one hundred miles from Lockerbie. It appears the Pan Am disaster is very similar to the Air India Boeing 747 disaster of June 1985, when a 747 en
route from Montreal, Quebec to London broke up over the
Atlantic. 1 photograph. 1 illustration.

9.013   **Brown, Peter J.**   "Should Americans Sit Still For Hijackers?" **Security Management** 30 (April 1986):   47-49.

A hypothetical account of how certain passengers on an
airplane might be able to overpower the airplane's hijackers. Author biographical information.

9.014   **Cary, Peter** and Sandra R. Gregg.   "Gaping Holes in
Airport Security." **U.S. News and World Report** 104
(April 25, 1988):   28-29.

The Federal Aviation Administration (FAA) has to police
400 airports, but has only 450 security agents to do
the job. In 1987 1.2 billion passengers were screened
by U.S. airlines. Three thousand weapons were seized
during screening. Also in 1987, there were four attempts to hijack planes. None of the four people involved were successful and none had a gun. One airport missed 66% of dummy weapons when federal auditors
tested x-ray procedures. Los Angeles International
Airport and Dulles International Airport could not account for 8000 employee identification badges during a
federal audit. In December 1987, a former employee of
Pacific Southwest Airlines (PSA) got aboard a PSA
flight with an old identification card and a gun. The
disgruntled employee fired the gun and caused the

plane to crash. Forty-three people died. 1 photograph. 6 illustrations.

9.015 "CCTV Helps Control Customs Clearance at the LA Air-
       port." **Communications News** 22 (December 1985):   38-
       39.

       Over one hundred people can pass through customs si-
       multaneously at the Tom Bradley International Terminal
       at Los Angeles International Airport. There is a
       closed-circuit television (CCTV) system, consisting of
       thirty-six cameras, to provide general security and
       specific surveillance. Up to 62,000 people can be mon-
       itored per day over a 125,000 square-foot area. Twen-
       ty-four of the cameras are color cameras used primar-
       ily for suspect-surveillance purposes. These cameras,
       enclosed in smoked-glass ceiling domes, have pan,
       tilt, and zoom capability. A suspect's actions can
       be recorded on tape with a time-lapse video cassette
       recorder, which has a built-in date/time generator. 1
       photograph.

9.016 **Clutterbuck, Richard.** "Airport Security." in **Kidnap,
       Hijack and Extortion: The Response,** by Richard Clut-
       terbuck, 75-77. New York, NY: St. Martin's Press,
       Inc., 1987.

       Every day approximately 3 million people board 30,000
       aircraft at 6700 airports. In 1985 the odds of being
       hijacked were about one in 500,000. It is the public-
       ity associated with hijackings that encourages other
       hijackings.

9.017 **Clutterbuck, Richard.** "Hijack to Mogadishu, 1977."
       in **Kidnap, Hijack and Extortion: The Response,** by
       Richard Clutterbuck, 187-188. New York, NY: St.
       Martin's Press, Inc., 1987.

       At 2:00 a.m. on October 18, 1977, German commandos
       stormed a Lufthansa Boeing 737 at Mogadishu, Somalia.
       There were eighty-four passengers and crew and four
       Arab hijackers on board. The airplane was wired with
       explosives. The hijackers—who had boarded the 737 at
       Palma, Majorca—wanted the release of prisoners and
       about $16 million. During a shootout, which also in-
       volved the use of stun grenades, three hijackers died
       and a fourth was severely wounded. None of the hos-
       tages or commandos received more than slight injuries.

9.018 **Clutterbuck, Richard.** "Hijacking." in **Kidnap,**

Hijack and Extortion: The Response, by Richard Clutterbuck, 19-21. New York, NY: St. Martin's Press,
Inc., 1987.

The motive for hijacking a plane between 1945 and 1952
was to escape from Eastern Europe. In the 1960s, however, the purpose of hijacking an airplane was to escape to or from Cuba. Of ninety-one hijackings in
1969, sixty-three were to Cuba. On January 5, 1973,
the U.S. introduced 100% search of passengers and baggage at boarding gates. There were, in 1985, sixteen
hijackings—the lowest number in eighteen years. 1
table.

9.019   **Cook, Nick.** "How to Guard the Airport." **Interavia**
40 (September 1985): 1014-1015.

On June 14, 1985, a Trans World Airlines (TWA) 727
was hijacked, after it left Athens, Greece. On June
23 of the same year, an Air India 747 crashed into the
Atlantic Ocean while en route from Montreal, Quebec to
London. Over 300 passengers and crew were killed.
Armed guards, thermal imagers, closed-circuit television (CCTV) surveillance cameras, perimeter fences, pa-
trolling guards with dogs, electrical intruder sensors,
bright floodlights, metal-detection gateways, and x-ray
machines are some of the ways to provide airport security. 3 photographs.

9.020   **Cooper, Nancy** and Richard Sandza. "Should the Pilot
Have Left the Plane?" **Newsweek** 108 (September 15,
1986): 24.

Both Martin Shugrue, Chief Operating Officer, Pan American (Pan Am) World Airways and Henry Duffy, President,
Air Line Pilots Association (ALPA), believe the pilot
did the correct thing, when he escaped, through an escape hatch, from his hijacked Pan Am Boeing 747.
Flight 73 was on the ground in Karachi, Pakistan when
the hijacking took place. All U.S. pilots now attend
a security course and are expected to attend follow-up
sessions annually. 1 photograph.

9.021   **Crenshaw, William A.** "Civil Aviation: Target For
Terrorism." **Annals of the American Academy of Political and Social Science** 498 (July 1988): 60-69.

Looks at the role of private security in protecting
U.S. domestic air transportation against terrorism,
and how private security might respond to Middle-East-
ern and European-type terrorism in the U.S. Abstract.

Author biographical information.

9.022   **Dorey, Frederick C.   Aviation Security.** London: Gra-
nada Publishing Ltd., 1983.

There are twenty-seven chapters in this book. Representative chapters pertain to the following topics:
(1) hijacking, (2) sabotage, (3) assassination, (4)
kidnapping/abduction, (5) car parks at airports, (6)
vehicle identification, (7) spectator areas, (8) security of airborne aircraft, (9) passenger searching,
(10) diplomatic personnel, (11) x-ray equipment, (12)
metal detectors, and (13) explosive detectors. Author
biographical information. Acknowledgements. List of
abbreviations. 17 figures. 12 tables. 6 plates.
Glossary.

9.023   **Drummond, James.** "It's a Bomb All Right." **Forbes** 144
(September 4, 1989): 41-42.

The Federal Aviation Administration (FAA) wants U.S.
airlines to purchase the thermal neutron analysis
(TNA) device—an explosives detector. Each unit weighs
nine tons, is the size of a Volkswagen bus, and costs
$1 million. The TNA device would scan for explosives
in checked baggage on U.S. international flights. However, there is considerable criticism of the TNA device. For example, it was not designed to detect bombs
weighing less than two pounds. Also, cheese and sau-
sage, which have high concentrations of nitrogen, can
set the TNA device off, as can heavy wool coats. Japan
Air Lines (JAL) has decided to purchase another device.
It is made by American Science and Engineering, Inc. in
Boston, Massachusetts and costs less than $250,000. 1
cartoon illustration.

9.024   **Eichler, Glenn.** "Airport Security and Other Oxymorons."
Esquire 110 (September 1988): 100.

Security at U.S. airports has to be improved in light
of certain developments in the recent past. Example
one: the General Accounting Office (GAO) issued a report in May 1987 about lax security. Example two: in
December 1987, a former employee of Pacific Southwest
Airlines (PSA) got on board a PSA jet and began shooting. Forty-three people died in the crash. Example
three: plastic and ceramic parts are being used in-
creasingly in the manufacture of handguns, making detection of these weapons virtually impossible at airport security. A positive development is the introduction of high technology identification badges, which

are almost impossible to counterfeit. The badges, which
contain computer-generated images of their owners, are
already in use in Los Angeles, California and Atlanta,
Georgia. 1 illustration.

9.025   "European Parliament Presses EEC to Strengthen Airport
        Security." **Aviation Week and Space Technology** 124 (April
        7, 1986):   34.

        The European Parliament, representing the twelve-mem-
        ber-nation European Economic Community (EEC), has ap-
        proved standards for improving airport security. Jean-
        Pierre Roux, a member of the European Parliament,
        drafted the resolution approved by the parliament.

9.026   **Farmery, R.**   "Security Problems at Airports." in **Pro-
        ceedings of the Fifth World Airports Conference on
        Technological and Economic Change, May 5-7, 1976,** ed-
        ited by Mary Monro, 199-205. London: Thomas Telford
        Ltd., 1976.

        Aviation terrorism—sabotage and hijacking—is ana-
        lyzed. How threats of sabotage and hijacking have
        been dealt with in the past, specifically in the United
        Kingdom, is discussed. The individual roles of airport
        security staff and police are also covered. It is em-
        phasized that future airport planning include security
        at the very beginning of the planning process. Author
        biographical information. Abstract.

9.027   **Feazel, Michael.**   "IFALPA Approves New Policies to
        Improve Airline Safety." **Aviation Week and Space Tech-
        nology** 124 (April 21, 1986):   32.

        The International Federation of Air Line Pilots Asso-
        ciations (IFALPA), which is comprised of forty-five
        national pilots associations, concluded its annual
        meeting in London on April 15, 1986. IFALPA wants
        boycotts against unsecure airports and countries that
        support terrorism. In 1985 approximately 928 people
        were killed and 1500 injured in terrorist attacks.
        Three hundred and twenty-nine people died when a bomb
        went off aboard an Air India Boeing 747 on June 23,
        1985.

9.028   **Fotos, Christopher P.**   "GAO Outlines FAA Shortcomings
        in Lockerbie Commission Hearings." **Aviation Week and
        Space Technology** 132 (January 1, 1990):   94-95.

        After the bombing of Pan American (Pan Am) World

Airways Flight 103 over Lockerbie, Scotland, the U.S. established the President's Commission on Aviation Security and Terrorism. The GAO (General Accounting Office) testified on December 18, 1989 regarding FAA (Federal Aviation Administration) security efforts. Although the FAA's security division has almost three times as many staff as in 1985, the GAO feels there are deficiencies in FAA security efforts.

9.029   **Fotos, Christopher P.** "Union Representatives Praise Pan Am Security." **Aviation Week and Space Technology** 130 (January 2, 1989): 32.

In spite of the downing by a bomb of Pan American (Pan Am) Flight 103 on December 21, 1988 over Lockerbie, Scotland, a representative of the Air Line Pilots Association Master Executive Council, and a representative of the Independent Union of Flight Attendants praised Pan Am security procedures.

9.030   **Funke, Douglas J.** "Perceptual Training Sharpens Baggage Inspection Skills." **Security Management** 23 (September 1979): 30-31 and 34.

Reports on research regarding airport baggage inspectors—"explosive trained," "gun trained," "control"—and percentages of weapons missed by subjects in each group. 1 photograph. 1 graph. Author biographical information. 15 references.

9.031   **Gilliam, Ronald R.** "An Application of Queueing Theory to Airport Passenger Security Screening." **Interfaces** 9 (August 1979): 117-123.

Security screening, equipment throughput capacities, passenger security screening rates, passenger arrival rate, and queueing analysis are the major topics covered. Author biographical information. Abstract. 2 tables. 4 references.

9.032   "Handling of Threats by Airlines, Governments Called Into Question After Pan Am Crash." **Aviation Week and Space Technology** 130 (January 2, 1989): 32.

On December 5, 1988, the U.S. embassy in Helsinki, Finland was warned anonymously, by telephone, that a Pan American (Pan Am) flight would be bombed within two weeks. The Federal Aviation Administration (FAA) informed a number of organizations about the threat,

including Pan Am. However, a public announcement was
not made. Paul Channon, British Transport Secretary,
ordered a review of security procedures at British airports, after the bombing.

9.033   **Higgs, D.G.,** P.N. Jones, J.A. Markham and E. Newton.
"A Review of Explosives Sabotage and Its Investigation
in Civil Aircraft." **Journal of the Forensic Science
Society** 18 (July/October 1978): 137-160.

The flight data recorder (FDR), cockpit voice recorder
(CVR), impact craters, radiophotography, fiber analysis, x-ray diffraction analysis, microscopic examination, and chemical identification of explosives are
some of the areas discussed. Author biographical information. Abstract. 24 figures. 15 references. 1
appendix.

9.034   "The Hijack War." **Newsweek** 76 (September 21, 1970):
20-21.

Commandos of the Popular Front for the Liberation of
Palestine (PFLP) hijacked four airliners and unsuccess-
fully attempted to hijack a fifth. Three of the airliners—worth $28 million—were flown to a rock-hard
strip of desert in Jordan, where they were blown up.
Another aircraft, a 747, was destroyed with explosives
in Cairo, Egypt. The hijackers held men, women, and
children hostage, demanding the release of captured
Palestinian guerrillas in Israel. The hijackers also
demanded release of prisoners in West Germany, Switzerland, and England. All fifteen members of the
United Nations (UN) Security Council voted against
the hijackers. 3 photographs.

9.035   "Hijacking in the Skies: 48 Planes This Year—So
Far." **U.S. News and World Report** 67 (September 22,
1969): 50.

Of forty-eight aircraft hijackings to date, around
the world, more than half have been U.S. planes diverted to Cuba. Airplanes have also been hijacked
in Mexico, Colombia, Ecuador, and Venezuela, then diverted to Cuba. Passenger planes have been shot up
on the ground in Zurich, Switzerland; Athens, Greece;
and other countries. On August 28, 1969, a Trans
World Airlines (TWA) aircraft landed in Damascus,
Syria and was destroyed by a bomb a few minutes later.
To protest the hijacking problem, the International
Federation of Airline Pilots Associations (IFALPA) is
considering a strike.

9.036   "How to End Skyjacking." **U.S. News and World Report**
        69 (October 12, 1970):   48-52.

        Interview with Charles C. Tillinghast, Jr., Chairman
        of the Board and Chief Executive Officer (CEO), Trans
        World Airlines (TWA). 6 photographs.

9.037   "How to Stop Air Piracy." **Newsweek** 76 (September 21,
        1970):   28-29.

        The first known hijacking of an airplane occurred in
        1930 in Peru. The U.S. will adhere to an antiskyjack-
        ing policy based on the Israeli model. When hijackers
        attempted to hijack five aircraft in September 1970,
        the only airline which foiled the hijackers was the
        Israeli airline, El Al. 2 photographs.

9.038   **Hubbard, David G. The Skyjacker: His Flights of Fan-
        tasy.** New York, NY: Macmillan Co., 1971.

        The author, a psychiatrist, states that the objective
        of his book is to examine skyjacking from a common
        sense point of view. The book is an expanded version
        of an article which was about the case histories of
        twelve skyjackers. The article was written for a med-
        ical audience; the book was written for the general
        public. An appendix is a master list of all hijack-
        ing attempts, updated July 29, 1970, worldwide, air
        carrier, and general aviation. Theft of aircraft or
        hijacking of military aircraft is not included.

9.039   **Hughes, David.** "Experts Pursue Systems Approach to
        Bomb Detection at Airports." **Aviation Week and Space
        Technology** 132 (April 30, 1990):   66-67.

        Lee Grodzins, Massachusetts Institute of Technology
        (MIT); John D. Baldeschwieler, California Institute
        of Technology; Raymond Salazar, Federal Aviation Ad-
        ministration (FAA); and Robert Quigley, Federal Bu-
        reau of Investigation (FBI) are some of the confer-
        ence attendees discussed.

9.040   **Jackson, Stuart E.** "Americans Get Queasier About
        Air Travel." **Business Week** (July 15, 1985):   37.

        Between 1970 and 1985, the number of Americans who
        believed flying was safer than five years earlier
        dropped from 60% of those surveyed in a Louis Harris
        poll (1970) to 16% (1985). Security measures are

hardly effective: 7% of respondents believed this in
1978, 19% in 1985. Eighty-three percent of those poll-
ed now want all checked baggage to be x-rayed or hand-
searched. 1 graph.

9.041   **Johnson, R.W. Shootdown: Flight 007 and the American
        Connection.** New York, NY: Viking, 1986.

        A Soviet SU-15 fighter shot down Korean Airlines (KAL)
        Flight 007 on September 1, 1983. The 747, with 269
        people on board, was shot down as it was leaving Rus-
        sian airspace over Sakhalin Island. The U.S. charged
        the Soviet Union with deliberate mass murder; the So-
        viet Union accused the U.S. of having sent the South
        Korean aircraft on an espionage mission. Flight 007
        originated in New York, touched down at Anchorage,
        Alaska, and resumed on its way towards Seoul, South
        Korea. There still does not appear to be a conclusive
        answer as to why Flight 007 was in Russian airspace.
        16 illustrations.   10 maps and figures.   79 abbrevia-
        tions and acronyms. 912 notes. References: 17 news-
        papers, 32 periodicals (magazines), 5 transcripts of
        broadcasts, 58 books, 11 documents. Another book-
        length account of the shooting down of KAL 007 is:
        KAL Flight 007: The Hidden Story (1985) by Oliver
        Clubb.

9.042   **Koch, Peter** and Kai Hermann. **Assault at Mogadishu.**
        London: Corgi Books, 1977.

        Four hijackers—two men and two women—held the pas-
        sengers and crew of a Lufthansa Boeing 737 hostage
        from October 13-18, 1977. The hijackers demanded re-
        lease of convicted terrorists from West Germany. The
        hijacked plane, Flight 181, was commandeered from Ma-
        jorca to Cyprus, Dubai, Aden, and finally to Mogadi-
        shu, Somalia. The West German government had begun
        preparing for this type of incident after Israeli
        athletes were massacred at the 1972 Munich Olympics.
        The result was the formation of the GSG-9, a crack
        antiterrorist commando force. In seven minutes, on
        the night of October 17-18, twenty-eight GSG-9 com-
        mandos raided the hijacked plane. Three terrorists
        were shot dead; one was severely wounded. The eighty-
        six hostages were not hurt. 10 photographs.

9.043   "L.A. Airport Blast Kills Two Employees." **Aviation
        Week and Space Technology** 101 (August 12, 1974): 43.

        On August 6, 1974, two persons were killed and thir-
        ty-six were injured at Los Angeles International Air-
        port, when a bomb exploded in the international

terminal building. The blast occurred in a luggage
locker. The facilities of several carriers, including
Pan American (Pan Am), received the most damage.
False bomb threat calls the same day interrupted the
operations of other airlines.

9.044   "The Lady Who Trained Tigers." **Newsweek** 76 (September
21, 1970): 25.

Leila Khaled, age twenty-four, a heroine to millions
of Arabs, grew up in Lebanon. Educated at the American
University of Beirut, and a member of the Popular
Front for the Liberation of Palestine (PFLP), she
trained Tiger Cubs (teenage commandos). She failed,
however, twice to successfully hijack an aircraft.
The first failure involved a TWA (Trans World Airlines)
jet. The second failure involved an El Al flight. 2
photographs.

9.045   **Laver, Ross.** "A New Reign of Terror." **Maclean's** 98
(July 8, 1985): 20-23.

An Air India Boeing 747, carrying 329 passengers and
crew, crashed into the sea off the coast of Ireland.
All aboard died. About an hour earlier—at Narita
Airport, in Tokyo, Japan—an explosion killed two baggage handlers. The Air India 747 had departed from
Canada and was bound for Bombay, India. The two Japa-
nese baggage handlers died when baggage from a CP Air
Flight from Vancouver, B.C. exploded. A bomb was the
most likely cause for the crash of Air India Flight
182. It is believed another Air India flight from Tokyo to Bombay was to be blown up, but the baggage handlers died accidentally. Sikh extremists are believed
to be responsible for the two crashes. 8 photographs.

9.046   **Marbach, William D.,** William J. Cook, Donna Foote and
Elizabeth O. Colton. "Building the Terror-Proof Airport." **Newsweek** 106 (July 8, 1985): 36-37.

Text and a two-page illustration describe the terror-
proof airport characterized by gadgetry and tight procedures.

9.047   **Marshall, Eliot.** "FAA's Bomb Scanner: An Awkward Go-
liath?" **Science** 245 (September 1, 1989): 926-927.

Isahi Gozani, a physicist, designed the thermal neutron analysis (TNA) device for Science Applications

International Corp., Santa Clara, California. TNA detects nitrogen in explosives and is used at JFK (John
Fitzgerald Kennedy) Airport in New York. A drawback
to using TNA is that increasing its sensitivity also
increases the number of false alarms. Wool, leather,
and some foods have nitrogen densities as high as plastic explosives. 2 photographs.

9.048   **Marx, Joseph Laurance.** "How Safe Is Safe? I. In the
Air." Chapter in **Crisis in the Skies,** by Joseph Lau-
rance Marx, 189-217. New York, NY: David McKay Co.,
Inc., 1970.

Retirement at age sixty, bombs, hijackings, collision
avoidance systems, fog, clear air turbulence (CAT), and
lightning are discussed.

9.049   **McArthur, W.J.,** P.J. Dean, J.R. Carroll, T. Holliday
and R.E. Stokes. "Handling the Hijacker." **Aerospace
Medicine** 43 (October 1972): 1118-1121.

Sociopathic, schizophrenic, and manic depressive persons are potentially violent and have a high potential
for hijacking aircraft. The fewer the number of people that deal with the hijacker, the better. Honesty
is important to gain rapport and to promote trust.
Short, simple, verbal statements should be used. If
necessary, be repetitious, but do not reveal impatience.
Avoid threatening, condescending, and sexual messages.
Maintain eye contact and keep hands in full view.
Avoid sudden or unnecessary movements. The hijacker
should not be given alcohol because it may disinhibit
him, making him even more dangerous. The hijacker
should not be restrained unless enough people can act
successfully in unison. Author biographical information. Abstract. 1 figure. 1 table. 14 references.

9.050   **Moore, Kenneth C. Airport, Aircraft and Airline Security.** Los Angeles, CA: Security World Publishing Co.,
Inc., 1976.

The five sections and examples of one or more chapters
in each section follow: (1) attacks against air traffic (skyjacking threat, skyjacking counteraction); (2)
aircraft security (predeparture screening, bomb threat
response); (3) airport security (perimeter security and
lighting, terminal and ramp security); (4) airline security (ticket fraud, credit card fraud, baggage handling and security); and (5) air freight security
(physical security of the freight terminal).

9.051   **Murphy, Gordon K.** "'A Brilliant Ball of Fire:' The
        Sabotage of United Airlines Flight 629." **American
        Journal of Forensic Medicine and Pathology** 7 (March
        1986):   59-61.

        United Airlines (UAL) Flight 629, a DC-6B, left Den-
        ver, Colorado on November 1, 1955, and was headed for
        Portland, Oregon.   There were five crewmembers and
        thirty-nine passengers on board.   An explosion oc-
        curred aboard the DC-6B and the aircraft crashed
        near Longmont, Colorado.   All forty-four persons on
        board died.   An investigation by the Civil Aeronau-
        tics Board (CAB), Federal Bureau of Investigation
        (FBI), and others revealed that John Gilbert Graham
        had placed a time bomb aboard Flight 629.   Graham,
        the son of one of the female passengers, wanted to
        collect $37,500 in life insurance.   After being con-
        victed of murder, Graham was executed.   Author bio-
        graphical information.   Abstract.   10 references.

9.052   **Nelms, Douglas.** "USA Plans Tighter Security." **In-
        teravia Aerospace Review** 44 (July 1989):   690-692.

        "Access to Secured Areas. of Airports" is a ruling by
        the Federal Aviation Administration (FAA) effective
        February 1989.   The ruling concerns access by air-
        line staff and other individuals to sensitive areas
        of airports.   Automated entry-control systems will
        be a key feature of the ruling.   Some critics of the
        ruling contend the ruling expects too much too soon.
        The Airport Operators Council International (AOCI),
        the American Association of Airport Executives
        (AAAE), and the Regional Airline Association (RAA)
        are the main opponents of the ruling.   Controlling
        access points will be very expensive, especially at
        major airports.   The three major airports in the New
        York area have the following number of access points:
        Kennedy (more than 1500 doors), Newark (about 1000),
        and La Guardia (about 750).   5 photogaphs.

9.053   **Norris, Guy.** "Security Concerns Across the Atlan-
        tic." **Interavia Aerospace Review** 44 (July 1989):
        693-694.

        Flights between member countries of the European
        Community (EC) will be considered domestic, after
        1992, when borders between these countries will be
        open.   Britain is already taking steps to counter
        terrorist action, which may take place after 1992.
        One step involves computer control of employee entry
        passes.   It will be possible to check passes against
        a database updated at least once every twenty-four
        hours.   All authorized persons entering restricted

areas will be searched as if they were passengers.
Aircraft will not only undergo security checks before
each flight, they will be guarded until departure.   2
photographs.

9.054   **Ott, James.**   "FAA Tightens Airport Security to Counter
Sabotage Threats." **Aviation Week and Space Technology**
124 (April 21, 1986): 31-32.

Because of the U.S. air strike against terrorist tar-
gets in Libya, the Federal Aviation Administration
(FAA) increased airport security measures to the maximum alert stage: passenger body searches, additional
x-raying of luggage, increased hand-examination of luggage, and holding selected cargo for at least twenty-
four hours.   In Canada, the government, airlines, and
labor unions are cooperating in increased airport security measures.   A chemiluminescent system ("sniffer")
has been developed by Thermedics of Woburn, Massachusetts.   This "sniffer" identifies explosives.

9.055   **Ott, James.**   "ICAO Upgrades Security Unit as Part of
Antiterrorist Effort." **Aviation Week and Space Technology** 130 (May 1, 1989):   109 and 111.

An interview with Shivinder Singh Sidhu, Secretary
General, International Civil Aviation Organization
(ICAO). 1 photograph.

9.056   "Passengers Have the Last Word." **Interavia Aerospace
Review** 44 (July 1989):   694.

Examples of passenger attitudes to airport security
from a questionnaire survey. The quality and motiva-
tion of airport security staff was the most important
concern of questionnaire respondents. International
cooperation in maintaining aviation security was per-
haps the second most important concern.

9.057   **Potter, Anthony B., Jr.**   "The Application of Peel's
Principles to Airport Security Forces." **Security Management** 21 (November 1977):   48-54.

Twelve principles pertaining to police officers are
discussed: (1) management; (2) control; (3) crime
prevention; (4) press relations; (5) patrol distribution; (6) conduct and the use of force; (7) appear-
ance; (8) personnel and training; (9) identification;
(10) headquarters; (11) probation; and (12) records.

Ten recommended airport police policies are included. Author biographical information. 45 footnotes.

9.058   **Ramon, Jacob.** "Terrorism Takes Off." **Security Management** 31 (June 1987):   62-64.

Presents a brief history of aviation terrorism and analyzes procedural security shortcomings at a major European airport. 1 illustration. Author biographical information.

9.059   **Rose, Richard N.** "Airport Security at Bangor International." **Security Management** 24 (April 1980):   16-18.

Profiles security at Bangor International Airport (BIA) in Bangor, Maine. This airport handles about 500,000 domestic and foreign passengers each year. This figure is expected to increase to one million by 1985. Bangor International is a refueling point and customs entry for approximately 3000 transatlantic flights annually. Author biographical information.   2 photographs.

9.060   **Salholz, Eloise,** Ray Wilkinson, Christopher Dickey, Fiona Gleizes and Sana Issa. "Terror at 30,000 Feet." **Newsweek** 114 (October 2, 1989):   30.

UTA (Union de Transports Aeriens) Flight 772 left Ndjamena, Chad and was en route to Paris, France, when a bomb aboard the DC-10 went off. The aircraft crashed in neighboring Niger. One hundred and seventy-one people died. Security was lax at Ndjamena. 1 photograph. 1 illustration.

9.061   **Siedlarz, John E.** and Jill A. Nelson. "Airport Security: A Prudent Approach." **Security Management** 31 (August 1987):   101-102.

Policy and procedures; personnel; facilities; and technology and equipment are examined in relation to the systems approach to airport security. Author biographical information.

9.062   "Skyjacking—What Causes It and a Way to End It." **U.S. News and World Report** 66 (February 17, 1969):   68-69.

There were 170,000 airline flights in and out of

Florida in 1968; thirteen were hijacked. Only about
one out of four hijackers who hijack an aircraft to Cuba are Cubans. The cost to an airline each time one of
its planes is hijacked to Cuba is approximately $15,000.
There were twenty-four planes hijacked from the U.S. to
Cuba between 1961 and 1968. 2 photographs. 1 table.

9.063   **Smith, Donald I.,** John D. Odegard and William Shea.
"Airport Security." Chapter in **Airport Planning and
Management,** by Donald I Smith, John D. Odegard and William Shea, 150-154. Belmont, CA: Wadsworth Publishing Co., 1984.

An airport security manual should include: an introduction; airport description (example: fenced areas);
organization of police or security personnel (example:
administrative staff); closed-circuit television system; and airport areas (example: passenger screening).

9.064   **Steacy, Anne.** "Security in the Skies." **Maclean's** 101
(January 11, 1988): 30-31.

A Canadian parliamentary committee, consisting of elev-
en MPs (Members of Parliament), studied European airports for three weeks, and decided that preboarding
screening in Canada is inadequate. The committee members want the government to assume full responsibility
for security checks of passengers and carry-on baggage.
Security companies which pay modest wages, and have
training programs lasting only several days, presently
provide screening staff on a contractual basis. These
employees earn only $6.25 per hour (Canadian dollars)
for highly responsible work. 2 photographs.

9.065   "Three Cases of Revolving Success." **Security Management** 31 (June 1987): 98-99.

How revolving doors contribute to security at three
U.S. airports: Daytona Beach, Florida; Mobile, Ala-
bama; and San Juan, Puerto Rico. 1 photograph.

9.066   "TWA Believes Explosive Device Caused Blast." **Aviation Week and Space Technology** 124 (April 7, 1986):
32-33.

An explosion occurred aboard Trans World Airlines
(TWA) Flight 840 on April 2, 1986, while the aircraft
was at 15,000 feet and a flying time of fifteen minutes from Athens, Greece. The explosion tore a 20-
square-foot hole at seating row ten. Although there

was moderate decompression, the pilot landed safely at
Athens. No fuel or oxygen lines could have contributed
to the explosion. Three people were confirmed as dead;
nine others were injured. The Arab Revolutionary Cells
claimed responsibility for the explosion.

9.067 **Wallace, Bruce.** "The Imposition of a State of Siege."
       Maclean's 98 (July 8, 1985): 24-25.

No country is immune to terrorism, in view of the June
23, 1985 Air India disaster and the explosion in baggage in Tokyo, Japan. The Air India flight had originated in Canada. The baggage which exploded was from
a CP Air flight which had also originated in Canada.
The myth that terrorists are not interested in Canada
was the weakest link in Canadian airport security.
Narita Airport in Tokyo is guarded by more than 1500
police officers and 400 private guards. Barbed wire,
electrified fences, and ground sensors are other security features at Narita. Athens International Airport
has allegedly the worst security in the world. 3 photographs.

9.068 "What Have We Learned? How Can We Fight Back?" **News-
       week** 108 (September 15, 1986): 27.

The comments of political violence expert Brian Jenkins, regarding the hijacking of TWA (Trans World Airlines) Flight 847 to Beirut, Lebanon in 1985, and other terrorism issues. 1 photograph.

10

Airplane Crashes

10.001   **Abramson, Howard S.** "Unsafe at Any Altitude." **Washington Monthly** 15 (April 1983): 42-46.

Inadequate seats, overhead compartments which have weak latches, and poorly-anchored galley equipment present serious safety problems to passengers and cabin crewmembers in an aircraft crash. Seats and other cabin furnishings were responsible for the deaths of over 600 passengers in eighty-eight major commercial airline crashes which occurred between 1970 and 1981.

10.002   "Accident Rate Continues Decline." **Aviation and Aerospace** 63 (May 1990): 12.

Canadian Aviation Safety Board data about aircraft accidents in Canada during the 1980s.

10.003   **Achiron, Marilyn,** Julith Jedamus and David Lewis. "Sitting Aft: Is It Really Safer?" **Newsweek** 106 (August 26, 1985): 16.

There do not appear to be any convincing statistics, which indicate that surviving an airline crash is dependent on sitting in a particular part of the airplane. Survivors and casualties have been found in every part of the fuselage. Robert Buckhorn of the National Transportation Safety Board (NTSB) suggests sitting near an exit. It is possible, however, to present arguments against sitting even there. 1 photograph.

10.004   "Air Safety—Why the Growing Worry." **U.S. News and World Report** 85 (October 9, 1978): 45-46.

A Cessna 172 and a Pacific Southwest Airlines (PSA) Boeing 727 collided on September 25, 1978, at 3000 feet, above a San Diego, California neighborhood. The Cessna was practicing instrument-landing approaches and the jetliner was preparing to land,

when the collision occurred. One hundred and fifty
people died, thirteen on the ground. The number of
private airplanes in the U.S. outnumbers commercial
aircraft seventy-five to one. The number of takeoffs
and landings is presently 64 million a year. This
figure is expected to become 118 million annually by
the year 2000. One of every three air travellers
travel by private aircraft. Frank Borman, Chairman,
Eastern Air Lines and Elwood Driver, Acting Chairman,
National Transportation Safety Board (NTSB), are concerned about the mixture of commercial and private
airplanes near airports. Yet commercial air travel
is more than thirty-three times safer than driving.
1 photograph. 2 illustrations.

10.005   "Aircraft Crashes Put Down to Human Error." **New Scientist** 109 (February 20, 1986): 20.

Airline accidents are still relatively rare events
and when they occur, about 70% are due to human error.
When a Lockheed L-1011 crashed in the Florida Ever-
glades in 1974, the crew was preoccupied with a
faulty light bulb. When a Western Airlines plane
crashed in Mexico City in 1979, the crew could have
been fatigued. In the U.S. the Aviation Safety Reporting System received 178 reports about fatigue between April 1982 and August 1984. In Britain the
Confidential Human Factors Reporting Programme received fifty-two reports regarding fatigue during a
year-and-a-half time period. 1 photograph.

10.006   **Anderson, Harry,** David Lewis, Melinda Liu, Doug
Tsuruoka and Wendie Lubic. "What Went Wrong?"
Newsweek 106 (August 26, 1985): 14-17.

What was to have been a routine flight became a disaster when Japan Air Lines (JAL) Flight 123 crashed
sixty-two miles northwest of Tokyo, Japan. The Boeing 747SR was en route form Tokyo to Osaka, when there
was a loud bang above the plane's aft section. The
plane could not return to Haneda Airport because parts
of the aircraft's vertical stabilizer and rudders were
missing. Four passengers survived; 520 people died.
2 photographs. 2 illustrations.

10.007   "Avionics Scrutinized in Delta DC-9 Crash." **Aviation
Week and Space Technology** 99 (September 3, 1973): 30.

According to the National Transportation Safety Board
(NTSB), avionics equipment may have contributed to
an accident involving a Delta Air Lines McDonnell

Douglas DC-9, which crashed at Boston, Massachusetts on July 31, 1973. Avionics equipment was modified after Northeast Airlines and Delta merged in April 1973.

10.008 **Barnett, Arnold,** Michael Abraham and Victor Schimmel. "Airline Safety: Some Empirical Findings." **Management Science** 25 (November 1979): 1045-1056.

The authors studied eighteen principal U.S. domestic airlines and forty major international airlines. The safety record of the U.S. domestic airlines was found to be excellent. None of these airlines was found to be especially safe or especially dangerous. Large airlines from westernized countries appear to be safer than airlines from most countries in Latin America, Eastern Europe, and the Middle East. During the last fifteen years, fatality rates dropped over 50% in all segments of the airline industry. Author biographical information. Abstract. 6 footnotes. 2 tables. 12 references.

10.009 **Barnett, Arnold** and Anthony J. Lofaso. "After the Crash: The Passenger Response to the DC-10 Disaster." **Management Science** 29 (November 1983): 1225-1236.

In May 1979 an American Airlines DC-10 crashed, as it was taking off from O'Hare International Airport in Chicago, Illinois. The authors, with the aid of market-share data, wanted to determine how many air travellers avoided flying on DC-10s because of the Chicago disaster. The authors were not able to find statistically significant evidence of passengers avoiding the DC-10. Author biographical information. Abstract. 1 figure. 2 tables. 3 footnotes.

10.010 **Beck, Melinda,** Richard Sandza, William J. Cook, Mary Hager, Holly Morris, Shawn Doherty and Madlyn Resener. "Can We Keep the Skies Safe?" **Newsweek** 103 (January 30, 1984): 24-31.

In 1983 U.S.-certified airlines carried 310 million passengers with only twenty-five fatalities. More Americans died from bee stings. Flying on scheduled U.S. carriers is still many, many times safer than travelling by automobile. Yet 35% of Americans have a fear of flying. 11 photographs. 1 illustration. 1 table.

10.011 **Bertin, Leonard.** "A New Clue to Those Big Jet

Crashes." **Maclean's** 79 (March 19, 1966):   2.

In 1963 an Air Canada DC-8, which took off from Dorval
Airport in Montreal, Quebec, crashed five minutes later. All 118 people aboard died in the crash. Dr.
Melvill Jones, John F. Martin, and Charles Bryan are
three people who have been studying the crash. Jones
is Director, Aeromedical Research Unit at McGill University; Martin is Senior Staff Scientist, Unica Research Co., and Bryan is affiliated with the Institute
of Aviation Medicine. Jones, Martin, and Bryan feel
the crash is related to the flight deck crew experienc-
ing misleading sensations caused by G forces. 1 illustration.

10.012   "The Blowouts That Plague the Big Jets." **Business
         Week** (July 31, 1978):   102 and 105.

During its takeoff roll from Los Angeles International
Airport on March 1, 1978, Continental Air Lines Flight
603 blew two tires. Two people aboard the DC-10 died
and twenty-eight were seriously injured. The same day
another Continental DC-10—this one in Honolulu, Hawaii—aborted its takeoff when its tires blew out.
There were fifteen reported blowouts on DC-10s between
January 1973 and April 15, 1978. Six tires blew on
Lockheed L-1011s and thirteen on Boeing 747s during
the same period. American Airlines had ten DC-10 tire
failures in 1975. American's solution to the problem
is strict monitoring of tire pressure. Most blowouts
are directly related to weight, taxi speed, and taxi
distance. 1 photograph.

10.013   **Brannan, Peter.** "Wanted: Improved Safety For the
         Supersonic Era." **Canadian Aviation** 37 (January 1964):
         5.

Longer runways will improve safety margins for the
takeoff and landing of big jets.

10.014   **Briggs-Bunting, Jane,** David Diamond, Jack Hayes,
         Staci D. Kramer, Steve Marsh and Stephanie Slewka.
         "Sitting at the Edge of Eternity." **Life** 12 (Septem-
         ber 1989):   28-32, 35 and 38-39.

United Flight 232, a DC-10 bound from Denver, Colorado to Chicago, Illinois crashed at Sioux City, Iowa
on July 19, 1989. There were 296 passengers and crew
aboard the 168-ton aircraft piloted by Captain Alfred
C. Haynes. One hundred and eighty-five people survived. Thirty-three survivors comment on their or-
deal. 22 photographs.

10.015   **Brown, David A.**   "Incorrect Computer Route Cited in
         Antarctic Crash."   **Aviation Week and Space Technology**
         114 (May 18, 1981):   26-27.

         On November 25, 1979, an Air New Zealand McDonnell
         Douglas DC-10-30 crashed in Antarctica. The aircraft,
         which had descended below the acceptable minimum alti-
         tude, flew into Mount Erebus. It appears the crew did
         not know the true position of the DC-10. The main
         cause of the accident, however, was navigational in-
         formation which was changed in the plane's navaigation-
         al system hours before the aircraft left New Zealand.
         The crew was not informed of the change. Both the New
         Zealand Ministry of Transport and a New Zealand Royal
         Commission investigated the accident.

10.016   **Burrows, William E.**   "Cockpit Encounters."   **Psychology
         Today** 16 (November 1982):   42-47.

         On January 13, 1982, Roger Pettit, copilot of Air Flor-
         ida Flight 90, told Larry Wheaton, pilot, four times
         that conditions for takeoff were not right. Seconds
         after the 737 left the runway at National Airport in
         Washington, DC, it dropped out of the sky, first hit-
         ting the Fourteenth Street Bridge, then slamming into
         the Potomac River. Seventy-eight people died, includ-
         ing Pettit and Wheaton. According to the National
         Aeronautics and Space Administration (NASA), 70% of
         all civil-aviation incidents, during a five-year-peri-
         od, were due to human error. Not only was this the
         case in the Air Florida crash, it was also the case
         in the crash of a Convair in 1971, when the Convair
         was approaching Tweed-New Haven Airport. Twenty-eight
         passengers and two crewmembers died. Some airlines—
         KLM, Eastern, Lufthansa, British Airways, and Swissair
         are examples—promote better cooperation on the flight
         deck by means of seminars, which deal with communica-
         tion, interaction, and decision-making. United Air-
         lines (UAL) has a three-phase program which includes,
         in part, videotaped role-playing and peer critique.
         1 illustration. Author biographical information.

10.017   "Canada 8th in Airline Safety."   **Canadian Aviation**
         58 (April 1985):   6.

         Between 1973 and 1984, Canadian airlines were involved
         in fourteen fatal accidents, resulting in 118 deaths.
         This placed Canada eighth in world airline safety for
         the last decade. Aircraft which can carry thirty or
         more passengers were included in this research.

10.018   **Carroll, Raymond,** Loren Jenkins and Janet Huck.

"Collision Course." **Newsweek** 89 (April 11, 1977):
48-51, 53 and 55.

After a terrorist bomb exploded at the airport on
Las Palmas, aircraft were diverted to Los Rodeos Airport at Tenerife, Canary Islands. Two of the aircraft
diverted to Los Rodeos were a KLM 747 and a Pan Am
(Pan American World Airways) 747. There were over 600
people aboard the two jumbo jets. Five hundred and
seventy-seven people died when the two airplanes collided on a runway. The KLM plane had begun to take
off in fog and had travelled approximately 4000 feet
before it lifted off, failing to clear the Pan Am jet,
which was on the same runway as the KLM, and was attempting to turn off onto the grassy shoulder. Everyone aboard the KLM plane died. Seventy-one Pan Am
passengers at the front part of the jumbo managed to
escape. 9 photographs. 3 illustrations.

10.019 **Carter, Ian.** "More Questions Than Answers Three
Years After Air Crash." **Atlantic Insight** 11 (March
1989): 10.

About twenty seconds after leaving the ground, an Ar-
row Airlines DC-8 crashed at Gander International Airport. All 256 on board died on that December morning
in 1985. Two hundred and forty-eight were members of
the 101st Airborne Division of the U.S. Army. The
soldiers were returning from Cairo, Egypt to Fort
Campbell, Kentucky, after peace-keeping duties in the
Middle East. Although the crash was investigated by
the Canadian Aviation Safety Board (CASB), the nine
members of the CASB do not agree on the exact cause
of the crash. Five members attribute the disaster to
ice on the sixteen-year-old DC-8's wings. Four members believe the plane crashed because of a fire and
explosion on board. A firefighter at the crash scene,
Fraser Hiscock, believes there is a coverup. 1 photograph.

10.020 "Cause of 707 Crash at Tahiti Eludes French Investigating Unit." **Aviation Week and Space Technology** 106
(May 30, 1977): 30.

Approximately one minute after taking off from Tahiti-
Faaa Airport, on July 22, 1973, a Pan American (Pan
Am) World Airways Boeing 707 crashed. The Pan Am
flight was travelling from Auckland, New Zealand to
Los Angeles, California via Papeete, Tahiti. Sixty-
eight passengers and ten crewmembers died in the
crash. One passenger survived. The 707 settled in
2300 feet of water and the flight recorders were nev-
er recovered. There is no indication of an incident

between birds and the aircraft. However, both the
captain and copilot were receiving treatment for hypertension.

10.021   **Collins, Richard L.** "Milestones." **Flying** 114 (June
          1987): 68-69.

          A table which supplements this article provides the
          following categories of information about seventeen
          airplane collisions in the U.S. between 1967 and 1987:
          date, location, aircraft, altitude, and distance from
          airport. DC-9s were involved in six collisions, 727s
          in three, and 707s in three collisions. All the col-
          lisions occurred within twenty-five nautical miles of
          an airport. Five collisions took place in California,
          two in Texas, two in North Carolina, and two collisions
          in Colorado. Five collisions took place in August and
          three in January.

10.022   **Cook, Robert H.** "Monroney Demands Action on Air Safe-
          ty." **Aviation Week** 74 (February 27, 1961): 41.

          Highlights remarks by Senator A.S. Mike Monroney (Dem-
          ocrat-Oklahoma), Chairman, Senate Aviation Subcommit-
          tee. Monroney spoke about cooperation between the
          Civil Aeronautics Board (CAB) and the Federal Aviation
          Agency (FAA) in the investigation of accidents. He
          also talked about the midair collision in New York of
          a Trans World Airlines (TWA) Super Constellation and a
          United Air Lines (UAL) DC-8.

10.023   "Crash Probe Spurs 1958 Finding Review." **Aviation
          Week and Space Technology** 80 (June 22, 1964): 29.

          Ice buildup is thought to have been involved in two
          airline crashes—one in 1958, the other in 1963. The
          1958 crash was that of a Capital Airlines Viscount;
          the 1963 crash was that of a Continental Air Lines
          Viscount. The Civil Aeronautics Board (CAB), in com-
          paring the two accidents, feels the 1958 crash was
          not due to a stall, but rather to undetected ice
          buildup.

10.024   "DC-9, Cessna Collision Assigned Combination of
          Probable Causes." **Aviation Week and Space Technology**
          91 (September 15, 1969): 122.

          On March 27, 1968, near St. Louis, Missouri, an Ozark
          Air Lines McDonnell Douglas DC-9 was making a visual

approach to Lambert Field. At the same time, a Cessna 150F trainer was also making a visual approach to
the same airport. The two airplanes collided and two
people in the Cessna were killed. The DC-9 landed
safely. None of the forty-nine persons aboard the
DC-9 were injured.

10.025 **Dille, J.R.** and M.K. Linder. "The Effects of Tobacco
on Aviation Safety." **Government Reports Announcements
and Index** 81 (March 13, 1981): 1014. NTIS AD-A091
510/8.

Smoking was not identified as a casual factor in 2660
fatal, general aviation accidents. The accidents occurred between 1973 and 1976. It is not likely smoking would precipitate dire consequences in commercial
flight operations.

10.026 **Doty, L.L.** "Sayen Charges FAA Program Causes Pilot
'Resentment, Anxiety.'" **Aviation Week** 72 (January 25,
1960): 38-39.

The remarks of Clarence N. Sayen, President, Air Line
Pilots Association (ALPA), when he testified before
the Senate Aviation Subcommittee. The subcommittee,
headed by Senator A.S. Mike Monroney (Democrat-Okla-
homa), is investigating airline safety. Sayen spoke
about airline accidents in 1959 (nine accidents, 212
deaths); rescue facilities; midair collisions; pilot
training; and copilot proficiency. Airline accidents
in 1959 were of two types: aircraft disintegrated in
the air and aircraft crashed while attempting to land.
Sayen emphasized that a pilot in charge of a particular aircraft is the best judge of how to handle an incident which may arise in-flight. Sayen was critical
of individuals who feel the pilot should always follow "the book."

10.027 **Eckert, William G.** "Fatal Commercial Air Transport
Crashes, 1924-1981." **American Journal of Forensic
Medicine and Pathology** 3 (March 1982): 49-56.

Covers milestones in commercial aviation in America.
Gives a chronological listing of fatal commercial airline crashes. Year, date (month and day), airline
and/or aircraft, location, and number of deaths are
included. Author biographical information.

10.028 **Eddy, Paul,** Elaine Potter and Bruce Page. **Destina-
tion Disaster: From the Tri-Motor to the DC-10: The**

Risk of Flying. New York, NY: Quadrangle, 1976.

This book, by three journalists from the London **Sunday Times**, is about the crash—on March 3, 1974 in the Forest of Ermenonville near Paris, France—of a Turkish Airlines DC-10. All 346 persons aboard died in the crash, which was caused by a faulty cargo door latch. This type of crash was predicted by an engineer in a memo written on June 27, 1972. The memo was written about a year after the DC-10 had been in service. The Turkish Airlines crash was the first crash of a fully loaded jumbo jet. 85 photographs. 17 figures. 5 tables.

10.029   **Eddy, Paul,** Elaine Potter and Bruce Page. "Is the DC-10 a Lemon?" **New Republic** 180 (June 9, 1979): 7-9.

In June 1972, over Windsor, Ontario, an American Airlines DC-10 lost a rear cargo door. Although the cabin floor collapsed, the captain managed to land the plane without fatal injuries to anyone. After this incident, F.D. Applegate, an engineer, predicted in a memo future such incidents. In 1974 there was an incident of this type: a Turkish Airlines DC-10 crashed outside Paris, France. Three hundred and forty-six people died in that crash. A National DC-10 disintegrated during takeoff from Kennedy Airport, New York in November 1975. None of the passengers were seriously hurt. Those aboard American Airlines Flight 191, which was taking off from O'Hare International Airport in Chicago, Illinois, on May 25, 1979, were not as fortunate. Two hundred and seventy-three people died in that crash. Author biographical information.

10.030   "FAA Adopts a Laissez-faire Attitude—For Now." **High Technology** 5 (July 1985): 52.

It was after an airline crash in 1974 that the FAA (Federal Aviation Administration) decided that a ground proximity warning system be mandatory for all large, civil, jet aircraft. On December 1, 1974, a TWA (Trans World Airlines) Boeing 727 crashed into a hill during adverse weather. Ninety-two people died in the crash, which took place near Dulles International Airport. If or when a midair collision occurs, the position of the FAA may no longer be that the use of TCAS (threat alert collision avoidance system) be optional. There are approximately 7000 airplanes in commercial service. Equipping them with TCAS could cost between $500 million and $700 million.

10.031   "Flying's Safer Than Ever, But Stress Is Increasing."

Nation's Business 75 (November 1987):   24.

According to the Federal Aviation Administration (FAA), fatalities per 100,000 hours flown declined to 0.92 in 1986, from 1.72 in 1978, the year of deregulation.   When a Northwest Airlines flight crashed at Detroit Metropolitan Airport on August 16, 1987, it was the first commercial accident in twenty-three months, involving loss of life.   One hundred and fifty-four people died.

10.032   "For Safer Flying: Stiffer Rules on Planes, Pilots, Control Towers." **U.S. News and World Report** 78 (June 2, 1975):   59-60.

William T. Coleman, Jr., Secretary of Transportation, wants a sweeping overhaul of the Federal Aviation Administration (FAA).   The agency is to improve its regulatory procedures via a nineteen-point program. The program was established after a special task force reviewed U.S. air safety.   There is concern because in 1974 the highest number of lives since 1960 were lost in air crashes.   Cockpit voice recorders are to be placed on all planes to monitor crew performance.   J.J. O'Donnell, President, Air Line Pilots Association (ALPA), views this move as a violation of pilot constitutional rights.   1 photograph.

10.033   **Ford, Barbara.**   "When an Airplane Crashes." **Technology Review** 87 (April 1984):   80.

Improving seats on aircraft in order to increase survivability in a crash is recommended.   Individuals who differ in their views regarding where to sit include the following: Dr. Richard G. Snyder, Transportation Institute, University of Michigan; Dr. Edmund J. Cantilli, Institute for Safety in Transportation; and Brad Dunbar, National Transportation Safety Board (NTSB).   Two examples of airline crashes: Allegheny Airlines DC-9, June 1976, Philadelphia International Airport and United Airlines (UAL) Boeing 737, December 1972, Midway Airport, Chicago, Illinois. Lap belts should be strengthened and supplemented with shoulder harnesses.

10.034   **Fromm, Gary.**   "Aviation Safety." **Law and Contemporary Problems** 33 (Summer 1968):   590-618.

Growth of aviation activity, comparative accident rates, accident costs, accident prevention and compensation for accident victims.   Author biographical

information. Acknowledgements. 58 footnotes. 8 tables. 1 figure.

10.035 **Gallagher, John.** "Investigators Find This Pilot Applied the Incorrect Rudder." **Canadian Aviation** 61
(February 1988): 14.

Offers an explanation for the cause of the crash of a
McDonnell Douglas DC-9-14 on September 6, 1985. The
Midwest Express aircraft took off in clear weather
from General Billy Mitchell Field at Milwaukee, Wisconsin. The plane's right engine disintegrated shortly after takeoff then the plane stalled. All aboard
died in the crash. The National Transportation Safety
Board (NTSB) concluded the pilot likely caused the
crash, when he applied incorrect rudder deflection.
1 illustration.

10.036 **Gavaghan, Helen.** "Failing Engines Puzzle Air Crash
Investigators." **New Scientist** 121 (January 14, 1989):
28.

Speculation regarding the crash in England of a Boeing 737-400, in which forty-six people were killed.
There were fires in both of the CFM56-3CL engines.
The 737 crashed while attempting to land with only
the port engine operational. Despite the reliabili-
ty of this type of engine, there have been problems
in the past. Both engines on two 737-300s failed.
One plane was flying in the U.S., the other in Greece.
Weather was very bad in each case. Norman MacCallum,
of Glasgow University and Cranfield College of Aeronautics, doubts that faulty maintenance is the reason
for the Heathrow crash. However, faulty maintenance
was thought to be the cause of all three engines
failing on a Lockheed L-1011 on May 5, 1983. 1
photograph.

10.037 **Gelman, David,** Richard Manning and Mary Hager. "The
Super-Sleuths of the Skies." **Newsweek** 93 (June 11,
1979): 37.

"Go teams" are comprised of approximately ten specialists—federal investigators—who investigate major accidents. Most go-team members are former pilots or mechanics who interview witnesses and sift
through wreckage. Go teams investigated the crash
of Flight 191, the American Airlines DC-10 which
crashed at O'Hare International Airport in Chicago,
Illinois in 1979. 1 photograph.

10.038   **Hawkins, Chuck** and Aaron Bernstein. "Is It Still
         Safe to Fly?" **Business Week** (March 31, 1986): 34-
         35.

         Although there were fifty-two deaths in the U.S. in
         airline crashes in 1984, the number for 1985 was 561.
         The Federal Aviation Administration (FAA) had 2012
         airline inspectors in 1979 for 237 airlines. In
         1985 there were 1400 inspectors and 526 airlines.
         Both near-misses and runway incursions have in-
         creased. The FAA has fined Eastern Air Lines $9.5
         million for safety violations—78,372 of them. Pan
         American (Pan Am) World Airways, Delta, Southwest,
         and United are to be inspected next. 2 graphs.

10.039   **Hickson, Ken. Flight 901 to Erebus.** Christchurch:
         Whitcoulls, 1980.

         The crash in the Antarctic at 1:50 p.m. on November
         28, 1979 of an Air New Zealand DC-10. A U.S. Navy
         helicopter—restricted by overcast weather, snow,
         and whiteout—landed less than five miles from the
         crash site fifteen minutes after the DC-10 crashed.
         A U.S. Navy Hercules search plane located the DC-10
         wreckage. There were no survivors. Two hundred and
         fifty-seven people had died. 33 illustrations.

10.040   **Hotz, Robert.** "Politics and Safety." **Aviation
         Week** 72 (April 25, 1960): 21.

         This editorial focuses on accidents involving the
         Lockheed Electra at Buffalo, Texas and Tell City, In-
         diana. It comments on the views of Senators Vance
         Hartke, Stuart Symington, and Warren Magnuson. It
         also looks at the different views of the Federal
         Aviation Agency (FAA) and the Civil Aeronautics
         Board (CAB) regarding the Electra.

10.041   **Hotz, Robert.** "The Safety Problem." **Aviation Week**
         72 (January 11, 1960): 21.

         This editorial contends that a tradition in the air-
         line industry has been not to publicly discuss air-
         line safety, the reason being that such discussions
         frighten the travelling public. However, after a
         collision over the Grand Canyon, involving a United
         and a Trans World Airlines (TWA) plane, some air-
         lines changed their policy about remaining silent.
         The Federal Aviation Agency (FAA) should be stringent
         and fair in its enforcement of safety regulations.

10.042 **Hurst, Ronald** and Leslie R. Hurst. Editors. **Pilot
        Error: The Human Factors.** Second Edition. London:
        Granada Publishing Ltd., 1982.

        M. Allnutt, M.K. Strickler, Jr., R.S. Jensen, E.L.
        Wiener, R.E. Curry, R.C.W. Weston, S.N. Roscoe, and R.
        Hurst are the contributors to this book. Accident
        prevention, pilot judgement, flight deck automation,
        terrain accidents, and midair collisions are some of
        the topics discussed. 19 figures. 5 tables. 248
        references.

10.043 "'I Had to Turn Away.'" **Newsweek** 114 (August 28,
        1989): 37.

        Excerpts of conversations between Captain Alfred
        Haynes of United Airlines (UAL) Flight 232, which
        crashed in Sioux City, Iowa and Kevin Bachman, a con-
        troller in Sioux City. One hundred and eleven pas-
        sengers died in the crash; 185 survived.

10.044 "'Incompetent Administrative Procedures' Cited in
        Crash Report." **Aviation Week and Space Technology**
        115 (July 6, 1981): 34-35.

        Gives opinions regarding the probable cause of the
        crash of an Air New Zealand DC-10 which crashed on
        Antarctica's Mount Erebus. Morris R. Davis, Chief
        Executive, Air New Zealand, subsequently resigned
        and a Royal Commission of Inquiry was held regarding
        the crash. Davis was replaced by John B. Wisdom.
        The commission felt that the cockpit crew were not
        responsible for the disaster. Incompetent adminis-
        trative procedures were the cause of the crash. Em-
        ployee transfers, police investigations, and legal
        action contributed to depressed morale at Air New
        Zealand.

10.045 "Investigators Cite Engine Failure in Polish Ilyu-
        shin II-62M Crash." **Aviation Week and Space Tech-
        nology** 127 (August 3, 1987): 57.

        A Polish Airlines Ilyushin II-62M crashed on May 9,
        1987 about three miles from Okecie International Air-
        port, Warsaw, Poland. The Soviet-made aircraft was
        attempting an emergency landing. All 183 passengers
        and crew were killed in the crash. Disintegration
        of the airplane's left engines was one of several
        reasons for the crash.

10.046   "Investigators Study Data, Voice Recorders in Search
          For Cause of Mexicana 727 Crash." **Aviation Week and
          Space Technology** 124 (April 7, 1986):   34.

          After it was airborne less than ten minutes, a Mexi-
          cana Airlines Boeing 727-200 crashed into a mountain
          northwest of Mexico City, Mexico. This was on March
          31, 1986 and neither weather nor visibility appear to
          have been factors in the loss of all 166 persons
          aboard. The last radio transmission from the captain
          was that he was losing altitude and having pressuriza-
          tion problems. Mexicana Airlines has lost three 727-
          100s: June 1969 (seventy-nine passengers and crew
          died in Monterrey, Mexico); September 1969 (twenty-
          seven fatalities in Mexico City); and October 1973
          (no injuries or fatalities in a crash at Mazatlan,
          Mexico). Boeing considers the 727 its second safest
          commercial airplane.

10.047   "'It Was a Miracle For Anybody to Have Lived.'" **News-
          week** 115 (February 5, 1990):   22.

          Avianca Flight 52, a Boeing 707, left Bogotá, Colom-
          bia and travelled towards New York. There were 161
          people on board. When the 707 was near John F. Kenne-
          dy (JFK) International Airport, the aircraft ran out
          of fuel. Although the plane fell out of the sky,
          there was no fire or explosion, after the plane struck
          a hillside in Cove Neck, New York. More than half the
          people aboard Flight 52 survived. 1 photograph.

10.048   **Jenish, D'arcy.** "A Blackened Year." **Maclean's** 102
          (October 2, 1989):   59.

          As of October 1989, more than 900 people had died in
          air disasters—one of the worst years ever. A DC-10,
          destined for France from Chad, exploded in midair
          over the Sahara Desert. All 171 people on board
          died. The following day, at La Guardia Airport in
          New York, the pilot of a USAir Boeing 737 aborted
          takeoff. The plane plunged into the East River and
          broke apart. Only two of the sixty-one people aboard
          died. The USAir flight, destined for Charlotte, North
          Carolina, was taking off four hours late because of
          rain in the New York area. Both the pilot and copilot
          were suspended. 1 photograph.

10.049   **Johnston, Moira. The Last Nine Minutes: The Story
          of Flight 981.** New York, NY: William Morrow and Co.,
          Inc., 1976.

          There were 334 passengers and twelve crewmembers

aboard Flight 981, a Turkish Airlines DC-10, which
took off from Orly Airport in Paris on March 3, 1974.
The weather was good and there was no indication of
trouble at noon, when the passengers were at Orly.
Nine minutes after takeoff, the DC-10's cargo door
blew out and the plane crashed into the Ermenonville
Forest. Everyone on board died in the first crash of
a wide body jet. Twenty-four countries were involved
in the subsequent investigation. 50 photographs. 3
diagrams. Glossary (23 items). Synopsis of each of
the 26 chapters.

10.050   **Lane, J.C.** and T.C. Brown. "Probability of Casualties
in an Airport Disaster." **Aviation, Space, and Environmental Medicine** 46 (July 1975): 958-961.

When the authors studied world airline accident statistics for the years 1960-1970, they learned the
number of seriously injured individuals is not likely
to be greater than 25% of the number of people the
largest airplane can carry. There is only a 5% chance
this number will be an underestimate. Author biographical information. Abstract. 5 tables. 1 figure. Acknowledgement. 8 references.

10.051   **Lefer, Henry.** "Changes Will Result From DC-10 Crash,
But They Won't Be Big." **Air Transport World** 16 (October 1979): 24-28.

After an engine fell off American Airlines Flight 191
over Chicago, Illinois, McDonnell Douglas DC-10 aircraft were grounded for five weeks. Before the DC-10
was certified, 18 million man-hours of engineering
were expended. Also, prior to certification, a production line DC-10 structure was subjected to the
equivalent of fatigue testing of approximately forty
years. After the DC-10 was certified, 17 million engineering hours were expended improving the plane.
Between 1959 and 1978, there were only ten fatal accidents in the U.S. involving certified planes. During the same time period, there were 521 accidents
involving certified U.S. jet transports. 5 photographs. 1 illustration.

10.052   "Let's Get Moving on Air Safety." **Life** 50 (March
10, 1961): 28.

The number of air carrier fatalities in the U.S.
rose from 144 in 1950 to 500 in 1960. There were
six major fatal accidents between October 1960 and
March 1961. One hundred and thirty-four died in the

collision over Staten Island of a United DC-8 and a
TWA (Trans World Airlines) Constellation. Improper
adherence to safety regulations is a definite problem. Lockheed was fined by the Federal Aviation
Agency (FAA) for not properly inspecting its Electra
aircraft.

10.053   **Long, Michael E.** "The Air-Safety Challenge." **Na-
         tional Geographic** 152 (August 1977):   206-235.

In 1976 in the U.S., 229 million passengers were
transported safely by air carriers. There were approximately 5 million flights, four fatal crashes,
forty-five people killed. There were twenty-five
fatal air carrier accidents in the U.S. in 1951, four
in 1976. Since 1959, 85% of all fatal accidents have
occurred at takeoff, approach, and landing. 26 photographs.

10.054   **Lowell, Vernon W. Airline Safety Is a Myth.** N.p.,
         Bartholomew House, 1967.

A summary in table form lists U.S. airline accidents
between 1960 and 1965. Date, location, airline, type
of service, airplane, damage, and total aboard are
given. 26 photographs.

10.055   **Lowther, William.** "The Instant Horror of Flight
         191." **Maclean's** 92 (June 4, 1979):   40-41.

Michael Laughlin, a businessman from Toronto, Ontario, was at O'Hare International Airport in Chicago,
Illinois on May 25, 1979. American Airlines Flight
191, a DC-10, had just taken off and was at an altitude of about 500 feet. The DC-10 was missing the
engine on the left wing. The engine had fallen off
seconds before. Laughlin watched in disbelief and
photographed the aircraft as it plunged to the
ground. Over 72,000 gallons of fuel burned instant-
ly in a ball of flame. Two hundred and seventy-one
people died. 1 photograph.

10.056   **MacBurnie, Eric.** "'Missing' Documents From PWA
         Crash Heightened Tensions Within DOT." **Canadian
         Aviation** 53 (May 1980):   48-52.

"Missing" documents pertaining to the PWA (Pacific
Western Airlines) 737 crash at Cranbrook, B.C., in
February 1978, heightened tensions within DOT (De-
partment of Transport). This was revealed in

Toronto, Ontario at the Commission of Inquiry Into
Aviation Safety. The Air Transport Association of
Canada, the Canadian Air Traffic Control Association,
the Canadian Bar Association, and the Canadian Flight
Attendants Association were a few of the parties par-
ticipating in the inquiry. Five individuals at the
inquiry: Francois Dubé, Luc LeGal, Harold Fawcett,
Walter McLeish, and Don Button. 2 photographs.

10.057   "Majority of Lives Lost in Crashes Can Be Saved."
         Science News Letter 88 (October 23, 1965): 265.

         Sixty percent of crash accident fatalities can be
         prevented. Head wounds are the most important cause
         of death in these accidents. John J. Swearingen, who
         conducted research for the Federal Aviation Agency
         (FAA), demonstrated that the human skull is much
         stronger than previously believed. Dr. Stanley Moh-
         ler, Director, Civil Aeromedical Research Institute,
         recommends design modifications in automobile interi-
         ors and pilot cabins. Use of softer metals and elim-
         ination of knobs are among the recommendations.

10.058   **Marske, Charles E.** "A Community of Fate: The Polit-
         ical-Economics of Risk in College Athletic Air Trav-
         el." **Journal of Sport and Social Issues** 10 (Summer/
         Fall 1986): 6-26.

         Primary focus is on the organization of knowledge and
         the structure of reality; a sociological explanation
         of air disasters; college athletic air travel: a
         case study; preliminary findings; and summary and
         conclusions. Author biographical information. Ab-
         stract. 5 tables. 1 figure. 5 notes. 19 refer-
         ences.

10.059   **Mathieu, R.** "Regional Statistics on Safety in Air
         Transport." **Government Reports Announcements and
         Index** 71 (May 25, 1971): 3. NTIS N71-18115.

         Aircraft accident investigation in a European con-
         text.

10.060   **McClement, Fred.** "Air Traffic—Control or Chaos."
         Chapter in **It Doesn't Matter Where You Sit,** by Fred
         McClement, 173-192. New York, NY: Holt, Rinehart
         and Winston, 1969.

         A Trans World Airlines (TWA) DC-9 and a Beechcraft

Baron collided near Dayton Municipal Airport, Dayton, Ohio, on March 9, 1967. There were twenty-one passengers and four crewmembers aboard the DC-9. The pilot was the only person aboard the Beechcraft. A North Central Airlines Convair collided with a small engine aircraft near Mitchell Field, Milwaukee, Wisconsin, on August 4, 1968. Three people died in this accident. On December 4, 1966, a TWA 707 collided with an Eastern Constellation over Carmel, New York. Four persons died. And on July 19, 1967, a Piedmont 727 collided with a small airplane near Ashville, North Carolina. Eighty-two persons died in this collision.

10.061   **McClement, Fred.** "The Death of Flight 304." Chapter in **It Doesn't Matter Where You Sit,** by Fred McClement, 159-172. New York, NY: Holt, Rinehart and Winston, 1969.

On February 18, 1964, an Eastern Airlines DC-8, Flight 304, took off from New Orleans, Louisiana and plunged into Lake Pontchartrain. The captain was William B. Zeng, forty-seven; the first officer was Grant Newby; and the pilot-engineer was Harry Idel. There were forty-nine passengers and four other crewmembers on board. The Civil Aeronautics Board (CAB) held a public inquiry into the crash on July 14, 1964. Representatives from Northwest Airlines, the Air Line Pilots Association, Douglas Aircraft Co., and other organizations testified at the inquiry. It was learned that the pitch-trim compensator was the cause of the crash.

10.062   **McClement, Fred.** "Flight Recorders." Chapter in **It Doesn't Matter Where You Sit,** by Fred McClement, 90-98. New York, NY: Holt, Rinehart and Winston, 1969.

Flight recorders are manufactured in the U.S. and England. Although American recorders measure five parameters, British recorders can measure up to 200 parameters. Each flight recorder costs approximately $5000. Sometimes it is not possible to recover flight recorders from accident scenes. One example: a Pan American (Pan Am) 707, Antigua, West Indies, September 17, 1965. Another example: an Eastern DC-8, Lake Pontchartrain, Lousiana, February 18, 1964. And a third example: an American Airlines 727, Cincinnati, Ohio, November 8, 1965. Intense heat from fire or mangling from impact can make a recorder useless for crash investigative purposes.

10.063   **McClement, Fred.** "Jet Roulette." Chapter in **It**

Doesn't Matter Where You Sit, by Fred McClement, 140-
158. New York, NY: Holt, Rinehart and Winston, 1969.

Various types of aircraft are involved in fatal accidents: Boeing, Douglas, Convair, Sud Caravelle. Between 1959 and 1965, in a survey of 153 jet airliner
accidents, 138 of the accidents took place during
takeoff, ascent, descent, and landing. Furthermore,
pilots are blamed for 80% of accidents. Marital problems, fatigue, and weather contribute to accidents.

10.064   McClement, Fred. "Safety and Acceptability." Chap-
         ter in It Doesn't Matter Where You Sit, by Fred McClem-
         ent, 220-224. New York, NY: Holt, Rinehart and Win-
         ston, 1969.

         The number of persons who die, in jet accidents on
         scheduled airlines, is not accurate, if figures sup-
         plied by the ICAO (International Civil Aviation Organi-
         zation) are used. These figures do not include crew-
         member deaths. For example, according to the ICAO,
         256 persons died in 1961. The figure is 310, if crew-
         member deaths are included. The figures for 1962 are
         424 (passengers only) and 610 (passengers and crew).
         For 1963 the figures are 347 (passengers only) and
         383 (passengers and crew).

10.065   McClement, Fred. "The 727 Story." Chapter in It
         Doesn't Matter Where You Sit, by Fred McClement, 122-
         139. New York, NY: Holt, Rinehart and Winston,
         1969.

         The Boeing 727 airliner rolled from the factory at
         Renton, Washington in November 1962. Four 727s were
         involved in disasters between August 16, 1965 and
         February 3, 1966. Two hundred and sixty-three passen-
         gers and crew died. An irony about the first crash,
         involving this type of aircraft, is that on board was
         Clarence N. Sayen, a former president of the Air Line
         Pilots Association (ALPA). A misreading of the altim-
         eter by the crew might have been the cause of the
         crash. On November 8, 1965, an American Airlines 727
         Astrojet crashed while approaching Greater Cincinnati
         Airport. And on February 3, 1966, an All-Nippon 727
         crashed near Tokyo, Japan claiming 133 lives.

10.066   McClement, Fred. "Survivability." Chapter in It
         Doesn't Matter Where You Sit, by Fred McClement, 99-
         121. New York, NY: Holt, Rinehart and Winston,
         1969.

         On November 11, 1965, United Air Lines (UAL) Flight

227 was en route from Denver, Colorado to Salt Lake
City, Utah—a fifty-seven-minute flight. The pilot
was Captain Gale C. Kehmeier, forty-seven; the first
officer was Philip E. Spicer, thirty-nine; and the
second officer was Ron Christensen, twenty-eight.
There were also on board eighty-five passengers and
three stewardesses. During the descent into Salt
Lake City, the Boeing 727 struck the ground 335 feet
short of the active runway. Forty-three people died
in the ensuing fire. On August 2, 1968, an Alitalia
Airlines DC-8 crashed and burned while approaching
Milan Airport. Pine trees cushioned the crash and
ninety-five persons survived because the fuselage
was broken up on impact. Also, there was little fuel
left as the airplane struck the trees. This contributed to passenger and crew survivability.

10.067   **McClement, Fred.** "'They're Going Down in Flames.'"
Chapter in **It Doesn't Matter Where You Sit,** by Fred
McClement, 1-16. New York, NY: Holt, Rinehart and
Winston, 1969.

The drama of aircraft, hazardous weather, and the
crash of a Pan American (Pan Am) 707 Jet Clipper on
December 8, 1963. Eighty-one passengers and crew
were aboard the 707. Paul Alexy was the air traffic
controller (ATC) communicating with airplanes in the
vicinity of the Clipper. Allegheny Airlines, United
Air Lines (UAL), and National Airlines had aircraft
in the area. Captain Malcolm M. Campbell and Captain Gerald Sutliff, piloting National Airlines
Flight 16, saw the Pan Am go down in flames.

10.068   "Medical Aspects Cited in Crash Testimony." **Aviation
Week** 72 (April 4, 1960): 45.

Oscar Bakke, Chief, Civil Aeronautics Board Bureau of
Safety, spoke about two airline crashes. The first
crash was that of a Piedmont Airlines Douglas DC-3
that crashed near Charlottesville, Virginia on October 30, 1959. The pilot had been depressed and had
been on tranquilzers. The second crash involved an
Allegheny Airlines Martin 202 that crashed near Wil-
liamsport, Pennsylvania in December 1959. The copilot of this plane had suffered a coronary occlusion
before the plane smashed into a mountain. Bakke
stated that the accidents were not necessarily
caused by tranquilzer use and coronary occlusion.

10.069   **Miller, Annetta** and Karen Springen. "A Bumpy Ride
For the Airbus A320." **Newsweek** 115 (May 21, 1990):
70.

The Airbus A-320 jetliner is made by Airbus Industrie,
a European consortium. Two of the highly-automated
and fuel-efficient aircraft have crashed since 1988.
The first crash occurred in France. Three passengers
died. The second crash took place in India. Ninety-
three people died. Northwest Airlines has eight A320s
and plans to add seventeen others. 2 photographs.

10.070   "Monitoring Air Safety." **Consumers' Research** 68 (Feb-
          ruary 1985): 4.

          The U.S. has 327 airlines and 95% of them follow fed-
          eral safety rules, according to the Federal Aviation
          Administration (FAA). This conclusion was reached
          after Transportation Secretary Elizabeth Dole ordered
          the FAA to conduct a survey of air safety. An Air Il-
          linois flight that crashed, killing ten people in Oc-
          tober 1983, was one reason the survey was conducted.

10.071   **Moore, Bill.** "The Secrets of the Black Boxes." **Dis-
          cover** 7 (August 1986): 68-72 and 74-76.

          Dennis Grossi, Billy Hopper, and Paul Turner are NTSB
          (National Transportation Safety Board) specialists,
          who examined the flight recorders which were on Air
          Florida Flight 90. Flight 90 crashed into the Poto-
          mac River in Washington, DC on January 13, 1982,
          about a minute and a half after the airplane took off.
          Captain Larry Wheaton and First Officer Roger Pettit
          were among the seventy-four on board the 737 who died.
          2 illustrations. 9 photographs.

10.072   **Morganthau, Tom,** Daniel Pedersen, Richard Sandza, Bar-
          bara Burgower and William J. Cook. "Delta 191:
          Death in Dallas." **Newsweek** 106 (August 12, 1985):
          30-32.

          Delta Air Lines Flight 191 was approaching Dallas-Fort
          Worth Airport, when the Lockheed L-1011 aircraft was
          struck by lightning, and plunged into the ground,
          smashing into two cars at the same time. Flight 191
          had been en route from Fort Lauderdale, Florida to
          Los Angeles, California—with 162 men, women, and
          children aboard. This was the first major crash at
          Dallas-Fort Worth Airport. The captain, Edward M.
          Connors, age fifty-seven, and most of his passengers
          died. Wind shear, sudden turbulence that can desta-
          bilize an airplane, is, along with lightning, believed
          to have caused the crash. The Federal Aviation Admin-
          istration (FAA) plans, beginning in 1988, to install
          wind-shear radar at 110 U.S. airports. 4 photographs.
          1 illustration.

10.073 **Needham, Richard J.** "Air Crash: The Lingering Cost
        of Disaster." **Maclean's** 78 (January 2, 1965): 20-
        21 and 26-27.

        Stephanie Szostak, Sharon Gostick, Maria Allemand,
        and Louisa Finkler became widows on November 29, 1963,
        when Air Canada Flight 831 crashed shortly after tak-
        ing off from Montreal, Quebec. How these widows are
        managing without their husbands, and the legal action
        they are taking, is discussed. One hundred and eigh-
        teen people died in the airplane disaster. 1 photo-
        graph.

10.074 "No Sabotage." **Aviation Week and Space Technology** 99
        (October 1, 1973):   31.

        Mrs. E. Howard Hunt, wife of Watergate principal, E.
        Howard Hunt, died in the crash of a United Airlines
        (UAL) Boeing 737 at Midway Airport, Chicago, Illinois.
        There were published rumors, following the crash, that
        it was linked to the Watergate hearings. However, the
        National Transportation Safety Board (NTSB) found no
        evidence of foul play or sabotage.

10.075 "NTSB Evaluates Factors in Detroit MD-82 Crash." **Avia-
        tion Week and Space Technology** 127 (August 24, 1987):
        18-20.

        On August 16, 1987, a Northwest Airlines MD-82 crash-
        ed, while attempting to takeoff from Metropolitan Wayne
        County Airport in Detroit, Michigan. The crash of the
        MD-82, Northwest Flight 255, claimed 155 lives. The
        only survivor is a four-year-old girl. She is in se-
        rious condition from multiple injuries. There was no
        warning, on the voice recorder of the Crew Aural
        Warning System (CAWS), that the aircraft's flaps and
        slats were set incorrectly. An incorrect setting,
        however, appears to have caused the crash of the air-
        plane piloted by a veteran crew. There was no severe
        weather in the area when Flight 255 took off, reach-
        ing a maximum altitude of forty-eight feet. 1 diagram.
        1 photograph.

10.076 "NTSB Studies Ozark FH-227B St. Louis Crash." **Avia-
        tion Week and Space Technology** 99 (July 30, 1973):
        26.

        Thirty-six people were killed on July 23, 1973, when
        an Ozark Air Lines Fairchild FH-227B crashed during
        final approach at Lambert Field in St. Louis, Missouri.
        There was a heavy thunderstorm at the time and wind

was gusting from twenty to thirty-eight miles per
hour. A flash fire broke out at the rear of the aircraft after impact. The eight survivors included both
pilots. There is a possibility a lightning strike and/
or faulty maintenance were responsible for the crash.

10.077   **Nurski, Janice.** "Promoting Air Safety." **Science Di-
         mension** 15, No. 1 (1983): 28-31.

         Bernard Caiger is Head of the Flight Recorder Play-
         back Centre, which analyzes data from flight recorders
         retrieved from Canadian aircraft crash scenes. Flight
         recorders contain up to twenty-five hours of data and
         as many as fifty parameters. Airspeed and magnetic
         heading are examples of two parameters registered by
         flight recorders. 3 photographs. 1 illustration.

10.078   **O'Donnell, John J.** "Seek the 'Why?' of Aircraft Acci-
         dents." **Air Line Pilot** 44 (April 1975): 6-9 and 43.

         Remarks by John J. O'Donnell, President, Air Line Pi-
         lots Association (ALPA), regarding the Trans World
         Airlines (TWA) crash on December 1, 1974. O'Donnell
         spoke on the last day of the NTSB (National Transpor-
         tation Safety Board) hearing. The crash involved a
         727 attempting to land at Dulles International Air-
         port. 4 photographs.

10.079   **Ott, James.** "Andes Climbers Obtain Eastern 727 Photo-
         graphs For Use in Crash Inquiry." **Aviation Week and
         Space Technology** 123 (September 9, 1985): 40-41 and
         45.

         An Eastern Airlines Boeing 727, several miles off
         course, crashed into Mount Illimani in the Bolivian
         Andes on January 1, 1985. The aircraft, Flight 980,
         was at an altitude of 19,600 feet when it crashed.
         The accident occurred twenty-six miles from La Paz
         International Airport. The flight recorders were not
         recovered. Judith Kelly, wife of a U.S. passenger
         who died in the accident, financed an expedition to
         the crash scene because she felt the accident inves-
         tigation was lagging. Two Bolivian teams visited the
         crash site prior to the Kelly team ascent. 3 photo-
         graphs.

10.080   **Ott, James.** "Investigators Find Reconstructed Tail
         of DC-10 Riddled With Damage." **Aviation Week and
         Space Technology** 131 (August 7, 1989): 22-23.

The main element in the National Transportation Safety Board (NTSB) investigation of the crash of a United Airlines (UAL) DC-10-10 over Iowa on July 19, 1989
is a 300-pound, first-stage fan disk of the Number
Two engine. The disk is still missing. Three hydraulic lines were severed at 37,000 feet by shrapnel
from the fan disintegration. The United crew used
thrust for control to guide the aircraft down for a
crash landing. One hundred and eleven of the 296 people aboard were killed. 2 photographs. 1 illustration.

10.081   "Pilots Protest CAB Crash Ruling." **Aviation Week** 72
(January 25, 1960): 39.

Sixty-eight people died in the crash of an American
Airlines Electra. The airplane was on final landing
approach to La Guardia Field in New York, when the
crash occurred. The Civil Aeronautics Board (CAB)
attributed the accident mainly to pilot error. C.N.
Sayen, President, Air Line Pilots Association, dis-
puted CAB's position, and would like part of the report revised. Oscar Bakke of CAB stated the accident
probably would not have taken place if the runway had
been illuminated with high intensity approach lights.

10.082   **Platenius, Peter H.** and Gerald J.S. Wilde. "Personal
Characteristics Related to Accident Histories of Ca-
nadian Pilots." **Aviation, Space, and Environmental
Medicine** 60 (January 1989): 42-45.

Approximately 70,000 Canadian pilots were sent a 302-
item questionnaire. The following were some of the
areas covered by the questionnaire: (1) life events
and preoccupations; (2) risk acceptance; (3) lack of
humor appreciation; (4) asocial or sedentary hobbies;
(5) medical symptoms; (6) perceiving oneself as un-
successful; (7) lack of initiative or self-control
and dislike of constraints; (8) social disability or
loneliness; (9) alcohol use; (10) accidents and violations in automobile driving; and (11) underattribu-
tion of accident causes. Discriminant analysis was
used regarding four types of pilots—airline transport, commercial, helicopter, and private—and six
variables relating to the pilots. This study is
based on questionnaire responses of 8819 English-
language male respondents. Author biographical information. Abstract. 1 table. 7 references.

10.083   "Poor Crew Coordination Cited in United 737 Crash at
Chicago." **Aviation Week and Space Technology** 99

(October 1, 1973):   31.

A United Air Lines (UAL) Boeing 737 crashed near Midway Airport, Chicago, Illinois, while attempting a go-
round. The aircraft's spoilers were extended when the
crash occurred on December 8, 1972. The go-round was
ordered by the Midway tower. Total dead in the plane
and on the ground numbered forty-five. Five homes
were also destroyed. Excerpts from the National Transportation Safety Board (NTSB) report on the crash are
included.

10.084   "Positive Visual Contact Lacking in DC-10 Crash."
         Aviation Week and Space Technology 111 (November 5,
         1979):   30.

         On October 31, 1979, shortly before 6 a.m., a Western
         Airlines DC-10-10 crashed at Benito Juarez Airport in
         Mexico City, while attempting to land. The flight,
         which had originated in Los Angeles, was carrying sev-
         enty-seven passengers and eleven crew. Seventy-three
         persons died—two on the ground. Captain Charles
         Gilbert landed on Runway 23L, but thought he was
         landing on Runway 23R. There was fog outside, 23L's
         runway lights were off, and 23L was closed for resur-
         facing. The DC-10 struck a truck then crashed into
         airport buildings. The International Federation of
         Airline Pilots Association (IFALPA) has rated the air-
         port as seriously deficient. 1 illustration.

10.085   **Purl, Sandy** and Gregg Lewis. **Am I Alive?: A Surviv-
         ing Flight Attendant's Struggle and Inspiring Triumph
         Over Tragedy.** San Francisco, CA: Harper and Row,
         Publishers, 1986.

         Sandy Purl, a Republic Airlines flight attendant,
         worked for Southern Airways in 1977 when, on April 4
         of that year, a Southern DC-9 she was on crashed at
         New Hope, Georgia. Flight 242 slammed into a highway,
         smashing utility poles and gas pumps, then exploded.
         Seventy-two people died. Purl heroically saved lives
         and walked through fire and smoke to reach bodies.
         Nightmares, flashbacks, and guilt were with her three
         years after the crash. 15 photographs. 1 diagram.

10.086   **Reingold, Lester.** "The Crashes of '79: The FAA
         Stalls Out." **Washington Monthly** 11 (December 1979):
         50-58.

         At any given moment there are more than 100,000 peo-
         ple airborne over the U.S. Since 1908 more than
         60,000 people have died in U.S. air disasters.

Through the Federal Aviation Administration (FAA)
the U.S. government spends, annually, over $2.5 bil-
lion to promote flight safety. 1 illustration.

10.087   **Richman, Alan.**   "Trapped in the Wreckage of Flight
1713, Robert Linck Survives to Fly Home Again."
People Weekly 28 (December 21, 1987): 98-102.

Twenty-eight passengers and crew were killed and
fifty-four survived, when a Continental Airlines DC-9
crashed seconds after taking off from Denver, Colorado en route to Boise, Idaho. The plane was about
fifty feet off the ground and was travelling about
170 miles per hour when it crashed. The pilot and
copilot were among the dead. Robert Linck, age sixty, who was sitting in row fifteen, was trapped in
the plane for ninety minutes before he was rescued.
The aircraft was sprayed with deicing fluid and took
off in a snowstorm. Nine days later Robert Linck,
recovering from injuries received in the crash, flew
on another Continental flight, his wife and members
of their family with him. This flight was complimen-
tary and first class. 6 photographs.

10.088   **Ridgeway, James.**   "Air Accidents." **New Republic** 157
(August 5, 1967): 12-14.

There are in the U.S. 2000 commercial airliners, 100,
000 general aviation planes, and fifty reported near-
misses each month. Although the airlines serve 547
airports, 434 airports do not have radar, and 285 do
not have control towers. Prior to September 1963,
the Federal Aviation Administration (FAA) did not
have any safety regulations regarding evacuation of
airplanes. In November 1964, forty-nine people could
not evacuate a TWA (Trans World Airlines) 707 in
Rome, Italy and died inside the aircraft after the
flight was aborted. Some of the twenty-four survivors complained that seats near emergency exits in-
terfered with evacuation. About a year later, forty-
one people died of smoke and fire when they could not
evacuate a United 727, which crash landed at Salt
Lake City, Utah.

10.089   **Roitsch, P.A.,** G.L. Babcock and W.W. Edmunds. **Human
Factors Report on the Tenerife Accident.** N.p., Air
Line Pilots Association, n.d.

On March 27, 1977, a Pan American (Pan Am) World Airways Boeing 747 and a KLM Royal Dutch Airlines Boeing
747 collided on a runway at the Los Rodeos Airport,

Tenerife, Canary Islands. An Air Line Pilots Association (ALPA) Study Group—comprised of P.A. Roitsch,
G.L. Babcock, and W.W. Edmunds—investigated the accident. The following are some of the factors studied:
time, weather conditions, political unrest, airport
facilities, language on the radio, crew management,
ambiguous words, and airline and air traffic control
(ATC) stress.

10.090   **Ruppenthal, Karl M.** "Tomorrow's Air Crash." **Nation**
         190 (January 30, 1960): 97-99.

         In 1959 in the U.S., the airline fatality rate per
         million passenger-miles was twice the rate in 1958.
         Three hundred and twenty-nine persons were killed in
         1959. There are six reasons why airline passengers
         will be killed in 1960: (1) inadequate airports for
         the jet age, (2) inadequate airport planning, (3) in-
         adequate approach lights, (4) inadequate traffic con-
         trol, (5) inadequate copilot training, and (6) inad-
         equate second officer training. Author biographical
         information.

10.091   "Safety Experts Study Successful Ditching." **Aviation
         Week and Space Technology** 77 (October 29, 1962): 42.

         On October 22, 1962, a Northwest Airlines DC-7, car-
         rying 103 persons was ditched by Captain Vinton R.
         Hanson near Sitka, Alaska harbor. The flight had
         originated at McChord Air Force Base (AFB), Washing-
         ton. The plane, after being ditched, stayed afloat
         for almost half an hour. During this time, those on
         board were transferred to life rafts. A Federal Avia-
         tion Agency (FAA) boat then picked up the passengers
         and crew. The Civil Aeronatuics Board (CAB) is par-
         ticularly interested in determining why the plane
         could not continue flying on three of its four engines
         before being ditched.

10.092   "Safety in the Air." **Forbes** 133 (January 16, 1984):
         8 and 10.

         A chart depicts the safest and least safe times, dur-
         ing a flight, for passengers in commercial airliners.

10.093   **Stark, Elizabeth.** "Wild Blue Blunders." **Psychology
         Today** 22 (October 1988): 30-32.

         According to the Federal Aviation Administration
         (FAA), between 60% and 80% of all aircraft accidents

are due to an error in the cockpit. This was the case
in 1987 with near-misses and accidents involving Delta
Airlines. It was also the case in 1972, when an Eastern Airlines aircraft crashed while approaching Miami
International Airport. H. Clayton Foushee, an aviation psychologist, reports that captains can intimi-
date other crewmembers to the point that the other
members dare not intervene in the captain's actions,
even when the actions are seriously wrong. Cockpit
Resource Management (CRM) is a program whose aim it is
to correct flight deck communication problems. United
Airlines (UAL), Pan American (Pan Am), Continental,
Alaska Air, and Delta are involved in CRM. 2 illustrations.

10.094 **Stich, Rodney. The Unfriendly Skies: An Aviation Wa-
tergate.** Alamo, CA: Diablo Western Press, 1978.

The author has been involved in aviation for almost
four decades. He was a pilot and flight instructor
during World War II. He has been a captain for Japan
Air Lines (JAL) and for U.S. air carriers. Stich was
also an FAA (Federal Aviation Administration) inspec-
tor. He has virtually every aviation certificate issued by the U.S. government. And he has over 20,000
hours of flight time. He attempts, in this book, to
expose scandal behind certain air carrier crashes.
Some of the crashes he discusses: United Airlines
(UAL) July 11, 1961; American Airlines at Cincinnati,
Ohio, November 8, 1965; United near Santa Monica,
California, January 18, 1969; and TWA (Trans World
Airlines) December 1, 1974. 16 photographs.

10.095 **Stockton, William. Final Approach: The Crash of
Eastern 212.** New York, NY: Doubleday and Co., Inc.,
1977.

A minute-by-minute, person-by-person account of the
crash of Eastern Airlines Flight 212 on September 11,
1974 at Charlotte, North Carolina. Ten of the
eighty-two people aboard survived when the DC-9
plunged to earth.

10.096 **Taylor, A.J.W.** and A.G. Frazer. **Psychological Seque-
lae of Operation Overdue Following the DC10 Air-
Crash in Antarctica.** Wellington: Victoria University
of Wellington Department of Psychology, 1981.

Two hundred and thirty-seven passengers and twenty
crew died on November 28, 1979, when an Air New Zealand DC-10 crashed into Mount Erebus on Ross Island,

Antarctica. The DC-10 was on a scenic flight when it
crashed. This was the fourteenth "Antarctic Cruise"
since 1977. This publication is about the psychological effects of stress on individuals involved in
body recovery and victim identification at the site
of the crash and, later, at the Auckland Mortuary.
The authors hope their research will aid in more adequate training of rescue workers facing similar cir-
cumstances in the future. Author biographical information. Acknowledgements. 111 references. 12 tables.
1 graph.

10.097   **Turque, Bill,** Tony Clifton and Richard Sandza.   "Hit
and Run at La Guardia." **Newsweek** 114 (October 2,
1989):   25-26.

Michael Martin, age thirty-six, was the pilot and
Constantine Kleissas, age twenty-nine, was the copilot
of USAir Flight 5050, which was travelling 140 miles
per hour down runway 13-31 at New York's La Guardia
Airport. Kleissas was making his first takeoff for
USAir. Both he and Martin tried to control the new
737-400. Martin thought he could safely abort the
takeoff, but the aircraft skidded off the runway and
into the East River. Sixty-one of the sixty-three
passengers and crew, bound for Charlotte, North Carolina, got out alive. Both Martin and Kleissas quickly disappeared after the accident. They reappeared
more than thirty-six hours later to talk to investigators. The Federal Aviation Administration (FAA)
suspended the pilots licenses of both men. 3 photographs.

10.098   **Wallace, Bruce** and William Lowther.   "Dangers in a
Crowded Sky." **Maclean's** 100 (August 31, 1987):   44.

There were 155 passengers aboard Northwest Airlines
Flight 255, a McDonnell-Douglas MD-80, when it left
Metropolitan Airport in Detroit, Michigan on August
16, 1987. Flight 255, which was departing for Phoenix, Arizona, climbed a hundred feet, when its engines stalled, and the plane plunged into the ground.
The only survivor was Cecilia Cichan, age four, from
Tempe, Arizona. The crash of Flight 255 is another
example of the decline in U.S. air safety. There
were 415 million airline passengers in the U.S. in
1986. Also in that year, there were 839 midair near-
collisions. Controllers claim air traffic has increased more than 25% since 1981, when President
Reagan fired over 11,000 striking controllers. 1
photograph.

10.099 "'We're Going to Crash.'" **Maclean's** 102 (March 20,
        1989): 14.

        On March 10, 1989, at Dryden, Ontario, Air Ontario
        Flight 363 crashed. The Dutch-built Fokker F-28,
        originally en route from Thunder Bay, Ontario to
        Winnipeg, Manitoba, had landed at Dryden to pick up
        additional passengers. It crashed and burned short-
        ly after leaving Dryden. Twenty-four people died;
        forty-five survived. Speculation regarding the
        cause of the crash centers on too much fuel and ice
        buildup on the wings. 1 photograph.

10.100 **Weston, Richard** and Ronald Hurst. **Zagreb One Four
        Cleared to Collide?** London: Granada Publishing
        Ltd., 1982.

        On September 10, 1976 over Vrbovec, Yugoslavia two
        aircraft were on a collision course at 33,000 feet.
        Then they collided—a British Airways Trident 3 and
        an Inex-Adria DC-9. The Trident 3 was bound from
        London to Istanbul, Turkey. The DC-9 was headed
        from Split, Yugoslavia to Cologne, West Germany.
        One hundred and seventy-six people died in the col-
        lision. The cause of the disaster was an error made
        by Gradimir Tasic of the Zagreb Air Traffic Control
        (ATC) Center. Tasic was sentenced to seven years in
        prison. 5 plates. 5 figures.

10.101 **Woolsey, James.** "Air Safety, the Press and the
        Public." **Air Transport World** 16 (August 1979):   88.

        When an American Airlines McDonnell Douglas DC-10
        crashed at O'Hare International Airport in Chicago,
        Illinois—and 273 people died—there was inadequate
        communication between the press and government of-
        ficials. The gap between air transport and the me-
        dia's ability to understand this means of travel is
        widening. FAA (Federal Aviation Administration) Ad-
        ministrator Langhorne Bond and NTSB (National Trans-
        portation Safety Board) Vice-Chairman Elwood Driver
        made incomplete and inaccurate statements regarding
        the Chicago accident.

10.102 **Work, Clemens P.** "How to Cut the Risk of Your Num-
        ber Coming Up." **U.S. News and World Report** 103 (July
        6, 1987): 65.

        Dick Livingston, International Airline Passengers As-
        sociation; Terry Denny, International Air Transport
        Association; and C.O. Miller, a safety consultant

comment on surviving airline crashes. Wearing the
right type of clothes (cotton or wool instead of synthetic fibers), crawling to an exit if there is smoke,
and sitting at the rear of the airplane can all make
a positive difference regarding survival. 1 cartoon
illustration.

11

Airline Deregulation

11.001   **Baggaley, Carman.** "A Matter of Faith." **Canadian
         Consumer** 18 (August 1988): 30-35.

         Airline deregulation in the U.S. and Canada is viewed
         critically by some individuals because they associate
         with deregulation older aircraft, maintenance cutbacks,
         less experienced crews, and more airplanes in the sky.
         The Federal Aviation Administration (FAA) fined Amer-
         ican Airlines, Continental Airlines, and Eastern Air-
         lines millions of dollars in 1986 for maintenance vio-
         lations. Near-misses and accidents in both countries
         are also of concern. On February 11, 1978, a Pacific
         Western Airlines (PWA) flight crashed at Cranbrook,
         B.C., when the pilot tried to avoid hitting a snow
         removal vehicle on the runway. Forty-two passengers
         and crew were killed. In August 1986 a Piper Chero-
         kee and an Aeromexico DC-9 collided near Los Angeles
         International Airport. 3 photographs. Author bio-
         graphical information.

11.002   **Duffy, Henry A.** "Deregulating Safety." **USA Today**
         (Magazine) 113 (July 1984): 54-56.

         Since 1978 twenty-six airlines in the U.S. have de-
         clared bankruptcy or ceased operations. Continental
         Airlines, for example, declared bankruptcy on Septem-
         ber 24, 1983. A "new" Continental continued to op-
         erate with one-third the former manpower. Most of
         the "new" employees were quickly-promoted junior of-
         ficers. One junior officer who was promoted was
         landing in Denver, Colorado on November 9, 1983 and
         completely missed the runway. The pilot who died in
         the Air Florida crash in Washington, DC in January
         1982 had little more than three years' experience.
         He had little familiarity with East Coast winters.
         Air Illinois quit service after an accident involving
         deaths. Author biographical information. 1 photo-
         graph.

11.003   **Engen, Donald D.** "Deregulation: Seven Years Later."
         Vital Speeches of the Day 52 (March 15, 1986): 335-
         337.

Text of a speech by Donald D. Engen, Administrator, Federal Aviation Administration (FAA), delivered before the Wings Club, New York, January 15, 1986.

11.004   "How Safe Is Air Travel?" **Consumers' Research** 69 (June 1986):   15-17.

Since deregulation of the U.S. airline industry in 1978, the air travel safety record has been steadily improving. 2 illustrations. 2 tables.

11.005   **McKenzie, Richard B.** and William F. Shughart, II. "Deregulation's Impact on Air Safety: Separating Fact From Fiction." **Consumers' Research** 71 (January 1988):   10-13.

Airline travel is not less safe now than before deregulation. This is the opinion of the authors both of whom are economists. They studied, statistically, the impact of deregulation on air safety. Two charts aid in explaining the research findings. One chart is about fatalities per billion passenger-miles flown for scheduled airlines, 1972-1986. The other chart is about reported near midair collisions and passenger-miles flown for scheduled airlines, 1972-1986. 1 illustration.

11.006   **Moses, Leon N.** and Ian Savage. "Air Safety in the Age of Deregulation." **Issues in Science and Technology** 4 (Spring 1988):   31-36.

By 1986 deregulation was saving airline passengers about $16 billion annually, but it was also reducing the quality of service and passenger comfort. Deregulation is blamed for more flight delays, more lost baggage, increased overbookings, and a decline in the number and quality of meals. Deregulation is also viewed as the reason for airline cost-cutting regarding safety equipment, crew training, maintenance, and aircraft replacement. Author biographical information. 9 references.

11.007   **Moses, Leon N.** and Ian Savage. Editors. **Tansportation Safety in an Age of Deregulation.** New York, NY: Oxford University Press, 1989.

Selected chapters: "Financial Influences on Airline Safety" (Nancy L. Rose) 93-114 (7 tables. 1 figure); "New Entrants and Safety" (Adib Kanafani and Theodore E. Keeler) 115-128 (6 tables); "Is It Still Safe to

Fly?" (Clinton V. Oster, Jr. and C. Kurt Zorn) 129-
152 (10 tables); "Congestion Pricing to Improve Air
Travel Safety" (Richard J. Arnott and Joseph E. Stig-
litz) 167-185 (1 figure. 9 notes); and "Economic Deregulation's Unintended But Inevitable Impact on Airline Safety" (John J. Nance) 186-205.

Author Index

Subject Index

O

About the Compiler

JOHN J. MILETICH is Reference Librarian at the University of Alberta, Canada. He is the author of *Retirement: An Annotated Bibliography; Work and Alcohol Abuse: An Annotated Bibliography;* and *States of Awareness: An Annotated Bibliography* (Greenwood Press, 1986, 1987, and 1988, respectively).